ABSTRACT ENTITIES

Think of a number, any number, or properties like *fragility* and *humanity*. These and other abstract entities are radically different from concrete entities like electrons and elbows. While concrete entities are located in space and time, have causes and effects, and are known through empirical means, abstract entities like meanings and possibilities are remarkably different. They seem to be immutable and imperceptible and to exist "outside" of space and time.

This book provides a comprehensive critical assessment of the problems raised by abstract entities and the debates about existence, truth, and knowledge that surround them. It sets out the key issues that inform the metaphysical disagreement between platonists who accept abstract entities and nominalists who deny abstract entities exist. Beginning with the essentials of the platonist–nominalist debate, it explores the key arguments and issues informing the contemporary debate over abstract reality:

- arguments for platonism and their connections to semantics, science, and metaphysical explanation
- the abstract–concrete distinction and views about the nature of abstract reality
- epistemological puzzles surrounding our knowledge of mathematical entities and other abstract entities
- arguments for nominalism premised upon concerns about paradox, parsimony, infinite regresses, underdetermination, and causal isolation
- nominalist options that seek to dispense with abstract entities.

Including chapter summaries, annotated further reading, and a glossary, *Abstract Entities* is essential reading for anyone seeking a clear and authoritative introduction to the problems raised by abstract entities.

Sam Cowling is Assistant Professor, Denison University, USA.

NEW PROBLEMS OF PHILOSOPHY
Series Editor: José Luis Bermúdez

> *New Problems of Philosophy* is developing a most impressive lineup of topical volumes aimed at graduate and upper-level undergraduate students in philosophy and at others with interests in cutting edge philosophical work. Series authors are players in their respective fields and notably adept at synthesizing and explaining intricate topics fairly and comprehensively.
>
> —*John Heil, Monash University, Australia, and Washington University in St. Louis, USA*

> This is an outstanding collection of volumes. The topics are well chosen and the authors are outstanding. They will be fine texts in a wide range of courses.
>
> —*Stephen Stich, Rutgers University, USA*

The New Problems of Philosophy series provides accessible and engaging surveys of the most important problems in contemporary philosophy. Each book examines either a topic or theme that has emerged on the philosophical landscape in recent years, or a longstanding problem refreshed in light of recent work in philosophy and related disciplines. Clearly explaining the nature of the problem at hand and assessing attempts to answer it, books in the series are excellent starting points for undergraduate and graduate students wishing to study a single topic in depth. They will also be essential reading for professional philosophers. Additional features include chapter summaries, further reading and a glossary of technical terms.

Also available:

Semantic Externalism
Jesper Kallestrup

Consequentialism
Julia Driver

Forthcoming:

Egalitarianism
Iwao Hirose

Imagination
Fabian Dorsch

Attention
Wayne Wu

Disjunctivism
Matthew Soteriou

ABSTRACT ENTITIES

Sam Cowling

LONDON AND NEW YORK

First published 2017
by Routledge
2 Park Square, Milton Park, Abingdon, Oxon OX14 4RN

and by Routledge
711 Third Avenue, New York, NY 10017

Routledge is an imprint of the Taylor & Francis Group, an informa business

© 2017 Sam Cowling

The right of Sam Cowling to be identified as the author of this work has been asserted by him in accordance with sections 77 and 78 of the Copyright, Designs and Patents Act 1988.

All rights reserved. No part of this book may be reprinted or reproduced or utilised in any form or by any electronic, mechanical, or other means, now known or hereafter invented, including photocopying and recording, or in any information storage or retrieval system, without permission in writing from the publishers.

Trademark notice: Product or corporate names may be trademarks or registered trademarks, and are used only for identification and explanation without intent to infringe.

British Library Cataloguing in Publication Data
A catalogue record for this book is available from the British Library

Library of Congress Cataloging in Publication Data
Names: Cowling, Sam, author.
Title: Abstract entities / by Sam Cowling.
Description: 1 [edition]. | New York : Routledge, 2017. | Series: New problems of philosophy | Includes bibliographical references and index.
Identifiers: LCCN 2016038051| ISBN 9781138827585 (hardback : alk. paper) | ISBN 9781138827592 (pbk. : alk. paper) | ISBN 9781315266619 (e-book)
Subjects: LCSH: Entity (Philosophy) | Abstraction.
Classification: LCC BD336 .C69 2017 | DDC 111—dc23
LC record available at https://lccn.loc.gov/2016038051

ISBN: 978-1-138-82758-5 (hbk)
ISBN: 978-1-138-82759-2 (pbk)
ISBN: 978-1-315-26661-9 (ebk)

Typeset in Joanna and Scala Sans
by Swales & Willis Ltd, Exeter, Devon, UK

"The curious task/economics is to demonstrate to men how little they really know about what they imagine they can design."
— Fredrich van Hayek —

For My Folks

"Be faithful in small things b/c it is in them that your strength lies."
— Mother Teresa —

CONTENTS

Acknowledgements		ix
Introduction		1
1	**The case for platonism**	23
	1.1 Platonism	23
	1.2 Semantic arguments	26
	1.3 Alethic arguments	38
	1.4 Indispensability arguments	47
	1.5 Metaphysical explanation	57
2	**The abstract–concrete distinction**	69
	2.1 The standard view	70
	2.2 Analyzing abstractness	74
	2.3 Primitivism	92
	2.4 Eliminativism	97
3	**Paradox, parsimony, and infinite regresses**	106
	3.1 Paradox	107
	3.2 Parsimony	114
	3.3 Infinite regresses	120
4	**Causal concerns**	130
	4.1 Epistemic access	130
	4.2 Ensuring epistemic access	138
	4.3 Semantic access	147
	4.4 Cognitive access	150
	4.5 Eleaticism	155

5	**Non-uniqueness**	**162**
	5.1 The non-uniqueness problem	162
	5.2 Living with non-uniqueness	169
	5.3 Metaphysical underdetermination	177
	5.4 Overcoming underdetermination	179
6	**Modal objections**	**189**
	6.1 Necessary existents	190
	6.2 Necessary connections	196
	6.3 Contingent platonism	201
	6.4 Abstracta and actuality	206
7	**Nominalist options**	**214**
	7.1 Nominalisms	214
	7.2 Meaning	216
	7.3 Truth	220
	7.4 Commitment	228
	7.5 Harvard nominalism revisited	234
	Conclusion	**247**
	Glossary	252
	References	256
	Index	273

ACKNOWLEDGEMENTS

Thanks to the many folks who provided helpful comments on various parts of this book. Among others, my thanks to Marc Alspector-Kelly, Chloe Armstrong, Wesley Cray, Gus Evans, Arthur Falk, Ed Ferrier, Barak Krakauer, Anthony Kulic, Kelly McCormick, Michaela McSweeney, Kevin Morris, Joshua Spencer, Chris Tillman, Jenn Wang, and audiences at the University of Massachusetts-Amherst, the 2015 Central division of the American Philosophical Association, the 2015 Canadian Philosophical Association, and the 2016 Junior Metaphysics Workshop. I am especially grateful to James Davies, Cameron Gibbs, Dan Giberman, Bradley Rettler, and Kelly Trogdon for providing extensive comments on the manuscript. Additional thanks are owed to my excellent colleagues at Denison University for their kind support. Thanks also to my editors at Routledge, Tony Bruce and Adam Johnson, and to four anonymous referees for their helpful comments.

This book project began during a seminar on abstract entities at Western Michigan University in 2013 and was helped along by a class on the same topic at Denison in 2015. My thanks to all the students involved in those courses. My good fortune in teaching those classes (or anywhere at all, for that matter) owes to the many professors who have taught me over the years. I am especially grateful to Phil Bricker and Ben Caplan in this regard. Given their remarkable philosophical acumen, the stark difference in their views is evidence enough that there are no easy answers when it comes to abstract entities.

Finally, thanks to my friends and family, and especially my parents, Janet and Doug, and dear wife, Stephanie, for their patience and encouragement.

Columbus, Ohio
August 2016

INTRODUCTION

This book is about abstract entities. Like most entities subject to serious philosophical scrutiny, it is controversial whether there are any such things. It is also controversial which things would be properly counted as abstract if they were to exist. Worse still, there is widespread controversy about what exactly it means for an entity to be abstract rather than concrete.

You might take this abundance of controversy to be philosophically ominous, suggesting that debates about abstract entities are spurious or defective. That would be a mistake. Debates regarding abstract entities are among the most important in metaphysics. Since paradigmatic abstract entities like the real numbers and the Pythagorean theorem figure in our best scientific theories, they force us to clarify how our scientific commitments ought to inform our metaphysical theories. And, given that abstract entities are usually taken to be imperceptible entities existing outside of spacetime, they serve as a proving ground for the application of epistemological theories. Since abstract entities like meanings and theories seem both oddly familiar yet ontologically peculiar, investigating them also demands that we carefully examine our ordinary worldview and its proper place within philosophical methodology.

This book aims to provide an opinionated introduction to the metaphysics of abstract entities. It will focus on the main arguments that structure the contemporary debate over their nature and existence. But, before heaping complications upon qualifications upon distinctions, we can begin with the basics. Following a somewhat contentious convention, we will take platonism as the thesis that abstract entities exist and, for the moment, follow orthodoxy in taking entities like numbers, properties, and propositions as paradigm examples of abstracta.[1] In opposition to platonism stands the thesis of nominalism, which holds that there are no abstract entities.[2] According to nominalism, the world is wholly concrete. It contains only concrete entities like canoes, caribou, and cosmic rays. Since platonism affirms the existence of both abstract and concrete entities, the point of disagreement between platonists and nominalists boils down to a single question: are there abstract entities?

Tackling this question requires that we first get a grip on the notion of an abstract entity. And, while pointing to examples provides one way to introduce the notion of an abstract entity, it will be useful to mark some features commonly albeit controversially held to distinguish the abstract from the concrete: (i) *Causation*. Abstract entities are usually claimed to lack any causal role in the world; they cannot be created, altered, or destroyed. In contrast, concrete entities are creatable, mutable, and destructible; they can come into and go out of existence and change over time. (ii) *Location*. Abstract entities are typically claimed to lack spatiotemporal location and so are timeless, shapeless, and without any position in space. In contrast, concrete entities occupy particular locations in space or time. (iii) *Accessibility*. Abstract entities are also commonly held to be cognitively or epistemically accessible in a way that concrete entities are not. This is because our ordinary epistemic access to concrete entities like canoes and caribou is perceptual and therefore involves causal relations, like seeing or touching, between entities located within spacetime. But, as just noted, abstract entities seem to lack causal roles and spatiotemporal locations. So, if mathematical entities like integers, properties like *goodness*, and propositions like the Golden Rule are not in spacetime and are beyond our causal access, our ability to think about and acquire knowledge of them seems to require some sort of special cognitive or epistemic access.

Although many platonists claim we have special cognitive access to abstract entities, this does not mean that abstract entities are mental entities like ideas or psychological representations. Instead, as Gottlob Frege (1918) memorably puts it, abstract entities occupy a "Third Realm," distinct from both physical entities and from mental entities like hallucinations or feelings. Physical and mental entities are therefore concrete, while abstract entities are neither mental nor physical entities.[3] And, unlike ideas and other mental entities, abstract entities are typically held to be *mind-independent*: their existence and nature is ontologically independent from the attitudes and mental states of individuals. Accordingly, abstract entities are not products of our cognitive activities. They would exist and have their essential features even if there were no one around to think, know, or speak about them.

The mind-independence of abstract entities is nicely illustrated by Frege's example of the Pythagorean theorem. Although you believe the Pythagorean theorem by virtue of having certain mental states, the Pythagorean theorem is not identical to your mental states or to the mental states of anyone else. According to most platonists, the Pythagorean theorem is true, was so before you existed, and would be so even if you (or anyone else) had never existed. This is because the Pythagorean theorem is an abstract entity—specifically, a proposition—that is the content of your mental state.[4] You and other thinkers can bear various propositional attitudes like belief and doubt to the Pythagorean theorem and other propositions (e.g., that dogs bark or that it's raining in Vancouver). And, in virtue of bearing these attitudes, your mental states have their respective contents and can be evaluated for their truth or falsity. Moreover, the truth or falsity of your beliefs depends upon the truth of the propositions you believe. So, for example, your belief in the Pythagorean theorem is true in virtue of the Pythagorean theorem being true. And, if you were to believe that pigs fly, your belief would be false in virtue of the proposition that pigs fly being false. For platonists who posit propositions, the truth or falsity of our beliefs is tidily explained by appeal to the truth or falsity of the propositions they have as contents.

The mind-independence of propositions like the Pythagorean theorem plays a key role in platonist explanations of how the mental states of different individuals can share a common content. For, while our respective mental states are distinct—yours are in your head, mine are in mine—the platonist holds that our capacity to believe or doubt the very same things owes to our ability to bear attitudes towards the very same propositions. And, as we'll see, this is just one of several ways in which platonists invoke abstract entities—in this case, propositions—to provide philosophical explanations.

The features just noted—causal inactivity, lack of spatiotemporal location, special cognitive accessibility, and mind-independence—are rough guides in our efforts to single out abstract entities, but it is controversial where to draw the line between the abstract and the concrete realms. Some platonists posit abstract entities that lack one or more of these features. Others claim that some special feature—perhaps causal inactivity or lack of location—adequately distinguishes abstract entities from concrete ones. So, while platonists are united by a shared commitment to abstract entities, few platonists agree about what makes entities abstract rather than concrete. Similar disagreement arises over which kinds of abstract entities there are. Some platonists admit properties, but balk at propositions. Other platonists posit propositions, but reject mathematical entities. The lengthy list of candidate abstract entities will receive closer attention in Chapter 2, but, throughout this book, our focus will be on three main kinds of abstract entities: (i) *mathematical entities* like numbers, sets, and functions; (ii) *properties*, which are sometimes called "universals" or "attributes," like *being human*, *redness*, and *mass*; and (iii) *propositions* like the Pythagorean theorem and the proposition that pigs fly.[5]

In narrowing our focus, we will mostly set aside other kinds of abstract entities such as types, possibilities, and fictional characters which are sometimes posited by platonists. Doing so is useful, in part, because the status of these other kinds is controversial and because such kinds are often thought to reduce to properties, propositions, or mathematical entities. For example, *types* such as the letter type "z" or *the common housefly* seem to be related to their instances or *tokens* in a manner much like the relationship between properties and their bearers. This has prompted some platonists to identify types with properties of a certain sort. In a similar vein, possibilities like the possibility that the North Koreans land on Mars or that triangles have three sides are often identified with propositions that have modal properties like *being possibly true*. In addition, Ahab, Aquaman, and other *fictional characters* are, on certain platonist views, rightly identified with complex constructions of properties and propositions.

By focusing our attention on mathematical entities, properties, and propositions, we can avoid recurring qualifications and complications while also leaving open which kinds of abstract entities might reduce to which other kinds. In addition, the three kinds of abstract entities we will focus on have a strong claim to being both the most commonly posited abstract entities and the most theoretically fruitful. For this reason, they serve as the best test cases in our survey of the arguments for and against platonism. That said, we will also consider the fate of other kinds of abstract entities at certain points in what follows.

An additional category of alleged abstract entities requires special comment at this point. Many platonists hold the domain of abstract entities to be far broader than just suggested. Alongside numbers, properties, and propositions, *expansive platonists* posit conventional or created abstract entities such as musical works, trade deficits, secret handshakes, and soup recipes. According to expansive platonism, these entities and others like them share sufficiently many marks of abstractness to be properly counted as abstract. For example, some appear to lack locations in space even while they seem to be created or located in time (or *vice versa*). And, although some might seem to stand in certain kinds of causal relations, their causal status seems markedly different from the one ascribed to concrete entities.[6] As a consequence, expansive platonists extend the domain of abstract entities far beyond the realm of paradigmatic abstracta like numbers, properties, and propositions.

For expansive platonists, soup recipes, musical works, and a motley assortment of other entities are properly counted as abstract, despite their apparent dependence upon human activities and their apparent location in space or time. Against this expansive view, *austere platonists* deny that conventional or created entities are a part of abstract reality. According to austere platonism, such entities are not properly classified as abstract or simply do not exist. Austere platonists will therefore hold that entities like musical works and recipes are reducible to certain concrete entities—e.g., the mereological sum of various musical performances or inscriptions—or claim, instead, that such entities are somehow identical with paradigmatic abstracta like properties, propositions, or mathematical entities.

The divide between expansive and austere forms of platonism is arguably the most significant division among competing versions of platonism. It is frustrating, then, that one sometimes finds arguments about abstract musical works or fictional characters that boldly assert all abstract entities lack spatiotemporal locations or are causally inert. For austere platonists, this is plausible enough, but, for expansive platonists, there is simply no good reason to assume such a generalization. Arguments that hinge upon such generalizations are therefore worthless unless paired with an explicit commitment to austere platonism or to a well-worked out version of expansive platonism that would support such claims. For this reason, a not insignificant amount of work on abstract entities is hindered by a failure to explicitly address this divide between expansive and austere versions of platonism and their conflicting views about the abstract realm.

In Chapter 2, in-house disagreements among platonists will be surveyed in some detail. For reasons noted there, the primary concern of this book is with the fate of austere versions of platonism, which uphold substantive generalizations about abstract entities—e.g., that they are causally inactive or without spatiotemporal location—and eschew the abstract entities posited by expansive platonists. Obviously, this is controversial, but the good news is that many of the issues addressed in this book can be broached in a way that is more or less orthogonal to the expansive/austere divide. Where this divide does matter, I have tried to note as much. For example, in Chapter 6, I will suggest that the case against expansive platonism is somewhat stronger than the case against austere platonism.

Having marked the disagreements between austere and expansive platonism, it should be clear that the very notion of an *abstract entity* resists any simple definition. In this respect, the category of abstract entities is little different from the rest of nature. Nevertheless, those disposed to anxiety in the face of any metaphysical ambiguity will find this murkiness troublesome. There is, however, no good reason for panic. As we'll see, there is a range of ways we can make the abstract–concrete distinction precise. And, while the adequacy of these accounts is controversial, there is still good reason for austere platonists to believe that the category of *abstract entity* is importantly unified. This is due, not only to the clustering of the distinctive features noted above, but also to the commonalities between the theoretical roles usually assigned to abstract entities. We will map out these roles in later chapters, but, for now, we can proceed with this preliminary characterization in hand and briefly explore the significance and history of the debate over abstract entities.

§Significance and history

The intuitive appeal of platonism can be captured rather easily: our thought and talk seems steeped in abstract entities, so, in denying such entities exist, nominalism threatens to undermine a vast wealth of commonly and closely held truths. For example, we know that three is a prime number. We also know that the Pythagorean theorem is true and that patience is a virtue. In each of these cases, our knowledge seems to have a subject matter and that subject matter seems to be independent from concrete reality. This seems easy enough to account for if we accept platonism, since the relevant subject matters would all be found within the abstract realm. So, when we correctly believe that the Pythagorean theorem is true or errantly believe that four is a prime number, we get things right or wrong to the extent our beliefs accurately represent a mind-independent abstract realm that is no less real or objective than the concrete realm of pancakes and potholes.

Contrary to the ambitions of nominalism, platonists claim that any effort to reinterpret our familiar thought and talk about abstract entities solely in terms of concrete entities is doomed. Although we can count and reason mathematically about concrete entities, we cannot plausibly identify mathematical entities like the integers with collections of concrete entities like tadpoles or totem poles. For, even if we had sufficiently many tadpoles and totem poles, such entities, unlike the natural numbers, eventually perish or topple over. Similarly, it seems that the Pythagorean theorem would be true even if there were no tadpoles, totem poles, or perhaps no concrete entities whatsoever. In the eyes of the platonist, the nominalist's ambition of doing away with abstract entities like numbers, properties, and propositions is a mistaken one. Any nominalist proposal for recasting our thought and talk will inevitably distort or undermine the content and objectivity of our discourse about mathematics, meaning, and other subject matters tied to the abstract realm.

So far, so good. But why think the resolution of the debate between nominalists and platonists matters terribly much? Perhaps the debate over abstract entities is much like ontological debates concerning holes or shadows: interesting enough, but of limited or mostly illustrative significance. With this worry in mind, it will be useful here to outline the considerable and often underestimated stakes of the nominalist–platonist debate before examining it in detail.

Even in its modest implementations, platonism is a striking thesis about the explanatory structure of our best theories. If true, our philosophical and scientific explanatory projects will involve, in part or at bottom, entities found "outside" the physical world. This is because metaphysical explanations offered by platonists, when followed to their end, invariably trace through a realm of entities like properties or propositions that are rarely viewed as explicit objects of scientific inquiry. Moreover, most platonists hold that concrete entities stand in special relations to abstract entities that explain, at least in part, the behaviour and nature of concrete reality. For instance, the behaviour of an electron bustling through a cloud chamber depends, says the platonist, upon the relationship between that electron and an abstract entity, electronhood. In a similar vein, platonist explanations of the meaning of our thought and talk appeal to propositions. So, for platonists, if thought, meaning, and communication are to be explained, it will be in virtue of facts, not just about brains, sound waves, and inscriptions, but about a realm of acausal, atemporal, abstract propositions as well.

Platonists take our explanatory projects to point well beyond the physical world. In contrast, nominalists believe our best philosophical and scientific explanations to be circumscribed by concrete reality. Properly viewed, then, platonism and nominalism are competing views about what our ultimate explanations of the world ought to look like. Platonists hold that such explanations point beyond the concrete to some other portion of reality; nominalists deny exactly this.

Given the generality of platonist explanations, most versions of platonism hold reality to be positively teeming with abstract entities like numbers, properties, and propositions. This is because, implicitly or explicitly, abstract entities figure into the explanation of almost any fact. Suppose, for example, that an individual, Edie, is mistaken about the square root of nine. A typical platonist explanation of this fact would hold that Edie bears the belief relation to a false proposition and that she instantiates a host of properties like *being capable of thought* and *being a human*. Moreover, Edie's mistake owes to the fact that she has misrepresented an objective mathematical realm by believing of, say, the number five that it bears the property *being the square root of nine*.[7] In offering explanations of the above sort, demands of consistency and uniformity force platonists to admit a truly staggering number of abstract entities. Platonism therefore envisions a world that will seem radically overpopulated when compared to that of the nominalist.

A world in which abstract entities are pervasive, explanatorily indispensable, and the proper targets of inquiry will strike many platonists as a philosopher's paradise. Among other things, it offers philosophy a surprising pride of place, situating metaphysicians and mathematicians as leading authorities on the abstract realm. But, for many nominalists, this seemingly good news is a sign that something has gone badly wrong. According to the nominalist, reality is not teeming with abstract entities. Worse still, the explanations proffered by platonists are defective. They invoke cooked-up creatures of darkness or "explain" phenomena only through philosophical sleight of hand. If philosophical and scientific explanations are to be found, nominalists contend that they must be found in the concrete world of which we are a frustratingly small part.

Unfortunately for nominalists, metaphysics without abstract entities can be a gruelling and laborious affair. Not only do nominalists owe some account of why the arguments for platonism fail, they also owe some explanation of why discourse that seems to require abstract entities—most notably, mathematics—is useful despite being badly mistaken about what reality is like. The list of additional burdens bearing down on the nominalist is dauntingly long. She must explain the resemblance of individuals without appeal to universals, the apparent objectivity of mathematics without numbers, and the meaningfulness of thought and talk without propositions.

These theoretical burdens pile up quickly. Meanwhile, platonists are quick to help themselves to what the nominalist views as ill-gotten ontological gains. All too often, frustration sets in and fair-weather nominalists eventually dismiss nominalism as a bull-headed pursuit of ontological economy or an untutored hostility to the subtleties of metaphysics.

The above considerations speak to the significance of the nominalist–platonist debate for metaphysics and show why no account of the structure of reality can simply ignore the status of numbers, meanings, and properties. The significance of abstract entities is also fairly clear when we look past metaphysics to disciplines like mathematics and logic, and their intersections with philosophy. In these disciplines, abstract entities such as models, integers, sets, and functions are explicit targets of inquiry. And, while the working mathematician can get by without worrying about whether numbers exist or what they're like, mathematical research programmes like intuitionism, constructivism, and formalism are crucially tied to the nature of the abstract realm. Similar remarks extend to the philosophy of language and linguistics, where abstracta like sets, functions, and propositions figure into leading semantic theories and views about the nature of communication. The consequences of the nominalist–platonist debate for other areas like epistemology and ethics are perhaps less obvious, but, again, no less serious. A quick glance at contemporary work on these topics shows the apparatus of propositions and properties to be almost universally assumed in most investigations of justification, knowledge, value, rationality, and other issues.

Even within increasingly specialized domains, the role of abstract entities remains substantial. In the philosophy of art, the question of whether fictional characters and musical works are abstract or concrete has implications for views about the bearers of aesthetic value and for the status of artistic creation. In the philosophy of science, the challenge of discerning genuine physical reality from the artifice of representation requires careful attention to where we ought to drawn the line between the abstract and the concrete. Yet more narrowly, in the philosophy of biology, debates over the nature of biological species turn, in part, on whether our metaphysical resources are limited to concrete individuals or include abstract properties, kinds, or sets of individuals.[8]

In these and many other domains, abstract entities play a crucial role in the development and formulation of theories, since philosophers frequently help themselves to the framework of properties and propositions in advancing and defending their preferred views. The final verdict in the nominalist–platonist debate is therefore guaranteed to have significant and wide-ranging consequences for those who help themselves to abstract entities like numbers, properties, and propositions even if only as conveniences or tentative working assumptions.

In addition to the regular use of abstract entities one finds across philosophical disciplines, the nature of philosophy itself is sometimes tethered to the status of platonism. According to certain versions of *methodological platonism*, philosophy consists, at bottom, in *a priori* reflection aimed at discovering the nature of abstract entities such as numbers and universals like *beauty* or *goodness*. For platonists of this rather extreme sort, there is a non-spatial province of reality that is properly investigated through *a priori* methods and to which we have special cognitive access. So, for those sympathetic to methodological platonism, the fate of philosophy itself hinges upon the existence of this abstract realm and the dismissal of nominalism. (On views of this sort, see Bealer (1987).)

Despite the stark divide between nominalism and platonism, some have attempted to downplay the stakes of this debate. Memorably, Hilary Putnam (1995: 44)—himself an important contributor to the debate—remarks that "grown men and women arguing about whether the number three 'really exists' is a ludicrous spectacle." Historically, however, this dim view of the nominalist–platonist debate is an outlier. The nature and existence of universals is at the core of philosophy in Antiquity and the Middle Ages, where a profound disagreement separates Platonist views, on which universals are outside of space and time, Aristotelian views, which locate universals within the broadly physical realm, and nominalist views that reject universals altogether. More recently, the debate between platonists and nominalists has been placed at the very heart of systematic philosophical inquiry. Cautioning against the perils of nominalism, the doyen of pragmatism, C.S. Peirce (1976: 295) calls nominalism "a protest against the only kind of thinking that has ever advanced human culture." Yet more strikingly, F.E. Abbott (1885: 9) pitches the history of medieval and modern philosophy as an on-going battle between nominalism, which he takes to be in cahoots with idealism, and platonism (here, "Scholastic Realism"):

> The great Roscellino-Kantian "revolution" by which Nominalism was made to supplant Scholastic Realism, and philosophy to transfer its fundamental standpoint from the world of things to the world of thought, was a revolution which logically contracts "human knowledge" to the petty dimensions of individual self-consciousness, renders it valueless as to

things themselves, and valuable only as to the *a priori* constitution of the individual's own mind and, in effect, reduces it to a grand hallucination. Like the French Revolution, the Nominalistic revolution can live only by the guillotine, and decapitates every perception which pretends to bring to the miserable solipsist, shut up in the prison of his own consciousness, the slightest information as to the great outside world. Defining knowledge as the mere contents of consciousness, it relegates to non-entity, as pseudo-knowledge, whatever claims to be more than that. Under its sway, philosophy is blind to the race, and beholds the individual alone.

This is strong stuff. And, while Abbott overstates the significance of the nominalist–platonist debate, there is still good reason to set it alongside other perennial metaphysical debates. Notice, however, that by doing so we assume, along with Abbott, that there is a central, more or less unified, and historically lengthy debate over abstract entities rather than a series of loosely connected debates with merely overlapping terminology. This assumption is a substantive historical thesis. Understandably, those who uphold the centrality of the nominalist–platonist debate typically emphasize its historical continuity while still granting that its focus might shift over time from, say, a preoccupation with cognition and concepts to a preoccupation with truth and predication. In contrast, others have denied that there is any robust, unifying philosophical thread running through these successive historical periods and therefore downplay the continuity that surface terminology suggests. By emphasizing the discontinuities, they take issue with the notion of a lengthy and unified history of the nominalist–platonist debate. As a result, they are more likely to call its present significance into question.

For those impressed by the historical continuities of the debate, its contemporary significance should be manifest: it concerns competing views of reality that have sweeping implications for thought, language, truth, and many other subjects. For those who deny there is a unified historical thread, contemporary disagreements over abstract entities might seem to be of a different sort than those historically at issue. In fact, some who reject the continuity of the debate, might see its present incarnation as a watered-down remnant of past philosophical glory. This dim assessment, hinted at in Putnam's remark above, is sometimes tempting, but mistaken nonetheless.

Philosophy's increasing specialization and careful apportioning of intellectual labour make it reasonable enough to bracket the nominalist–platonist debate and to simply assume a platonist or nominalist metaphysics when focusing one's philosophical attention elsewhere. Perhaps understandably, this attitude can mislead those with their intellectual vision trained narrowly on other domains to dismiss the significance of abstract entities. And, while this book takes no side on the difficult historical questions regarding the continuity of the debate, it should be clear that, regardless of its historical trajectory, a final verdict comes with serious consequences. Despite this, challenges to the substantive character of the nominalist–platonist debate are still regularly offered up. In the next section, we will briefly note some of these challenges and, in doing so, mark some methodological assumptions of what follows.

§Naysaying

A tradition of metaphysical naysaying haunts almost every ontological debate, and, in keeping with Putnam's remark above, some claim that the disagreement over abstract entities is a defective or empty one. Certain of these naysayers paint with an extremely broad brush, undercutting debates about the metaphysics of abstract entities along with most other metaphysical disagreements. Unsophisticated verificationist naysayers will, for example, dismiss the nominalist–platonist debate on the grounds that both nominalism and platonism fail to meet implausibly stringent demands for being genuinely meaningful assertions. Other naysayers seek to dismiss the debate by alleging that no compelling arguments can be offered for either side and so conclude that the debate must be an empty one.[9] These sweeping kinds of metaphysical naysaying are of least concern here. Not only do they turn on contentious (and, I think, false) theses about disagreement, meaning, and evidence, they are better viewed as general challenges to metaphysics rather than the specific debate regarding abstract entities. Note, however, that no general defence of metaphysics from naysayers will be advanced here. Instead, I will simply mark as a working assumption that, despite their complexity and potential intractability, debates regarding abstracta are nevertheless substantial.

Inquiry into abstract entities, like other projects in metaphysics, consists in a carefully reasoned effort to answer tough questions by drawing upon a diverse range of considerations. These considerations include, but are not limited to, theoretical virtues and vices, compatibility with our best scientific theories, and coherence with our ordinary beliefs. Viewed this way, questions regarding abstract entities are no more or less defective than other metaphysical questions about, say, the reality of spacetime or the nature of minds.

Although we are simply assuming the tenabilty of metaphysical inquiry, it is worth examining the more worrisome forms of naysaying that try to seize upon some distinctive features of the nominalist–platonist debate and undermine its particular significance. Among such varieties of naysaying, the most influential owe directly or indirectly to Rudolf Carnap's "Empiricism, semantics, and ontology." The Carnapian brand of naysaying denies that the kinds of ontological questions at issue between nominalists and platonists—e.g., whether there are numbers—can be successfully posed, much less correctly answered. On the Carnapian view, different linguistic frameworks like the framework of arithmetic, the framework of spacetime points, or the framework of physical objects constitute our cumulative theory of the world. Each framework imposes certain semantic and syntactic rules on the relevant bodies of theoretical discourse. Some of these rules facilitate, among other things, the introduction of ontological commitments distinctive to these frameworks like numbers, ordinary objects, and spacetime points. For instance, it is a rule of the framework of mathematics that, for any natural number, there is a unique successor of that number. So, granted the existence of a number, this rule allows us to infer, within that framework, that there are infinitely many such numbers, each with a unique number as a successor. If this and other rules are analytic truths of their respective frameworks, it looks like certain facts about what exists are correspondingly analytic. So, for example, in the case of the mathematical framework, the very rules of the framework immediately settle the question of whether there are numbers. So, when we ask whether there are numbers, our question is most naturally taken as a "framework-internal question" which is concerned with whether, according to the mathematical framework, there are numbers. And, if taken as an "internal" question, the answer to this question is a trivial "yes," since, according to the framework of numbers, it is an analytic truth that there are numbers.

Unsurprisingly, those interested in the metaphysics of abstract entities typically deny that the existence of numbers is a trivial matter. Instead, nominalists and platonists alike take the question of whether there are numbers as a substantive one about the nature and existence of abstract reality. For this reason, those who treat this question with "metaphysical seriousness" insist that it is not properly taken as a framework "internal" question. It must therefore be taken as a framework "external" question, properly asked outside of the framework of numbers. But—and here's the key Carnapian move—the Carnapian naysayer denies that any sense can be made of an alleged "external question" that asks whether there are numbers in a way independent of the number framework. At best, this question can be charitably recast as a kind of prudential inquiry concerning whether we should adopt the number framework on pragmatic grounds. But, once again, this will leave the nominalist and platonist unsatisfied. For, in asking whether there are numbers or abstract entities, the nominalist and platonist are not interested in whether the number framework is pragmatically expedient. Indeed, it seems perfectly possible that a given framework might be incredibly useful to adopt despite being badly mistaken about the way the world is. Those who hold the nominalist–platonist debate to be substantial are therefore pressed to successfully pose the question of whether there *really* are numbers or, for that matter, any abstract entities whatsoever.

Answering the Carnapian naysayer is no small matter. It requires, among other things, explaining why the nominalist–platonist debate is not properly assimilated to a debate over the usefulness of certain linguistic frameworks. And, if Carnap's demand is a reasonable one, it likely requires that nominalists and platonists spell out, in some cognitively significant sense, what questions like "Are there numbers?" mean in a way importantly different from the internal or merely prudential readings.

In facing down this challenge, defenders of the intelligibility of the nominalist–platonist debate can pursue different strategies. They might, for example, attempt to spell out the connection between pragmatic virtues and the truth of theories in a way that carves out conceptual room for substantive external questions. Another option for defending the nominalist–platonist debate recommends that we dig in our heels and reject Carnap's demand for some independent, novel explanation of what the relevant metaphysical questions mean. For, although it would be nice to have a rich account of what questions like "Are there numbers?" mean in the mouths of nominalists and platonists, we have no good reason to believe such questions are more or less substantive than questions about whether there are caribou or cable-knit sweaters. Moreover, we have no compelling reason to believe that these questions are merely prudential. On the contrary, they are about what the world is like and what inhabits it. So, too, are the questions posed when we undertake metaphysics. According to this response, we have no good reason to think that, prior to tackling these questions, some framework-independent account of their content is required. Granting Carnap's initial assumption that such questions are either trivial or merely prudential therefore runs contrary to the substantive status we can reasonably ascribe to questions about what there is. And, absent compelling reason to believe that questions of ontology devolve into

INTRODUCTION

either of Carnap's two readings, we should simply refuse the burden the Carnapian naysayer tries to foist upon us.

Importantly, this unapologetic response to Carnap should not be taken as the suggestion that ontological disagreement is orderly or easily resolved. On the contrary, a recurring moral of this book is that there are few, if any, easy answers to questions about abstract entities. (Cf. Thomasson (2015).) Almost always, the grounds for preferring one metaphysical theory to its rivals are remarkably slim margins of evidence. Even so, this response contends that questions about what exists are in good standing and neither trivially settled nor mere matters of linguistic prudence.

Carnapian naysayers will be unimpressed by the preceding, and rightly so, given that the digging in of heels just suggested falls short of a full-fledged response. But even when we grant that ontological disagreement is substantive, the question still remains of whether the specific debate over abstract entities is defective or empty. If we hold that quantifier expressions like "there is" and ontological vocabulary like "exists" are in good working order, those who disagreement claims like "There are abstract entities" to be defective will try to single out the notion of abstract entity as the troublemaker. Of course, if the notion of abstractness or abstract entity is indeed meaningless or unintelligible, this would be very good reason to think that the nominalist–platonist debate is itself defective. But is it plausible that the notion of an abstract entity is so problematic that the entire nominalist–platonist debate proves to be nonsense?

Probably not. As we'll see later, it is an open question whether the notion of an abstract entity can be adequately defined or is instead an irreducible piece of theoretical vocabulary. But, either way, there is no compelling reason to think it is defective, empty, vague, or otherwise problematic enough to leave disagreement about abstract entities insubstantial. For those who claim that the notion of abstractness can be reductively analyzed—e.g., by taking abstractness to be shorthand for lacking spatiotemporal location or causal powers or whatever—abstractness is problematic only to the extent that the notion to which it is reduced is problematic. Since the latter notions are presumably in good standing, those who seek to reduce the notion of abstractness shouldn't be worried. And, for those who hold that abstractness is a primitive notion, a reasonable application of the principle of charity—roughly, the injunction to treat discourse as rational, absent good evidence to the contrary—requires that we accept the notion of abstractness as an intelligible theoretical concept. To fail to do so is to make an utter mystery of the systematic and complex interactions that fall under the heading of the "nominalist–platonist debate." Moreover, the introduction of predicates "is abstract" and "is concrete" involves a perfectly standard bit of methodology. Examples are supplied in the form of numbers, properties, and propositions. A cluster of characteristic features—e.g., lack of spatiotemporal location or causal inactivity—is provided. Disagreement and deliberation ensues. And, although no (non-tendentious) necessary and sufficient conditions for abstractness are supplied, it is methodologically capricious to demand them here even while we demand them almost nowhere else.

The good news, then, is that there is no compelling reason to think that debates regarding abstract entities are worse off than most other metaphysical debates. The bad news, which has prompted some to lose their nerve about the substantial character of this debate, is that there is a vast horde of competing, overlapping, as well as neither-clearly-competing-nor-overlapping versions of platonism and nominalism. As contemporary versions of nominalism and platonism have multiplied, key points of disagreement have become progressively harder to distinguish and hinge on a host of background assumptions. At the same time, conciliatory versions of nominalism have promised to deliver all the benefits of realism without ontological commitment to abstracta. Conversely, watered-down forms of platonism have tried to dodge the costs that nominalists associate with abstract entities. The result is a rich space of theoretical options but one that resists any broad generalizations or simple taxonomies. As a consequence, it is difficult to say much more about the general nature of abstract entities without extensive qualifications or settling a host of metaphysical questions by fiat. An organizational challenge in what follows is therefore to isolate various arguments and open questions about abstract entities while still offering a useful overview of key issues, arguments, and objections. To this end, it will be helpful to set out the plan for what follows.

§Overview

As an opinionated introduction to the metaphysics of abstract entities, this book has three primary aims. The first aim is to explain the nature and appeal of platonism as a metaphysical thesis. This is undertaken primarily in Chapter 1, which surveys the case for platonism by presenting a host of arguments in defence of abstract entities, and Chapter 2, which examines the nature and significance of the distinction between abstract and concrete entities.

The second aim of this book is to present and assess the case against abstract entities. This inquiry into the merits of nominalism is pursued in Chapters 3 through 6, which are mostly self-contained. Chapter 3 surveys regress arguments as well as appeals to parsimony and paradox sometimes offered in defence of nominalism. Chapter 4 explores arguments involving causation and abstract entities—most notably, epistemological arguments employing causal constraints on knowledge or justification but also Eleatic arguments that claim causal activity as a prerequisite for existence. Chapter 5 focuses on the non-uniqueness problem, which generates worries about arbitrariness and underdetermination for certain versions of platonism. Chapter 6 then examines modal objections to platonism, which find fault with the necessary connections posited between abstract entities. Taken together, these chapters survey the main arguments in favour of nominalism.

The third aim of this book is to provide a helpful overview of nominalist options. To this end, Chapter 7 surveys nominalist proposals, ranging from hard-nosed error theories to more conciliatory metaontological views. Given the vast number of competing nominalist options, this chapter is mostly aimed at orienting readers within a wide terrain of potential views.

As an opinionated introduction, my assessment of the specific arguments surveyed and the cumulative verdict on the nominalist–platonist debate will be partisan. By way of preview, I will suggest that most arguments for nominalism provide rather little reason to worry about abstract entities, but that modal arguments afford a slight advantage to nominalism so long as one accepts a Humean conception of modality. Still more controversially, I will suggest that certain heterodox versions of nominalism—most notably, nominalist possibilism—have rather under-appreciated virtues that warrant their inclusion among the best available nominalist options. Although these are measured assessments and the positive case in their favour is not the primary aim of what follows, they are still departures from full neutrality. That said, the presentation of the arguments and objections throughout this book is representative of fairly standard views in the relevant literature.

Taken together, the aims set out above are far from modest. Each could easily take up a book of its own, so, at various points, sins of omission are committed. Perhaps most notably, rather little attention is given to the nature and merits of Neo-Fregeanism and closely related views about the epistemology and metaphysics of abstraction. This reflects some methodological sympathies of the author, but omissions here are best remedied by reading one of the many exemplary discussions of these approaches.[10] Other regrettable omissions are also necessary—e.g., examination of the metaphysics of fictional characters, agnosticism regarding abstract entities, the metaphysics of structure, and structuralist realist views within the philosophy of science.

It is, I think, a good time to take stock of the nominalist–platonist debate. Currently influential lines of argument in specialized sub-disciplines like the philosophy of mathematics are fairly well trod but only occasionally considered in light of broader metaphysical controversies. Advances in ontology and metaontology have also clarified the finer points of debate over what there is. But, as will become clear, there are still no knockdown arguments to be offered on behalf of platonists or nominalists. A reasoned assessment of the fate of abstract entities therefore requires close and careful consideration of a battery of considerations drawn from diverse domains.

Throughout this book, chapter summaries and additional readings are provided in hopes of pointing the reader towards useful resources that expand upon, inform, or run contrary to the present discussion. These include many canonical resources as well as some less familiar discussions pertinent to the metaphysics of abstract entities. In offering these pointers, I've tried to limit redundancy in recommendations and offer up as wide a range of suggestions as possible. For this reason, some resources recommended in earlier chapters—e.g., general overviews noted just below—are omitted in subsequent recommendations although they are quite profitably consulted regarding specific matters discussed later. Given the style constraints of this series, this book has endnotes rather than footnotes, so, for the readers' convenience, I have tried, whenever possible, to avoid endnotes and to place references in the Recommended Reading sections.

Finally, some quick remarks about terminology. My preference for the terminology of nominalist–platonist (instead of anti-realist–realist, anti-platonist–platonist, or nominalist–anti-nominalist) is mostly aesthetic but partly prudential. After all, there are a lot of realisms out there to keep straight and I see no good way to choose between platonist–anti-platonist and nominalist–anti-nominalist. (The lone exception to this policy is the book's brief conclusion.)

A second terminological matter: in what follows, "entity" will serve as a general metaphysical "catch all," picking out absolutely anything there is, irrespective of its ontological category. On this usage, all objects are entities, but if there are universals or events as well objects, not all entities are objects. This particular terminological choice also accounts for why this book is advertised as an inquiry into abstract entities like universals and sets rather than the narrower category of abstract objects, which includes sets but not universals.

A final point: a nearby debate over the existence of universals rather than the broader class of abstract entities is sometimes referred to as "the nominalist–platonist debate." On this usage, "nominalists" are those who deny there are universals and "platonists" are those committed to the existence of universals.[11] This debate over universals crosscuts the one of present interest, since a commitment to universals is usually held to entail the existence of at least some abstract entities. But, in what follows, this alternative usage of "nominalism" and "platonism" is entirely avoided.[12] A bit more contentiously, I will assume throughout what follows that properties are abstract entities. As we'll see in Chapter 2, this clashes with at least one conception of the distinction on which abstracta are outside of spacetime but universals are, in fact, spatiotemporally located. So, just as much of what follows focuses on austere rather than expansive platonism, the platonism of interest is one that takes properties to be paradigmatic abstracta. Despite room for disagreement here, those who reject this assumption should still find what follows intelligible even if they remain unconvinced.

Summary

In this introduction, we surveyed the general features of the nominalist–platonist debate and offered a preliminary characterization of abstract entities. After explaining the significance of the debate over abstract entities, its historical pedigree was briefly discussed. Objections to the intelligibility of ontological disagreement over abstract entities were then presented along with some methodological assumptions of the discussion to follow. An overview of subsequent chapters was provided.

Recommended reading

Burgess and Rosen (1997) is the preeminent survey of nominalist views about mathematics and includes an excellent overview of the nominalist–platonist debate. A short but very good survey of the debate is provided in Szabó (2003). The *Stanford Encyclopedia of Philosophy* also offers numerous articles, often overlapping in content, which serve as ideal starting points. (The useful entries are too numerous to list here, but Rosen (2014), Balaguer (2015), and Rodriguez-Pereyra (2015) are of particular relevance.) General introductions to metaphysics with useful sections on abstract entities include Jubien (1997), Loux (1998), and Effingham (2013).

There are many useful discussions focused upon specific kinds of abstract entities. On mathematical entities, see Maddy (1990), Lewis (1991), Shapiro (1997), and Balaguer (1998); on universals, see Armstrong (1978), Jubien (1989), Lewis (1983a), Bealer (1982, 1993), van Inwagen (2004); on tropes, see Campbell (1990) and Ehring (2011); on propositions, see Bealer (1998), King et al. (2014), Merricks (2015), Stalnaker (1984); on types, see Wetzel (2009); on fictional entities, see van Inwagen (1977), Thomasson (1999), and Everett (2013); on possible worlds, see Divers (2002), Lewis (1986), Forrest (1986a), Melia (2003), and Plantinga (1974); on facts, see Armstrong (1997) and Olson (1987).

On the history of debate regarding universals, see Normore (1987). On Plato's metaphysics with an eye towards contemporary metaphysics, see Harte (2008). See also Penner (1987), Devereux (1994), Fine (1993), and Nolan (2015). On Frege's views, see Burge (1992), Currie (1982), Dummett (1973), and Wright (1983). On Peirce's views, see Forster (2011).

On Carnap's challenge for ontology and various responses, see Alspector-Kelly (2001), Eklund (2013), and Yablo (1998). For recent discussion of deflationism about ontological disagreement, see Yablo (2005), Hirsch (2009), Hofweber (2009), and Chalmers (2009). On Quinean metaontology, see van Inwagen (2009) and Hylton (2001). On the possibility of substantive ontological disagreement, see Schaffer (2009), Sider (2009), and Bennett (2009). For a partial survey of epistemic stances regarding platonism and nominalism, see Rosen (2001).

Notes

1 This name owes to an historical association with Plato's metaphysics, but, for various reasons, it is contentious whether Plato is a platonist in this contemporary sense. On the connection between Plato's views and (lower-case) platonism, see this chapter's recommended readings.
2 Here and throughout, Pythagoreanism, according to which *only* abstract entities exist, is mostly ignored. On Pythagoreanism in its contemporary guise, see Quine (1976a).
3 This is not to say that properties cannot be divided into physical properties, which are had exclusively or primarily by physical entities, and mental properties, which are had exclusively or primarily by mental entities. After all, a familiar distinction in the philosophy of mind separates mental properties like *being in pain* from physical properties like *having mass*. This familiar

usage of the term "mental property" is perfectly acceptable provided we are not misled into thinking properties themselves to be mind-dependent entities like hallucinations.

4 More accurately, Frege takes the Pythagorean theorem to be a *thought*, where Fregean thoughts are entities naturally taken to be propositions as currently understood. Similar complications arise given Frege's commitment to what he calls "concepts" and "value-ranges," which bear many similarities to more familiar abstract entities like properties and sets. On Frege's views, see this chapter's recommended readings.

5 In what follows, "that"-clauses are used to refer to propositions like *that pigs fly*, though where context is unclear I will sometimes italicize names of propositions. Similarly, I will use italics to distinguish properties like *being human* or *being an electron* or, when appropriate, adopt the convention of using "-ness," "-ity," and "-hood" suffixes to name properties like *humanity* and *electronhood*. Additionally, I will sometimes speak of "numbers" as shorthand for the broader category of mathematical entities, which includes sets, functions, topological spaces, equations, and mathematical entities of any other variety.

6 The case for viewing entities like musical works, novels, and other "repeatable" entities as abstract is controversial, but often concerns the peculiar features that seem to set them apart from ordinary concrete entities. Consider, for example, that no performance of *Happy Birthday* is numerically identical with the work itself, but, despite this, we seem able to hear *Happy Birthday* even if we have listened to only a single one of its vastly many performances. The same goes for someone else who might listen to a numerically different performance. Similar generalizations hold for other apparently "repeatable" entities like dance moves, recipes, and handshakes. It seems, for instance, that one can truly be said to have "done the Twist" without having participated in absolutely every dancing of the Twist.

7 At various points in what follows, talk of facts is assumed to be compatible with nominalism. As we'll see in Chapter 3, this is not the only way to treat talk of facts. For some platonists, facts are abstract entities, which might be identified with true propositions, and are often held to be constructed from or generated by properties and objects.

8 On the metaphysics of artworks as it relates to the abstract–concrete distinction, see Caplan and Matheson (2006) and Mag Uidhir (2013). On competing metaphysical views of species as abstract entities or concrete individuals, see Hull (1976) and Okasha (2001).

9 One sophisticated version of pessimistic naysaying, defended in Balaguer (1998), is specific to the nominalist–platonist debate and denies there is a fact of the matter about whether abstract entities exist, given the evidential equivalence of the best nominalist and platonist options.

10 On Neo-Fregean approaches to the metaphysics of abstract entities, see Hale (1987, 2013), Wright (1983), Dummett (1973, 1991), MacBride (2003), and the essays in Hale and Wright (2003).

11 Since universals are general entities—typically instantiable by many things—and non-universals are particulars, this debate is sometimes taken to concern the reality of *general* entities in addition to *particular* entities. On the ultimate status of the universal–particular distinction, see Ramsey (1925), MacBride (2005a), and Ehring (2011: 19–45).

12 There is an additional usage of "nominalism," courtesy of Goodman (1956), which takes nominalism to be the denial that distinct entities can be constructed or "generated" out of the same basic elements. This far less common usage is avoided throughout what follows. On Goodman's "nominalism," see Goodman (1956), Dummett (1956), Oliver (1993), Hellman (2001a), and Cohnitz and Rossberg (2006).

1

THE CASE FOR PLATONISM

1.1 **Platonism**
1.2 **Semantic arguments**
1.3 **Alethic arguments**
1.4 **Indispensability arguments**
1.5 **Metaphysical explanation**

§1.1 Platonism

Ontological categories like object, event, and property mark the world's most fundamental distinctions. They divide up reality at its highest levels of generality and, according to Plato's well-worn metaphor, carve nature at its deepest joints. A successful metaphysical theory will therefore accurately describe the world's *categoreal structure*—i.e., the nature and number of ontological categories—and, in doing so, provide a full metaphysical inventory of the world. So conceived, the world's categoreal structure fixes which entities, if any, fall within ontological categories like *universal*, *state of affairs*, *event*, *type*, and *proposition*. The status of these ontological categories, in turn, determines the kinds of explanations a metaphysical theory can provide. For example, if there are no propositions, propositions cannot be used to

THE CASE FOR PLATONISM

explain facts about meaning. And, if there are no universals, universals cannot be used to explain facts about resemblance.

Since discerning the world's categoreal structure is a central aim of metaphysics, competing views about categoreal structure abound. These views vary in myriad ways, disagreeing about both the nature and the number of ontological categories. Some views admit only a single ontological category like, say, tropes or facts. Others admit more than one ontological category but disagree over which ones figure into the world's categoreal structure—e.g., while some admit universals or propositions, others do not. Additional disagreements about categoreal structure concern which categories are more or less fundamental and whether certain categories are, in fact, one and the same. For example, much disagreement about the nature of spacetime turns on whether there is a distinctive ontological category of spatiotemporal region separate from categories like material object and relation. In a similar vein, metaphysical disagreement about the nature of minds and persons frequently hinges on whether there is an ontological category of mental substance separate from that of material substance.

The debate between nominalists and platonists is inextricably connected with two ontological categories: abstract entity and concrete entity. This is because platonism asserts, while nominalism denies, that there are entities falling within the former ontological category. For our purposes, it will be useful to divide a commitment to platonism into two "components." The first component is primarily ontological: it posits the existence of entities like numbers, properties, and propositions. The second component is primarily categoreal: it affirms that these entities are abstract rather than concrete.

By distinguishing the ontological and categoreal components of platonism, we can isolate two kinds of disagreements that arise in connection with platonism. The first kind of disagreement concerns platonism's ontological component. Consider, for example, a disagreement over whether propositions exist. Strictly speaking, such a disagreement concerns what exists, not what ontological categories entities belong to. After all, nominalists and platonist can agree that, if there were such things, they would be abstract. As a result, there can be ontological disagreement even in the face of agreement about categoreal matters, since nominalists, unlike platonists, deny the antecedent of such conditionals.[1]

A different kind of disagreement revolves around categoreal structure and, in particular, which entities fall under the category abstract entity. Consider, for example, a radical nominalist view on which numbers exist but are concrete rather than abstract. Taken at face value, this view accepts an ontological thesis endorsed by the overwhelming majority of platonists—namely, that numbers exist. At the same time, this radical nominalist view is in direct categoreal disagreement with the platonist, since only the radical nominalist believes numbers to be concrete. So, unlike an ontological disagreement over whether numbers exist, this disagreement is primarily categorical; it concerns the ontological category of numbers.

There are difficult questions about how to model (much less resolve) these disagreements between (and among) nominalists and platonists. But, by distinguishing these components, we can single out two projects critical for sustaining platonism. The first, ontological project seeks to defend the existence of entities like numbers, properties, and propositions. The second, categoreal project seeks to show that such entities are properly held to be abstract and to explain what distinguishes abstract entities from concrete ones. Since a successful defence of platonism requires the successful completion of each project, arguments against platonism will seek to undermine either one of these projects. On the ontological side of things, nominalists can attempt to show that that entities plausibly viewed as abstract do not, in fact, exist. While, on the categoreal side of things, nominalists might try to show that platonists are mistaken about categoreal structure, since entities claimed to be abstract are, in fact, concrete.

In the next chapter, the categoreal component of platonism is our primary focus. There, the nature of the abstract–concrete distinction is closely scrutinized. This chapter focuses on the ontological component of platonism and surveys arguments for paradigmatic abstract entities. There is no shortage of such arguments and, given their dependence on myriad background assumptions, the distinctions between them are murky at best. For this reason, our aim in outlining these arguments is not to rank their respective merits. Instead, our main aim is to make clear why platonism enjoys widespread support. In our survey, it will be useful to impose a rough taxonomy on these arguments and, in turn, on the ways one might defend platonism. And, while this taxonomy makes no claim to being canonical or exhaustive, most platonist arguments can be located within or across it without too much trouble. Our survey should therefore serve as a handy map of most platonist arguments one is likely to encounter.

To preview: we will divide platonist arguments into four species. Semantic arguments and alethic arguments will be examined in the next two sections. We will then consider indispensability arguments, which appeal to the seemingly indispensable role of abstract entities in our best scientific theories, and arguments from metaphysical explanation, which aim to show that abstract entities are required by our best explanations of "metaphysical" phenomena like resemblance, necessity, and laws.

§1.2 Semantic arguments

Despite the peculiar character of abstract entities, platonism is often claimed to be a commonsensical view well supported by our ordinary standards of judgment. This is likely because many arguments for platonism proceed from the plausible assumption that the following kinds of sentences are true:

(1) Thirteen is a prime number.

(2) Dogs and wolves share many biological properties.

(3) The Pythagorean theorem is uncontroversial.

By ordinary standards, these sentences seem true, and, according to platonists, their truth requires the existence of abstract entities like the number seven, biological properties, and the Pythagorean theorem. The main challenge for would-be platonists consists in spelling out precisely why the truth of these sentences requires the existence of abstract entities. To this end, most platonists seek to provide a plausible method for extracting the *ontological commitments* of these and other apparently true sentences—roughly, what the truth of these sentences requires the existence of—and then show that abstract entities are among these ontological commitments.

In the next section, we will examine alethic arguments, which defend platonism by appeal to theses that connect the truth of sentences with an ontological commitment to abstract entities. Prior to considering alethic arguments, we will begin by examining arguments that proceed from an even weaker initial assumption. These *semantic arguments* merely claim that sentences like (1)–(3) are meaningful and leave open whether these sentences are actually true. In this way, such arguments seek to establish platonism solely by appeal to facts about meaningfulness. As we'll see, these arguments divide into *direct semantic arguments*, which rely on theses that connect meaningfulness and ontology, and *explanatory semantic arguments*, which claim that abstract entities figure in our best explanations of the meaningfulness of these and other sentences.

§1.2.1 *Direct semantic arguments*

Direct semantic arguments take the meaningfulness of sentences like (1)–(3) as their starting point. This is a plausible assumption and made even more plausible by our standard method for characterizing the nominalist–platonist debate. This standard characterization holds that platonists believe sentences like (1)–(3) to be true, while nominalists believe these sentences to be false or somehow misleading. Since false or misleading sentences succeed in *misrepresenting* the world, they must be meaningful and, for this reason, even nominalists seem obliged to grant the meaningfulness of sentences like (1)–(3). The far more controversial part of direct semantic arguments is the move from the meaningfulness of these sentences to the platonist conclusion that there are abstract entities. If successful, direct semantic arguments would therefore show that our very capacity to think and speak about putative abstract entities guarantees such entities exist. Unsurprisingly, however, direct semantic arguments depend upon highly contentious theses about the connection between the meaningfulness of our thought and talk and the entities our thought and talk seems to concern.[2]

Despite some commonalities, there is considerable variation among potential direct semantic arguments. Two key axes of variation are worth noting. First, direct semantic arguments might focus on the meaningfulness of our mental states or, instead, on the meaningfulness of our utterances. Arguments that focus on mental content square well with theories of meaning that assert the primacy of mental content over linguistic content. That said, our particular focus suggests we would do best to sidestep this debate and leave open whether platonists ought to focus on mental content or the content of utterances. To this end, we will help ourselves to some loose terminology and speak about "thought and talk" here and throughout what follows.

Second, direct semantic arguments vary with respect to which semantic "units" are singled out as meaningful. We might focus on the meaningfulness of entire sentences or instead on the meaningfulness of individual expressions like "redness" or "the Pythagorean theorem." Focusing on expressions like proper names or predicates potentially simplifies matters, since the resulting arguments would involve a relatively simple recipe for extracting ontological commitments. For example, we might hold that, for any meaningful proper name, p, the referent of p exists. There is, however, good reason to worry about whether we can successfully isolate the meaning of expressions like proper names or predicates independently of the sentences in which they occur.[3]

Focusing on the meaningfulness of entire sentences would allow us to avoid this concern, but also raises challenges of its own.[4]

A full-scale defence of a direct semantic argument requires fixing upon certain kinds of meaningful expressions and providing a systematic treatment of the tie between their meaningfulness and their ontological commitments. We won't pursue that formidable challenge here. Instead, we can leave open how it might be done and focus on the broader issues raised by direct semantic arguments. With this in mind, consider the following direct semantic argument, which invokes a complete sentence, and seeks to establish the existence of its apparent subject, the number thirteen.

The direct semantic argument

P1. "Thirteen is a prime number" is meaningful.

P2. If "Thirteen is a prime number" is meaningful, then the number thirteen exists.

C1. Therefore, the number thirteen exists.

In the eyes of nominalists and many platonists, this argument attempts to somehow pull a metaphysical rabbit out of a purely semantic hat. Its peculiarity owes largely to the implicit principle linking meaning and ontology that motivates P2. Roughly speaking, such a principle asserts that meaningful thought and talk about a putative entity is possible only if that entity exists. If true, this principle renders ontological questions remarkably easy to answer. We simply need to run through sentences involving contentious posits and assess whether they are meaningful. If they are meaningful, we can safely conclude the entities in question exist. For this reason, direct semantic arguments provide a readymade strategy for defending a staggering range of contentious posits. We are able to think and speak meaningfully of aliens, Atlantis, Ares, Aquaman, and the Fountain of Youth. So, if the direct semantic argument is sound, the existence of these contentious entities is easy enough to demonstrate. In this way, our very capacity to describe or misdescribe the world provides a means for settling profoundly difficult questions about what there is. This result should trouble anyone who takes ontological questions to be non-trivial.

Proponents of the direct semantic argument will be quick to note that arguments like the one above leave the nature and ontological category of entities almost entirely unsettled. For, while these arguments do require the existence of the entities about which we can meaningfully speak and think, they do not entail that the entities in question are concrete rather than abstract, actual rather than merely possible, or that such entities have any especially interesting features. Proponents of direct semantic arguments might therefore claim that, while the Fountain of Youth exists, it is not, in fact, a fountain, magical, or anything more than a featureless abstract entity.[5] Despite this important concession, the direct semantic argument comes with sweeping metaphysical consequences. Given quite modest assumptions about which sentences are meaningful, it yields a vast wealth of ontological commitments. And, since entities like Aquaman and the Fountain of Youth are not plausibly held to be concrete, it almost certainly leads to the swift and immediate overpopulation of the abstract realm.

Explaining where direct semantic arguments go wrong is harder than voicing one's righteous and profound conviction that they are unsound. But, among their more objectionable consequences is the fact that, if sound, they foreclose the very possibility of overestimating what there is. For, provided that one can meaningfully think or say that a is F, the existence of a is thereby guaranteed. This runs contrary to the common conviction that failed theoretical posits like phlogiston, miasmas, and Atlantis simply do not exist. In a similar vein, since direct semantic arguments affirm the dependence of meaningfulness on the existence of subject matters, they seem to impose a bizarre necessary connection between two separate domains: what there is and what we can represent. This proposed connection is surely more controversial than platonism itself, since it requires belief in a vaguely magical correspondence between facts about ontology and facts about meaning. And, if our pre-theoretic intuitions count for anything, we have reason to reject any view which takes our mere capacity to represent the Fountain of Youth in thought or talk to settle whether it exists. In ruling out our capacity to overestimate what there is, the direct semantic argument seems flatly mistaken about the metaphysical demands that meaningfulness places on the world.[6] And, since the principles required to get the direct semantic argument off the ground are markedly less plausible than platonism itself, platonists must look elsewhere for a convincing semantic argument.

§1.2.2 Explanatory semantic arguments

The strongest semantic arguments for platonism retain the meaningfulness of our thought and talk as a starting point, but defend abstract entities by way of an abductive argument or an "inference to the best explanation." Like other abductive arguments, these *explanatory semantic arguments* seek to show that a given explanation of some phenomena—in this case, meaningfulness—is the best available and, in light of its explanatory credentials, conclude that the proposed explanation is true (or at least very probably so). Since the proposed explanations invoke abstract entities, the superiority of these explanations is held to establish platonism. Unlike direct semantic arguments, these explanatory semantic arguments do not seek to show that we must believe in the apparent subject matter of meaningful claims. Instead, the explanatory arguments contend that the best *general* explanation of the meaningfulness of claims requires that there are abstract entities. This section examines two such arguments: one for propositions and another for properties.

The first of these arguments—the explanatory semantic argument for propositions—was presented in rough outline in the introduction. There, we introduced propositions by detailing some of the theoretical roles they are typically held to play. Most notably, propositions are thought to serve as the objects of psychological attitudes like belief and desire. So, if you believe that spies sleep lightly, you bear the relation *believes* to a mind-independent abstract proposition, *that spies sleep lightly*.[7] Propositions are also thought to serve as the semantic content of ordinary declarative sentences. For instance, a sentence of English like "Obama presides" is held to express the extra-linguistic abstract entity *that Obama presides*. If propositions are indeed the semantic contents of such sentences, they are the entities that come closest to answering to our ordinary notion of the "meaning" of a sentence.

This straightforward explanation of the meaningfulness of sentences dovetails with an equally straightforward explanation of how sentences bear their truth-values: propositions are the primary bearers of truth-values and sentences inherit their truth-value from the propositions they express. For example, the proposition *that spies sleep lightly* has the property *being true* if the world is a certain way—namely, such that spies do sleep lightly—and lacks this property otherwise.[8] In turn, the sentence, "Spies sleep lightly," is true (or false) in virtue of whether the proposition *that spies sleep lightly* is true (or false).

Platonists implicate propositions in a diverse range of semantic explanations. But, for those who hope to avoid commitment to propositions, it is tempting to believe that they can be dispensed with somehow. A natural thought in this regard is that we might be able to get by with merely a commitment to sentences. Unfortunately for nominalists, it looks as though sentences are incapable of playing the key theoretical roles assigned to propositions. This is clearest when we consider semantic phenomena like translation. Intuitively, speakers of different languages are perfectly capable of believing and saying the very same things even while using words and sentences drawn from different languages. If, however, the objects of our attitudes and contents of our utterances are identified with sentences of specific languages, our capacity to believe and say the same things in different languages seems inexplicable.[9] But, once granted the apparatus of propositions, sentences of different languages can be held to have the same meaning in virtue of expressing the very same language-independent proposition. In this way, propositions provide an elegant explanation of translation: French-speaking Ben and English-speaking Carl each believe the same language-independent proposition, *that the canal is frozen*, in virtue of bearing relations to sentences in their own respective languages. Translation is therefore a matter of fixing upon the sentences of different languages that express the same propositions.

Along with semantic phenomena, propositions also provide platonists with the resources to explain certain platitudes about truth. For example, it seems that some truths obtained prior to the advent of thought or language and that truths would obtain in worlds without thinkers or speakers. It also seems that some truths, perhaps on account of their complexity, cannot be expressed within any language. Views that identify meanings with concrete entities like inscriptions, sounds, or mental states face serious challenges in upholding such platitudes. In contrast, platonists are ideally positioned to explain how there might be truths in the absence of thinkers and speakers or truths that are inexpressible in languages. In each case, such explanations naturally draw upon a realm of mind-independent, eternal, and necessarily existing propositions.[10]

Sentences are generally thought to be inadequate surrogates for propositions, but it is worth noting that certain appeals to sentences also run contrary to the requirements of nominalism. This is because *sentence types* like "Socrates is mortal" are repeatable entities with various instances scattered through books and conversations and spread across time and space. In contrast, *sentence tokens*—e.g., this particular pattern of black on this very page or a specific puttering of vibrations in the air—are perfectly ordinary concrete entities. So, depending upon one's view of types, sentence types are either properties or entities sufficiently similar to worry would-be nominalists. Unlike appeals to sentence tokens, appeals to sentence types therefore come with an implicit commitment to abstracta. For many platonists, this provides good reason to believe that, in serious theorizing about language, any viable approach requires at least some abstract entities. As Church (1951: 104) remarks, after describing his platonist view of propositions: "To those who find forbidding the array of abstract entities and principles concerning them which is here proposed, I would say that the problems which give rise to the proposal are difficult and a simpler theory is not known to be possible."

Given the explanatory riches that come with propositions, the abductive argument in their favour is a powerful one. Even so, it is not the most influential explanatory semantic argument. That honour goes to the One over Many argument. (On some interpretations, the One over Many argument concerns the nature of resemblance rather than meaning. We'll consider arguments of that sort below.) When understood as an explanatory semantic argument, the One over Many argument aims to show that properties are needed for our best explanation of predication, where predication is a cognitive activity that underwrites the meaningfulness of our thought and talk. When we say, for example, that Xanthippe is wise, a property-driven explanation holds that there is a property, *being wise*, that we predicate of Xanthippe. In perhaps its most famous incarnation, Aristotle attributes this argument to Plato, as Alexander of Aphrodisias reports:

> If each of the many men is [a] man, and each of the many animals [an] animal, and similarly in the other cases; and if in the case of each something is not predicated of itself, but there is something which is predicated of all of them, and is not the same as any of them, then there must be something besides the particulars which is separated from them and eternal. For it is always predicated in the same way of the succession of numerically different particulars. But what is a one over many, separated from them, and eternal is an idea. Therefore there are ideas.
>
> Fine (1980: 199)

Setting aside interpretive debate, this passage can be read as an argument that, in order to explain predication, we must posit entities distinct from but predicable of particulars. (Here, "Ideas" are taken to be properties, not mental particulars in the familiar sense of "idea.") But, since these predicable entities are eternal and "separate from particulars," they must be radically different from particulars and so are properly viewed as Platonic forms or, in their contemporary guise, abstract universals.

Presented with this argument, one nominalist response claims that it merely establishes that there are linguistic entities like the predicate "is wise." Note, however, that the notion of predication intended here is supposed to be independent of both any particular language and of predicates *qua* bits of language.[11] Unlike predicates, the "Ideas" predicated of entities are claimed to be eternal, not created. Moreover, we seem able to use different languages to predicate the very same entity of things. We might, for example, predicate the same universal—*wisdom*, say—of some particulars whether using English or Cantonese. So, while the activity of predication might involve linguistic items like predicates, it is the entities that we predicate via these linguistic items that are alleged to be eternal, extra-linguistic abstract entities.

The force of this argument depends on the role we take predication to play in our thought and talk. After all, the task of explaining predication is a pressing one only if there is good reason to believe that predication is a distinctive or foundational part of our best semantic theory. Understandably, this is controversial. In large part, it turns on whether our best semantic theory appeals to the notion of predication or instead some more fundamental semantic notions—e.g., the notion of function application in contemporary semantics. For this reason, contemporary defenders of explanatory semantic arguments for properties typically pursue the general strategy of the One over Many argument by focusing, not on the distinctive activity of predication, but on how to best explain the meaningfulness of predicates. And, just as the explanatory semantic argument above takes propositions to figure into our best semantic explanations, contemporary incarnations of the One over Many argument hold that properties supply us with the best explanation of the meaningfulness of predicates.[12]

On most platonist semantic theories, predicates like "is human" are held to *express* properties like *being human*. In this way, properties serve as the meanings or "semantic values" of predicates. This sets the stage for a straightforward explanation of the meaning and truth of subject-predicate sentences like "Gus is a polar bear." The truth-value of such sentences is determined by whether or not the property—in this case, *being a polar bear*—expressed by the predicate, "is a polar bear," is *instantiated* by or "true of" the subject of the sentence—namely, Gus. In a similar vein, the meaning of sentences like "Redness is more like orange than blue" seem most naturally explained by taking the relevant expressions to refer to properties like *redness* and *blueness*. A commitment to properties therefore supplies us with a powerful resource for explaining the meaningfulness of much of what we say and think. At the same time, this commitment raises the critical question: what exactly are properties?

Since we will return to concerns about properties throughout this book, it will be useful here to distinguish among three leading views about the nature of properties. These views differ with respect to the ontological category they assign properties, but, in each case, properties are held to fall within the category *abstract entity*.[13]

According to *universal theory*, properties are universals. Intuitively, such entities are the "one over the many," since a single universal is held to be instantiable by a plurality of entities. The universal *humanity* is held to be instantiated by Obama, Trudeau, and billions of other humans and it is in virtue of instantiating humanity that these entities are human. Beyond this schematic characterization, there is little that is uncontroversial about universals. As we'll discuss in Chapter 2, some hold that universals are "transcendent" or *ante rem* entities, existing outside of spacetime; others hold that universals are "immanent" or *in re* entities, wholly located wherever instantiated.

Where universal theory holds a property like *humanity* to be a single entity shared by many particulars, *trope theory* denies there is a numerically identical entity common to all humans. There is instead a plurality of particular property instances or *tropes*; one for each human. According to trope theory, our talk of "humanity" is really shorthand for talk of the plurality of particular *humanity* tropes, where resemblance or some other relation unites these tropes together as a common kind.[14] For trope theorists, our thought and talk about properties is ultimately analyzable in terms of collections of particularized property instances like the *redness of this very shirt* or the *bitterness of this very drop of coffee*.

According to set-theoretic views, properties are sets.[15] We will spend much of Chapter 5 discussing such entities. Here, we need only note that sets are abstract collections. So, according to the set-theoretic view, a property like *humanity* is just the set of all humans.[16] Just as sets are commonly held to provide a metaphysical and conceptual foundation for mathematics, defenders of the set-theoretic view claim that sets are suited to serve as properties and, in particular, as the semantic values of predicates. Among other things, this means that there are *impure sets*, which have concrete entities like Socrates as members (or members of members and so on). These include singleton sets such as {Socrates} with exactly one member. There are also *pure sets* such as {{∅}} and {∅, {{∅}}}, which have no non-sets as members (or members of members and so on), and are constructed from the empty set, $\emptyset$.[17]

The explanatory semantic argument for properties is largely neutral between universal, trope, and set-theoretic views, but it does require taking sides in one critical debate regarding the nature of properties. This debate concerns the "abundance" of properties. For, if properties are to serve as the semantic values of all predicates, then, for any given predicate, there must be some property that predicate expresses no matter how complex, bizarre, or unfamiliar it may be. (An allegedly principled exception: predicates that generate paradoxes—e.g., "is non-self-membered" or "is non-self-instantiating"—are commonly held to express no properties.) The proposed platonist explanation of the meaningfulness of predicates therefore requires the existence of "gerrymandered" properties like *being a bucket or a goat* alongside more familiar properties like *wisdom* and *being human*.

Abundant conceptions of properties are in opposition with "sparse" conceptions, according to which only certain privileged predicates express properties—e.g., those like "is an electron," drawn from our best physical theories. And, since those who reject the abundant conception deny there are properties expressed by predicates like "is a donkey or a wet cat", they must deny that the stock of properties mirrors the vast array of meaningful predicates. Instead, which properties exist is reflected in facts about which predicates figure into the laws of physics or in metaphysical explanations. Opponents of the abundant conception are therefore in no position to offer an explanatory semantic argument for properties. Consequently, explanatory semantic arguments square poorly with trope theory and versions of universal theory that posit only sparse properties. (Typically, views like *in re* universal theory and trope theory typically reject the abundant conception, since such views seem to implausibly require holding properties like *being a bucket or a goat* to be constituents or parts of individuals.)

We've now outlined the leading views about the nature of properties and spelled out their role in the explanatory semantic argument. How, then, should nominalists address the explanatory semantic argument? I take the strongest nominalist response to be one that finds fault with the explanatory ambitions of the platonist. According to this response, the meaningfulness of predicates does not require positing properties to serve as semantic values. Instead, the meaningfulness of predicates is a kind of explanatory ground floor, resisting further explanation in terms of additional ontology. Quine (1948: 29) sketches this line of response as follows:

> The words "houses", "roses", and "sunsets" are true of sundry individual entities which are houses and roses and sunsets, and the word "red" or "red object" is true of each of sundry individuals entities which are red houses, red roses, red sunsets; but there is not, in addition, any entity whatever, individual or otherwise, which is named by the word "redness", nor, for that matter, by the word "householhood", "rosehood", "sunsethood". That the houses and roses and sunsets are all of them red may be taken as ultimate and irreducible, and it may be held that [the platonist who posits properties] is no better off, in point of real explanatory power, for all the occult entities which he posits under such names as "redness".

This Quinean response disavows properties, while granting that predicates are meaningful. (Colourfully enough, nominalists who opt for this Quinean response are pejoratively labelled as "ostrich nominalists" for burying their heads in the metaphysical sand.[18]) But, while the nominalist who sides with Quine denies that the meaningfulness of predicates requires additional ontological commitments, she concedes that undefined or "primitive" predicates do contribute to the overall commitments of a theory. In particular, the primitive predicates that figure into a theory determine the ideology of that theory. To see what this means, we need to clarify the relevant notion of ideology. And, since the distinction between ontology and ideology will recur throughout this book, it will be useful to say a bit more about it here.

As Quine takes pains to point out, theories that furnish us with explanations are not exhausted by their ontological commitments. They also require ideological commitments, which Quine (1951: 14) describes as follows:

> Given a theory, one philosophically interesting aspect of it into which we can inquire is its ontology: what entities are the variables of quantification to range over if the theory is to hold true? Another no less important aspect into which we can inquire is its ideology (this seems the inevitable word, despite unwanted connotations): what ideas can be expressed in it? ... It is clearer, I think, to recognize in ontology and ideology two distinct domains of inquiry.

The ideology of a theory, whether in the form of predicates or operators, determines its representational power. In the broadest sense, any concepts or claims expressible within a theory are part of its ideology. In a narrower sense, ideology concerns only *primitive* notions, which are those predicates or operators that resist definition in terms of other concepts.[19] This narrow sense, which will be the one relevant for most of what follows, is typically of greater interest than the broader sense. This is because only primitive ideology comes at a cost to theories, since non-primitive ideology admits of definition in terms of primitive ideology and therefore "comes for free" once granted the relevant primitives. We can, for example, define the material conditional by way of negation and disjunction, so, granted the latter primitives, the former is readily analyzed and so not required as an additional bit of ideology. These connections of definability and analysis typically make for good theories: an explanatorily fecund theory that invokes only a small number of primitives is, other things being equal, superior to a similar theory that invokes a host of undefined notions all of which resist further analysis. There is therefore *prima facie* reason to avoid gratuitous ideology and pursue ideological parsimony. (More on this in Chapter 3.) For this reason, the key questions about the ideological commitments of a theory are questions about what *primitive* ideology it requires. But what exactly is the metaphysical status of primitive ideology?

For Quine, ideology is a matter of psychology, since the ideology of a theory concerns the particular mental items possessed by individuals who deploy a theory. In contrast, Sider (2011), following Lewis (1986), defends a view on which ideology is not a subjective matter but, instead, an objective concern that is indispensable for inquiry into the structure of reality. On this objective conception of ideology, ideology is no less a part of the world's metaphysical structure than ontology. Metaphysical inquiry therefore aims to provide a kind of match between the ontology and ideology of our best theories and the ontological and ideological structure of the world.

The objectivity of ideology is perhaps easiest to capture by considering a dispute like the one between *modal eliminativists*—those who deny there are modal facts—and *modalists*—those who hold that irreducible modal operators like the box ($\Box$necessarily) and diamond ($\Diamond$possibly) are needed to describe the world.[20] Modal eliminativists and modalists might be in perfect ontological agreement about what there is. Nevertheless, they starkly disagree about the ideological structure of reality, because the eliminativist, unlike the modalist, denies any truths are necessary or contingent. Put differently: while the modalist accepts that primitive modal ideology is a part of the world's structure, the eliminativist denies that the structure of world has any modal component and so denies we require the $\Box$ and $\Diamond$ to state any truths about the world. Crucially, this disagreement does not depend upon any facts about individual psychology or the meanings of theories. It is a substantive disagreement that persists even in the face of ontological agreement and, in this way, nicely illustrates how ideological commitments might be just as objective as ontological ones. Throughout this book, I assume the objectivity of ideology. Accordingly, I will typically use "ideology" in the narrow sense that applies only to the primitives (e.g., predicates or operators) of a theory, which are objective yet non-ontological aspects of the world's metaphysical structure.

For those who endorse the Quinean response to the explanatory semantic argument, making sense of predication comes at an ideological cost but requires no further ontological commitment. Such a view is in rough analogy with the modalist view, which takes modal operators as primitive and so incurs ideological costs without ontological ones. In marked contrast, platonist theories of properties absorb a considerable ontological commitment to properties and perhaps a small stock of property-related ideology (e.g., a primitive predicate like "instantiates").

The explanatory semantic argument for properties faces its stiffest opposition from those who deny ontology is required or recommended for explaining meaningfulness. The merits of this opposition largely depend on the coherence and qualifications of the Quinean view that expands ideology to make sense of meaningful predicates. For this reason, the ultimate fate of this argument turns on careful evaluation of the ideology-driven metaphysics of nominalism and, in particular, whether we ought to prefer minimal ontologies over minimal ideologies. We'll return to this issue in Chapter 3. For now, we can turn to alethic arguments, which are concerned with the truth of our ordinary (and not-so-ordinary) claims rather than merely their meaningfulness.

§1.3 Alethic arguments

In this section, we will consider arguments for platonism that proceed from the assumed truth of sentences like (1)–(3), which requires a commitment to platonism. While this might seem rather obvious, the specifics matter greatly here, since any platonist that pursues this strategy owes some account of how to extract ontological commitments from true sentences. Among other things, any proposed recipe for extracting ontological commitments will have wide-ranging consequences for the kinds of abstract entities platonists end up positing. To this end, we'll consider three different kinds of alethic arguments: Quinean arguments, Fregean arguments, and truthmaker arguments. As we'll see, each of these offers a somewhat different route for defending platonism on the basis of the truth of sentences like (1)–(3).

§1.3.1 The Quinean alethic argument

To see how the Quinean argument works, we first need to introduce the central features of Quine's view of ontology and ontological commitment. Since many of these features enjoy the status of orthodoxy and are assumed throughout much of this book, an overview of Quine's conception of ontology is also useful for our purposes.

The Quinean view of ontological commitment holds our ordinary discourse to be a questionable guide to what there is. For Quine (1981a: 9), "[o]ntological concern is not a correction of a lay thought and practice; it is foreign to the lay culture, though an outgrowth of it." So, while our best scientific theories do aim to discern what exists, it is the business of ontology to ensure that these theories are properly regimented in order to determine their genuine ontological commitments. In light of its simplicity and other virtues, Quine claims that the correct language for regimentation is first-order predicate logic with identity. As Quine (1968b: 112) puts it: "Classical quantification theory enjoys an extraordinary combination of depth and simplicity, beauty and utility. It is bright within and bold in its boundaries." So, only after translating our best physical theories into first-order logic can we determine what entities they are committed to. In particular, Quine takes the ontological commitments of a theory to consist in all and only those entities its quantifiers must range over in order to be true.[21] Expanding on the familiar slogan: for Quine, to be is to be the value of a bound variable that occurs in a true and properly regimented sentence.[22]

Quine's focus on quantification as a guide to ontology is bound up with his now-orthodox view about the connection between quantification and existence. This view holds that quantifier expressions like "there is" and claims about what exists are each properly interpreted in terms of the existential quantifier of first-order logic. On the resulting view, the claims "There is an F" or "An F exists" are more or less notational variants of one another. Each is properly regimented within first-order logic as "$\exists x Fx$" and any theory regimented in this way is ontologically committed to at least one F. As a result, to say that Fs exist is just to say that there are Fs and vice versa.

Quine's view of the relationship between quantification and existence is commonly held but not universally accepted. Most famously, it conflicts with Meinongian views on which quantification and existence can come apart.[23] For Meinongians, nonexistent entities are perfectly admissible values of bound variables, so no contradiction results from claiming that there are round squares, but that round squares do not exist. Meinongians therefore admit a vast realm of entities over which we can quantify, but hold that only a select few of these entities exist. For example, Meinong himself claims that there is a golden mountain, but that no golden mountain exists.

In the eyes of a Quinean, this Meinongian doubletalk leads to immediate and outright contradiction. Throughout this book we will side with Quine and against Meinong. In doing so, we will simply assume the interchangeability of claims about what *exists* and what *there is*. This requires us to take sides in a foundational debate about the nature of ontology. It would therefore be nice to have especially compelling reasons for doing so, but the case against Meinongianism is, I think, somewhat inconclusive.[24] Fortunately, we are justified in ignoring Meinongianism here largely because it is of no real help to nominalists. For one thing, it is unclear how to transpose nominalism into the Meinongian framework. Is it a claim about what there is or a claim about what exists? And, while we'll briefly return to this point in Chapter 7, we can set aside Meinongianism for the time being.

The final feature of the Quinean conception of ontology is a requirement that singular terms like "Obama" and definite descriptions like "the tallest man" be analyzed away in terms of first-order quantifiers. So, when assessing the ontology of a theory, any names are to be replaced with the bound variables that carry ontological commitment. In this respect, Quine sides with Russell's Theory of Descriptions by eliminating names, whether referring or non-referring, through careful deployment of the quantifiers of first-order logic.[25] The result, for Quine, is that ontological commitment is exhaustively determined, not by what entities names refer to, but solely by the values of the bound variables that occur with the canonical regimentation of the theory.

To see the Quinean conception of ontology in action, let us assume the following sentence is part of a physical theory we believe to be true:

(4) Sparky is a proton.

The first step in the Quinean procedure is to properly regiment (4) in order to determine its ontological commitments. (4) is therefore translated into first-order logic and the name "Sparky" is eliminated by introducing the (somewhat spurious) predicate "S" (read as "Sparky-izes") along with the predicate "P" (read as "is a proton"). The former predicate allows us to dispense with the name, "Sparky." Canonically regimented, (4) now runs as follows:

(4*) ∃x(Sx∧Px)

Regimented in this way, (4*) is true if and only if there is something that is a proton and Sparky-izes. And, since (4*) is part of the proper regimentation of our best theory, we are thereby ontologically committed to the proton in question.

According to the Quinean, we can employ the above procedure to show that we are also ontologically committed to abstract entities, since sentences like (1)–(3) are true. Consider, once again, the following sentence:

(1) Thirteen is a prime number.

Regimented in Quinean terms, (1) holds that there is some entity to which the predicates "N" (read: "is a prime number") and "T" (read: "thirteen-izes") apply.

(1*) ∃x(Nx∧Tx)

For Quineans, (1*) requires ontological commitment to something that is a prime number. So, in accepting the truth of (1), we take on a commitment to numbers. And, since such entities are standardly held to be abstract, platonism is a near-immediate consequence. The Quinean alethic argument can now be put more explicitly as follows:

The Quinean alethic argument

P1. (1) is true.

P2. If (1) is true, then there is something that is a prime number.

P3. If there is something that is a prime number, then numbers exist.

C1. Therefore, numbers exist.

The distinctive feature of the Quinean alethic argument is its rationale for P2, which issues from the Quinean conception of ontology just outlined. Granted this conception, the truth of sentences like (1) requires the existence of numbers and, given standard assumptions about the ontological category of *abstract entity*, platonism is all but unavoidable.

While we just saw how a Quinean might argue from the truth of (1) to the truth of platonism, it is noteworthy that Quine himself rejects a commitment to properties or propositions. This owes to Quine's views about the nature of meaning and his rejection of "intensional entities" such as universals and propositions.[26] Despite Quine's own views, the Quinean alethic argument does provide a recipe for defending the existence of abstracta like universals, propositions, and possibilities. The resulting arguments involve a fairly straightforward regimentation of claims like (2) and (3) which requires quantification over properties, propositions, and possibilities. Additional support for these commitments is commonly offered by pointing out that no nominalist paraphrase of sentences like "Redness is more like orange than green" seems readily available. In a similar vein, the truth of claims like "There are shapes that are never exemplified" or "There are possibilities that do not actually obtain" seems to require quantification over properties or possibilities.[27] For Quine and others who seek to avoid these particular commitments, such claims must either be denied or, instead, regimented in a way that preserves some of their content without allowing quantification over properties and possibilities. Success in this regard would be a clear indication that sentences of ordinary language need not wear their genuine ontological commitments on their sleeves. In any case, it raises the difficult issue of whether and to what extent ordinary judgments about meaning, truth, and commitment are suitable guides to ontology.

§1.3.2 *The Fregean alethic argument*

The Quinean alethic argument hinges on theses about quantification, but not all views of ontological commitment proceed along these lines. As a result, not all alethic arguments require a detour through quantification. In this section, we will briefly survey an alternative alethic argument roughly associated with Frege and certain Neo-Fregeans. Implementations of this argument differ in formulation and emphasis, but share a common commitment to taking certain syntactic and semantic facts as the proper guides to ontological commitment. And, given these guides, they take the truth of seemingly ordinary claims to entail platonism.

While the Quinean alethic argument dispenses with proper names when regimenting theories to determine what exists, the Fregean alethic argument takes the semantic function of names and other singular terms to play a key role in ontology. This traces back to Fregean theses regarding the relation between semantico-syntactic categories like *singular term* and ontological categories. On the Fregean view, if an expression functions as a singular term in a sentence, then, if the sentence is true, the expression refers to an object. (Frege's Context Principle denies the meaning of a word can be given in isolation from a sentence, so questions about the meaning of an expression are sensible only insofar as they concern the meaning of an expression in a sentence.) So, once we've determined that an expression functions as a singular term in a given true sentence, there is no further question about whether it *really* refers to an object. In this way, we can settle ontological issues by attending to facts about the semantic function of the various parts of true sentences.

The Fregean alethic argument takes the syntactic structure and semantics of true sentences as a guide to our ontological commitments. In doing so, it rules out any view on which "thirteen" functions as a singular term in sentences like (1) but on which there is no object, thirteen. In fact, Frege and other Neo-Fregeans typically hold the notion of an object to be inseparable from the notion of a singular term: objects are just those things that singular terms are capable of referring to. In contrast to the Quinean view, we cannot simply regiment away reference to the number thirteen, if we take (1) to be true.

So, while the Quinean conception of ontology permits us considerable latitude in regimenting true sentences in order to discern their genuine ontological commitments, the Fregean takes the truth of sentences like (1) to guarantee existence of abstract entities. We can present the Fregean alethic argument as follows:

The Fregean alethic argument

P1. (1) is true.

P2. In (1), "thirteen" functions as a singular term.

P3. If something functions as a singular term in a true sentence, then it refers to an object

C1. Therefore, the number thirteen exists.

Along with alethic arguments for abstracta like numbers, similar arguments can be offered for other kinds of abstract entities. For example, Frege's preferred semantic theory can, by parallel reasoning, deliver an argument for Fregean *concepts* (again, entities very close to properties) and for Fregean *thoughts* (again, entities very close to propositions). This is because Frege takes predicates like "is human" to have a distinctive semantic function tied specifically to concepts and Frege's preferred semantics of attitude reports (e.g., "Hans believes that pigs fly") also requires reference to thoughts.

In each case, the semantic features of certain linguistic expressions, when coupled with the truth of certain sentences, carry a commitment to abstracta. And, even if one balks at the Fregean semantic picture, the alethic argument above provides a direct way to defend the existence of numbers on the strength of fairly intuitive assumptions about the nature of singular terms.

The Fregean alethic argument is likely to generate a far richer ontology of abstract entities than its Quinean rival. For, if we take claims about dance moves, GDPs, directions, and symphonies to be true, such entities would seem to be commitments alongside properties, propositions, and mathematical entities. And, since we typically take sentences like "The Watusi is a dance" to be true, a commitment to the Fregean alethic argument points towards an expansive rather than austere version of platonism. Fregeans who would prefer an austere rather than expansive ontology will therefore be forced to deny the truth of the relevant sentences regarding dance moves and sonatas, since the Fregean alethic argument takes a commitment to abstract entities to be required only given the truth of the relevant sentences.

Fregean and Quineans disagree about how sentences mandate platonism, but they each make good on the intuitive thought that the truth of certain claims makes ontological demands of the world—namely, that numbers and other abstracta exist. But, as we'll now see, there is an additional option for advancing alethic arguments, which appeals to the decidedly metaphysical notion of a "truthmaker."

§1.3.3 *The truthmaker argument*

The truthmaker version of the alethic argument departs from the Quinean and Fregean arguments. Where those arguments appeal to semantic and syntactic features of sentences like (1)–(3), the truthmaker argument appeals to the metaphysical thesis that each truth has a *truthmaker*: an entity that necessitates or is somehow sufficient to guarantee its truth. So, in mounting a case for platonism, the truthmaker theorist holds either that sentences like (1)–(3) require abstract entities as their truthmakers or that truthmaking in general requires a commitment to abstracta.

The notion of a truthmaker is part and parcel of truthmaker theory, which is itself a distinctive view about the proper method for ontological inquiry. For the truthmaker theorist, each and every truth must be properly "grounded in reality" by virtue of having one or more truthmakers. Methodologically, truthmaker theory stands in stark and pointed opposition to theories that involve "ontological cheats"—i.e., theories that include truths not grounded in what exists. A staple example of the ontological cheater is the unrepentant presentist who holds that only presently existing entities exist, but still affirms truths about past and future entities while providing no account of what grounds such truths. Such a view runs contrary to the demand that truthmakers be supplied for each and every truth. So, absent some account of which entities ground truths about past and future entities, truthmaker theorists will dismiss unrepentant presentism as untenable: there can be no truths that "float free" of what there is.

Variations on truthmaker theory are numerous. And, on some versions, a commitment to abstract entities is built into the theory itself. This is because many versions of truthmaker theory claim that the crucial truthmaking relation holds between propositions (the things "made true"), which are paradigmatic abstracta, and states of affairs (the truthmakers), which are held to be abstract complexes of objects and properties. The need for states of affairs—conceived of as special abstract entities—owes to the observation that neither Socrates nor the property *being short* are suitable truthmakers for the claim that Socrates is short. After all, both of these entities could exist without Socrates being short—e.g., if Socrates is tall and Crito is short. It looks, then, like only a complex state of affairs, built up out of Socrates and *being short*, guarantees the truth of Socrates being short. It is therefore the only viable candidate for being the truthmaker of the claim in question. And, since states of affairs are abstract complexes built up partly out of properties, any truthmaker theory that invokes such entities is, by its very nature, incompatible with nominalism.

There is something intuitively compelling about the ambitions of truthmaker theory. Despite this, I know of no satisfactory way to develop a full-fledged truthmaker theory without recourse to abstract entities. (In some rare cases, concrete entities do suffice as truthmakers—e.g., Socrates is an adequate truthmaker for the bare existential "Socrates exists.") For diehard truthmaker theorists, this will suggest a kind of transcendental argument for abstract entities: the very nature of truth and ontology requires the apparatus of abstract entities. But, for those of us not already in the grip of truthmaker theory, a more promising alethic argument for platonism will proceed by showing that truths like (1)–(3) require a commitment to abstract ontology. To see how such an argument might go, let's briefly set aside the implicit appeal to abstracta that truthmaker theory requires and simply assume that a nominalist version of truthmaker theory is available.

Now, consider, once again, sentence (1), according to which thirteen is a prime number. At first glance, this has a rather obvious truthmaker:

thirteen. And, if thirteen is the truthmaker for (1), platonism follows. Notice, however, that truthmaking, as glossed above, requires only that we provide some entity that necessitates the truth of the claim in question. And, since (1) is a necessary truth, absolutely any entity is such that, necessarily, if it exists, then (1) is true. Should the nominalist therefore be delighted, since she can take any old concrete entity to serve as the truthmaker for (1) (and any other necessary truth)? Not by a long shot. Not only are there many contingent claims about abstract entities that still require truthmakers (e.g., that there are fewer dogs than prime numbers), such a view betrays an unwritten rule of truthmaking: truthmakers necessitate the truth of the claims they make true, but they must also be *about* those truths in some rough sense. A truthmaker theory that assigns (1) the same truthmaker as the claim that there are no round squares will therefore be untenable in virtue of betraying any intuitions regarding what the relevant truths are about.

Faced with these difficulties, the most promising strategy for truthmaker theorists is to take truthmakers to be those entities that claims are "grounded in" or those upon which they "metaphysically depend." This relation of metaphysical dependence is more fine-grained than that of necessitation and has a plausible chance of capturing our judgments of aboutness. It seems, for example, that the proper truthmaker for (1) is in the metaphysical vicinity of the number thirteen. In contrast, the proper truthmaker for the claim that "Humility is a virtue" is probably the property of humility. So, although these claims seem necessarily true, we cannot assign them arbitrary concrete entities as truthmakers; their truthmakers must be the abstract entities they are intuitively about.

There is no guarantee that a theory of truthmaking—especially one without propositions or states of affairs—will do justice to absolutely all of our intuitions regarding aboutness. (What, for example, does the truth that there are no round squares *really* seem to be about?) There is also no guarantee that a satisfactory accounting for absolutely all truths can be provided. But, if we accept the general framework of truthmaking and assume that it squares with our intuitions regarding aboutness, it provides a third route for defending the existence of abstract entities. For our purposes, we can formulate the truthmaker alethic argument as follows:

The truthmaker alethic argument

P1. (1) is true.

P2. If (1) is true, the number thirteen is the truthmaker of (1).

P3. If the number thirteen is the truthmaker of (1), then the number thirteen exists.

C1. Therefore, the number thirteen exists.

The fate of the truthmaker alethic argument turns on the general adequacy of truthmaker theory and the extent to which the number thirteen must serve as a truthmaker for (1). But, as we've already noted, nominalists are all but certain to dismiss this argument as question begging in light of truthmaker theory's implicit commitment to abstracta. Alternatively, nominalists might grant that truthmaker theory can be developed in general compliance with nominalism but then still take issue with P2. One option here is to claim that truthmaker theory is only in the business of accounting for truths about concrete reality and so does not apply to claims like (1). A second option is to hold that sentences like (1) are properly thought to have no distinctive truthmakers. The former option will, of course, run contrary truthmaker theory's ambition to systematically explicate the relation between truth and reality. After all, it is difficult to see why one might accept truthmaker theory only to disavow its application to the host of apparent truths regarding the abstract realm. (Cf. Melia (2005).) The latter option is more plausible and seems mostly unproblematic when applied to necessary truths, which are often claimed to "demand nothing of the world." It is, however, quickly confounded by contingent truths that involve abstract entities—e.g., that thirteen is Edie's favourite number.

Ultimately, the background metaphysical assumptions required by truthmaker theory are far less modest than those required for Quinean and Fregean arguments. And, since the Fregean alethic argument requires considerably stronger semantic and syntactic assumptions, it looks as though the Quinean alethic argument is the one most likely to underwrite a dialectically forceful case against nominalism. The central challenge for the Quinean is, however, to show that it is incumbent upon us to accept claims like (1) that require a commitment to abstract entities. With this concern in mind, we can turn to indispensability arguments for platonism that build upon the foundation of the Quinean alethic argument in an effort to show that (1) cannot be plausibly denied.

§1.4 Indispensability arguments

Semantic and alethic arguments aim to settle the question of whether abstract entities exist by appealing to *a priori* theses that connect meaning, truth, and existence. In the eyes of the ontological naturalist, this strategy is badly misguided, since ontology is not an *a priori* matter. On the contrary, ontological naturalism holds that the proper guides to ontology are our best scientific theories, which are products of sustained *a posteriori* inquiry into the world. So, if the question of whether there are abstract entities can be settled, it will be by carefully scrutinizing our best scientific theories to determine whether abstract entities are among their ontological commitments.

For those who accept platonism on the basis of ontological naturalism, the main line of argument runs as follows. Absent principled reasons to the contrary, our willingness to take on the ontological commitments of our best scientific theories should extend, not only to the concrete entities that figure into these theories, but to any abstract entities they include. And, since abstract entities such as numbers and functions figure into our best scientific theories, nominalism and ontological naturalism are in direct conflict. This places a heavy burden on ontological naturalists who might hope to be nominalists: they must explain why our best scientific theories do not require abstract entities, despite their apparent commitment to numbers and other abstracta. Moreover, this explanation must be motivated by considerations internal to science, since any appeal to extra-scientific *a priori* considerations would contravene a commitment to ontological naturalism, which holds our scientific theories to be the final word on what we ought to believe exists.

There are several ways to make this argument from ontological naturalism more precise. The most influential of these has come to be known as the indispensability argument, which is often taken to be, not just the strongest *naturalistic* argument for platonism, but the strongest of *any* argument for platonism. (Hartry Field (1980: 4), a leading nominalist, remarks that the indispensability argument for mathematical entities is "the only non-question begging argument" against nominalism.)

The indispensability argument is often attributed to Quine and Putnam and traced back to the following passage in Putnam (1971: 347):

> So far I have been developing an argument for realism along roughly the following lines: quantification over mathematical entities is indispensable for science, both formal and physical; therefore we should accept such quantification; but this commits us to accepting the existence of the mathematical entities in question. This type of argument stems, of course, from Quine, who has for years stressed both the indispensability of quantification over mathematical entities and the intellectual dishonesty of denying the existence of what one daily presupposes.

Some take Putnam's remarks here to constitute an argument for platonism which ties together a naturalistic view about the proper deference of metaphysics to science and the indispensability of mathematics to our best scientific theories. How exactly we ought to spell out such an argument is controversial, but a standard version supplements these general commitments with two Quinean ontological theses to produce the following argument for mathematical entities:

The indispensability argument

P1. *Ontological naturalism.* Our best guides to what exists are our best scientific theories, so we ought to believe in the ontological commitments of our best scientific theories.

P2. *Quine's criterion.* The ontological commitments of a theory are all and only those entities that are the values of bound variables occurring within that theory.

P3. *Indispensability.* Our best scientific theories involve indispensable quantification over mathematical entities.

P4. *Confirmational holism.* Support for a scientific theory accrues holistically to all of its ontological commitments, so belief in a given scientific theory requires belief in all of its ontological commitments.

C1. Therefore, there we ought to believe in the existence of mathematical entities.

This version of the indispensability argument, which concerns exclusively mathematical entities, involves four key premises. P1 is intended to capture the ontological naturalist's commitment to science as the proper guide to what there is. P2 is a rough formulation of the now-familiar Quinean recipe for extracting ontological commitments. P3, when combined with Quine's criterion, makes explicit that our best scientific theories are ontologically committed to abstract entities, which seems evident once we note that standard formulations of physical laws involve quantification over squares of distance, coefficients of friction, and topological spaces. Finally, P4 asserts a Quinean thesis about the epistemic evaluation of theories, which holds that theories are confirmed or disconfirmed holistically. This means that the epistemic evaluation of theories and their commitments is not a piecemeal affair. We cannot, for example, pick and choose which posits within a theory to treat with ontological seriousness. So, when endorsing our best scientific theory, we are rationally compelled to endorse each and every one of its ontological commitments. There is, then, no principled basis on which we could, say, disregard ontological commitment to numbers any more than we could disregard a commitment to electrons.

The indispensability argument makes trouble for those who would hope to dismiss platonism as a flight of metaphysical fancy or the postulation of "spooky" abstracta. On the contrary, it suggests that hard-nosed naturalists who take science to be on firmer footing than *a priori* metaphysics are, somewhat surprisingly, doing their best to respect scientific consensus when they stump for platonism. According to the ontological naturalist, the pervasive involvement of mathematical entities in physical theory renders any opposition to abstracta, not just unmotivated, but contrary to a well supported deference to the authority of science. So, just as we take our best scientific theories to require a belief in the existence of Neptune, genes, and polymers and to undermine belief in Vulcan, humors, and phlogiston, ontological naturalism requires that we admit the abstract entities that figure into our best scientific theories. Depending upon one's preferred version of naturalism, this will almost certainly include mathematical entities but might extend beyond physical theories to scientific domains that require an even broader swathe of abstracta.

Before considering nominalist objections, note how this naturalistic variety of platonism parts company from more traditional versions. Historically, platonism is defended on *a priori* grounds, but those who appeal to our best scientific theories in defending platonism opt for a naturalistic epistemology of abstract entities. On such a view, justified belief in abstracta is parasitic upon the *a posteriori* success of science. This is in stark contrast with traditional platonist views, which take the existence of numbers to be pretty much obvious, since it is justified *a priori* and independently of our best scientific theories. As Parsons (1971: 151) puts it, any view that defends platonism via the indispensability argument "leaves unaccounted for precisely the *obviousness* of elementary mathematics." So, for platonists of the traditional *a priori* variety, this suggests that the indispensability argument might be unsound despite its true conclusion.

Versions of platonism supported by the indispensability argument also inherit a second peculiarity concerning the scope of their commitment to mathematical entities. This peculiarity arises once we note that the mathematical entities of interest to working mathematicians—e.g., the strongly inaccessible cardinals of set theory—might lack any application within our best scientific theories. As Maddy (1992) notes, this leaves the ontological status of some mathematical entities rather uncertain. For, while the indispensability argument suggests that we must believe in mathematical entities, our commitment to mathematical entities is parasitic on their role in physical theory. And, although the posits of "recreational mathematics"—roughly, mathematics without scientific application—seem to be perfectly legitimate subjects of mathematical inquiry, they cannot earn their ontological keep by figuring into our best scientific theories. This puts the ontological naturalist in an awkward position. Either the entities studied in recreational mathematics and left "unapplied" must be disavowed, which would do violence to mathematical practice, or the indispensability argument's epistemic detour through physical theory seems pointless, since mathematical theories can, on their own, justify our commitment to abstract entities. Deciding which option to pursue is one among many critical concerns for proponents of the indispensability argument.

Setting these issues aside, how should nominalists respond to the indispensability argument? One direct response is to deny the central thesis of ontological naturalism, which underwrites the indispensability argument and similar defences of platonism. Those who wish to deny that science is the proper arbiter of ontology might do so because they reject commitment to those entities required by our best scientific theories. Alternatively, some might accept *supernaturalism* and believe in entities *in addition* to those required by our best scientific theories. Interestingly, some varieties of supernaturalism have been used to defend nominalism—e.g., by positing a divine being whose various features allow for an alternative to platonism. In doing so, such views simultaneously go beyond and fail to meet the requirements of ontological naturalism. Either way, in rejecting the ontological verdicts of our best scientific theories, such nominalists thereby reject the centrepiece of the indispensability argument.

Settling the fate of ontological naturalism would require an examination of the successes and failures of science and the relative merits of other forms of inquiry. We'll undertake no such effort here, but, despite leaving the status of ontological naturalism undecided, we can usefully note two tensions already hinted at above.

First, although ontological naturalists can leverage the impressive track record of science to defend abstract entities, this strategy fits rather poorly with other platonist arguments that depend upon *a priori* metaphysical, epistemological, or semantic theses. For those who might offer the indispensability argument, it is an open and important question which other arguments can be given without straying outside the limits of naturalism. But, as we'll see in the next section, it is unlikely that the methodological assumptions that underwrite arguments from metaphysical explanation are compatible with a serious commitment to ontological naturalism, given that metaphysics falls outside of science proper.

Second, it is crucial for proponents of ontological naturalism to be explicit about which kinds of scientific theories are to serve as guides to ontology. Some naturalists might hold that only our best physical theories (or perhaps even just our fundamental physical theories) are proper guides to ontology. Other ontological naturalists will be content to accept the ontological commitments of chemistry, biology, astronomy, and other "hard sciences." More restrictive versions of ontological naturalism point towards sparser ontologies. In contrast, liberal versions of ontological naturalism that count linguistics, cognitive science, and pure mathematics as proper arbiters of ontology provide readymade arguments for more diverse abstract entities like propositions. But, regardless of which version of ontological naturalism one adopts, an explanatory burden is incurred, since we are owed some account of why and where to draw the line between which scientific theories to treat with (or without) ontological seriousness.

Compared to ontological naturalism, P3, which asserts the indispensability of mathematical entities, seems fairly modest. It says that no version of our best physical theories can avoid quantification over and subsequent ontological commitment to abstract entities like numbers, functions, and coefficients. Against the indispensability premise, an influential nominalist response, mounted in Field's *Science Without Numbers*, contends that mathematical entities are in fact dispensable commitments. To this end, Field develops a version of Newtonian gravitational theory using exclusively nominalistic resources and suggests that comparable methods can, in principle, suffice for a nominalistic reconstruction of our best physical theories.

The fate of Field's suggestion is uncertain, especially given the challenges in providing genuinely nominalistic reconstructions of richer physical theories; however, it is fair to say that nominalists and platonists seem generally pessimistic.[28] But, as some platonists have suggested, even if Field's programme could be carried out, the resulting nominalist reconstructions would still fall short of qualifying as our best physical theories. They would, for example, be unduly complex or inelegant in light of the extensive modifications needed to avoid quantification over mathematical entities. And, even if nominalistic reconstructions were tolerably simple and reasonably elegant, other platonists maintain that the resulting theories would still be inferior by the standards of contemporary physics, since these standards involve little, if any, interest in avoiding commitment to abstract entities. On this front, Burgess and Rosen (1997: 210) half-seriously suggest that, given a naturalistic commitment to the authority of scientific standards, one could test the merits of nominalistic reconstructions *qua* alternative physical theories by submitting them to physics journals. (For all their trouble, nominalists should probably expect only baffled rejection letters from the editors.) Put more directly, Burgess and Rosen's concern is that, once one accepts ontological naturalism, there is no naturalistically legitimate reason to prefer physical theories that avoid abstract entities, since this alleged virtue is not prized by the standards of contemporary physics. The project of nominalistically reconstructing physical theories would therefore be wholly unmotivated in the eyes of many naturalists.

For the reasons just noted, indispensability has a fair claim to being the strongest premise of the indispensability argument. In contrast, P4, confirmational holism, advanced by Quine in "Two dogmas of empiricism" and elsewhere, is the most widely rejected. Not only is Quine's focus on confirmation rather than, say, justification controversial, there is no compelling reason to believe that epistemic credit must be distributed equally across the commitments of a theory. In this vein, Sober (1993) suggests that the mathematical commitments of our best scientific theories receive no additional support from successes of the theories that include them, since they are a common assumption of all competing theories. And, in advancing the case for a more "selective" naturalism, Maddy (1997) argues that careful attention to the attitudes and practices of scientists suggests that they do, in fact, treat different posits within the same theory with varying degrees of ontological seriousness—e.g., in the case of obvious albeit indispensable idealizations. For naturalists, this suggests that confirmational holism is mistaken and, worse still, in direct conflict with the actual practices and attitudes that constitute our preeminent authority: scientific inquiry.

Proponents of the indispensability argument might hope the argument can succeed even after confirmational holism is rejected. (For discussion, see Resnik (1997).) But, once we reject confirmational holism, we leave open the possibility of claiming that justified ontological commitment extends to concrete entities like electrons but not to abstract entities. The key issue that arises at this point is the one noted by Burgess and Rosen: even if naturalists have epistemic licence to disavow abstract entities, they must still provide a suitably naturalistic rationale for doing so. Otherwise, nominalism cannot be reconciled with naturalism, since it crucially appeals to extra-scientific, philosophical standards. So, if there is no principled and naturalistically acceptable reason to reject such entities, platonism looks all but mandatory for ontological naturalists. The challenge of finding scientific grounds for suspicions about abstracta has therefore prompted would-be nominalists to investigate the theoretical roles played by abstract entities. As we'll now see, this requires that we reassess whether indispensability might come in importantly different forms.

§1.4.1 Enhancing indispensability

An influential challenge to the indispensability argument builds upon the preceding concerns about confirmational holism. It seeks to show that, although mathematical entities are theoretically indispensable, they are not theoretically indispensable in the same way as, say, proteins and electromagnetic fields. Additionally, this nominalist challenge seeks to show that the kind of indispensability exhibited by mathematical entities does not provide good reason to view them as genuine ontological commitments. Roughly speaking, this challenge seeks to show that quantification over abstract entities is merely *expressively* indispensable: we only require it for articulating and applying our best physical theories. Such entities are not *explanatorily* indispensable in the manner of electrons and fields and it is only entities that are explanatorily indispensable that warrant ontological commitment.

To illustrate how quantification over certain entities might be merely expressively indispensable, suppose that we had good reason to believe that the average star is orbited by four planets. If we take this claim to be part of our best scientific theory, it is tempting to think we are thereby committed to the existence of an entity, the average star. And, while talk about the average star makes the formulation and application of our best theory easier, we can, when pressed, dispense with quantification over this entity by asserting a massively disjunctive claim such as: either there is one star orbited by four planets or two stars orbited by eight planets or three stars orbited by twelve planets... and so on *ad infinitum*. So, given a language that admits infinite disjunctions, quantification over the average star is expressively dispensable. Notice, however, that our best physical theories might very well be formulated in a language that does not permit infinite disjunctions. Under such circumstances, quantification over the average star would be expressively indispensable, but, even so, we ought not admit the existence of such an entity. With this in mind, the opponent of the indispensability argument contends that we can rightly reject ontological commitment to the average star as its indispensable role is merely a kind of representational artifact. Unlike genuinely warranted ontological commitments, we do not require the average star to provide the explanations the theory purports to supply. Returning to the case of mathematical entities, the indispensability of the average star within an impoverished language can be likened to our quantification over mathematical entities: such entities enrich our expressive wherewithal, but play no ineliminable explanatory role.

Granted the distinction between expressive and explanatory indispensability, nominalist opponents of the indispensability argument have a novel strategy for facing down the charge of naturalistic incoherence. In the terminology of Melia (2000), the ontological naturalist will seek to "weasel" out of ontological commitments. As Melia (2000: 467) puts it:

> Taking back or tailoring part of what we have said before is not unknown in everyday practice. "Everybody who Fs also Gs. Except Harry—he's the one exception." These are certainly sentences of English and it is clear what is being said. First, we assert that all the Fs are also G. Then we go on to retract an implication of this sentence ... Why indulge in such weasely behavior if we can avoid it? Taking back things we have said before is often unhelpful and misleading, and is indeed somewhat weasely. Why not say exactly what we want to say first time around? ... Because sometimes we have to. Sometimes, we just cannot say what we want to say first time around.

Platonists who opt for confirmational holism are not likely to accept a distinction between expressive and explanatory indispensability. But, for nominalists, this is a welcome distinction that puts the pressure on platonists to show that mathematical entities make a genuine explanatory contribution to our theories and are not mere presentational conveniences. So, if we admit this distinction, platonists must establish that mathematical entities occupy an indispensable explanatory role akin to that occupied by fields and photons and are unlike mere "notationalia" like periods and plus signs. With an eye towards meeting this challenge, platonists can revise the indispensability argument in an effort to face down the threat of weasely naturalists. The resulting revision of the indispensability argument qualifies the indispensability premise and yields what Baker (2009) and others call the *enhanced indispensability argument*:

> P3*. *Enhanced indispensability*. Our best scientific theories involve explanatorily indispensable quantification over mathematical entities.

The proponent of the enhanced indispensability argument need not take issue with the general coherence of the weaselling strategy. Instead, she can concede that the nominalist is within her rights to disavow entities even while formulating theories that quantify over them. But this is permissible only in the case of entities that occupy no explanatorily indispensable role. So, while explanatorily indispensability saddles us with ontological commitments, expressive indispensability does not. And, of course, the proponent of the enhanced indispensability argument contends that numbers are, in fact, explanatorily indispensable.

Assessing P3* requires close attention to the inner workings of scientific explanation and the role of mathematics in physical theory. It also plausibly requires a full-fledged account of what exactly explanatory indispensability is. But, for proponents of the enhanced indispensability argument, a natural strategy is to offer examples that bolster the explanatory status of mathematical entities. One such example, discussed in Baker (2005), concerns facts about the lifecycle of cicadas, insects that spend either 13 or 17 years underground in a larval stage and then emerge as adults. A proposed explanation for the length of these larval periods is that, since thirteen and seventeen are prime numbers, cicadas' lifecycle reduces overlapping interactions with predators that emerge from their own larval stages at, say, 2-, 4-, and 8-year cycles. Interestingly, this explanation of biological phenomena about cicadas seems to make direct appeal to a theorem regarding primes and their limited overlap with other numbers. Roughly put, it is only by looking to the status of mathematical reality that we can account for why it would be adaptive for cicadas to behave in a certain way. For defenders of P3*, this suggests that mathematical entities and facts about them are explanatorily indispensable and not just tools for indexing or representing concrete reality.

Committed nominalists will, of course, deny that such examples establish P3*. And, for those committed to naturalism, this is precisely where the key point of disagreement between nominalists and platonist ought to fall. For, if ontological naturalism is true, the fate of the enhanced indispensability argument and, in turn, the status of mathematical entities is rightly thought to hinge upon the role of abstract entities within scientific explanations. If there is no marked asymmetry between numbers and particles, naturalists should countenance both. But, if our scientific explanations treat the abstract and the concrete in strikingly different ways, the prospects for accepting particles while rejecting numbers leaves the door open for nominalism.

Before turning to another batch of arguments for platonism, one final complication is worth marking. If we suppose that the enhanced indispensability argument is successful, it is very tempting to think that a commitment to abstract mathematical entities follows therewith. Notice, however, that the explanatory indispensability of mathematics owes to the truth of mathematical claims rather than the specific nature of mathematical entities. There is, for example, no special explanatory role that mathematics plays on account of numbers being, say, non-spatiotemporal or acausal. For this reason, as Pincock (2011: 190–200) and others have noted, a committed ontological naturalist could, in principle, accept a non-platonist but still realist interpretation of mathematics so long as they can provide the requisite mathematical explanations. For this reason, the indispensability argument is not, in isolation, a full-fledged argument for platonism. It requires supplementary theses—some of which look distinctively metaphysical in nature—to show that the indispensability of mathematics is best accounted for by platonism. In this way, some nominalist views, which sustain the truth of mathematics, might also claim the indispensability argument as a source of support. (See, e.g., Section 7.4.)

§1.5 Metaphysical explanation

In the previous section, we considered naturalistic arguments for abstract entities based upon their role in scientific theories. This section surveys arguments for abstract entities based upon their role in what we will call "metaphysical explanations." Roughly put, these arguments proceed by targeting some "metaphysical" phenomenon like resemblance, modality, or lawfulness and then arguing that abstract entities figure into its best available explanation. In structural terms, these arguments have much in common with the indispensability argument, since they are broadly abductive in nature. But, while the indispensability argument defends abstract entities on the basis of their role in our best scientific explanations, these arguments defend abstract entities on the basis of their role in metaphysical explanations, which fall outside the purview of science. And, since these metaphysical explanations are extrascientific in character, arguments that rely upon them run contrary to any naturalism that takes scientific theories to be our *exclusive* guides to ontology.

Of necessity, our survey of these arguments will be brief, but it should still provide some sense of how familiar metaphysical projects have been used to support platonism. In particular, we will consider two leading arguments—one concerning resemblance, the other concerning modality—that seek to show our best metaphysical explanations require abstract entities. These two arguments by no means exhaust the list of potential arguments from metaphysical explanation. Not only can various semantic and alethic arguments be plausibly assimilated into this category, there is a wealth of further metaphysical phenomena that platonists have sought to explain by invoking abstract entities. Some of these phenomena are listed at the end of this chapter. Note, however, that responses to these arguments—in particular, efforts to develop superior nominalistic explanations—will receive no sustained attention at this point.

§1.5.1 *The argument from resemblance*

Resemblance is ubiquitous. Oranges resemble apples. Rhinos resemble elephants. And, while oranges also resemble elephants, they resemble apples far more than they resemble elephants. Generally speaking, any given thing resembles any other thing to at least some minimal extent insofar as they are each things. The interesting facts about resemblance are, however, typically facts about comparative resemblance or degrees of resemblance. But, regardless of the specific facts about resemblance, it is fairly uncontroversial that the world has at least some *resemblance structure*—i.e., a distribution of resemblance relations and corresponding facts about resemblance.

The argument from resemblance defends platonism by showing that our best explanation of the world's resemblance structure requires a commitment to abstract entities. In its most familiar form, the argument from resemblance seeks to show that resemblance structure is properly explained by positing the existence of properties. (As we saw in Section 1.2, there are several competing views about the nature of properties, but, given our schematic presentation of the present argument, we can remain neutral here.) Several additional choices are also required in advancing the argument from resemblance. In particular, we need to fix upon the relevant aspect of the world's resemblance structure that we hope to explain by appealing to properties.

For present purposes, our best bet is to focus on facts regarding *perfect resemblance in a certain respect*. To see why these facts are especially natural candidates for explanation via an ontology of properties, notice that, with respect to our biological species and ontological category, you and I perfectly resemble one another: we are each humans and, let us suppose, material objects. In contrast, we do not perfectly resemble one another with respect to mass or age: one of us will be more or less massive and one of us will be older or younger. Properties therefore provide a straightforward analysis of facts about perfect resemblance in a certain respect: we need only posit the existence of some entities that you and I both "share" or instantiate—in the present case, the properties *being human* and *being a material object*. Our sharing of these properties is thereby held to explain both the fact we are human and the further fact that we perfectly resemble one another with respect to our species and ontological category.

Equipped with an explanation of facts about perfect resemblance in a certain respect, facts about *imperfect* resemblance—e.g., facts about whether, all things considered, you resemble me more than Hillary Clinton—are often held to admit of explanation in terms of these more basic facts about perfect resemblance. This is, in part, why a metaphysical explanation of perfect resemblance in a certain respect is commonly held to underwrite an explanation the world's broader resemblance structure. As such, properties provide us a promising resource for explaining facts about resemblance. So, in light of their explanatory credentials, the argument from resemblance concludes we are justified in accepting an ontology of properties.

The argument from resemblance

P1. Some entities perfectly resemble one another in a certain respect.

P2. The best metaphysical explanation of the fact that some entities perfectly resemble one another in a certain respect is that there is some entity—a property—in virtue of which those entities perfectly resemble one another in a certain respect.

C1. Therefore, there are properties.

The success of the argument from resemblance depends on whether a better explanation that does without properties is available. It also depends on whether properties are up to their explanatory assignment. A central project for theories of properties is therefore to spell out precisely how properties account for resemblance facts. This is no small undertaking. Opponents of property-driven explanations of resemblance might claim, for example, that there are simply too many facts about resemblance to explain, since the resemblance relations that hold among properties also demand some explanation—e.g., the fact that *being an ape* resembles *being human* more than *being a bucket or a goat*. The standard platonist response here is to admit "higher-order" properties—properties had by other properties—which would, in principle, leave no resemblance facts without some explanation (even though they might require an infinitely ascending hierarchy of properties of properties). But, even if such a view is satisfactory, several potential objections remain.

Setting aside full-scale scepticism about resemblance, the most promising nominalist response contends that our best explanation of resemblance requires expanding our ideology rather than positing properties.[29] This nominalist response extends the Quinean suggestion that we admit primitive predicates rather than posit properties and applies it to the case of resemblance. So, rather than analyzing resemblance in terms of the sharing of properties, the nominalist introduces a primitive resemblance predicate—e.g., a three-place predicate like "*x resembles y more than z.*"[30] On such a view, resemblance structure is to be accounted for without any abstract ontological commitments.

Primitive resemblance predicates allow the nominalist to state facts about what resembles what while still eschewing abstract ontology. And, while this primitive ideology allows the nominalist to state facts about resemblance among objects, platonists will claim that certain facts are left unaccounted for. Specifically, claims like "Humility is more like kindness than wickedness" seem to require that there are properties of which such resemblance claims are true. The apparent ease with which platonism accommodates the translation and truth of resemblance claims seemingly about properties is a point in its favour. Nominalists who introduce the primitive ideology of resemblance in order to describe the world will, however, either deny the sentences in question or seek to provide some suitable nominalist replacement. But, in doing so, they are likely to concede a minor advantage to platonism.

§1.5.2 *The argument from modality*

Like resemblance, modality is ubiquitous. Modal notions like necessity and possibility infuse our ordinary talk and our reasoning. They figure explicitly in our claims about what we could or cannot do and in counterfactual conditionals like "If Oswald hadn't killed JFK, someone else would have." They are also implicit in our covertly modal talk about capacities, abilities, and dispositional properties like *fragility* and *dependability*. Modal notions also play myriad theoretical roles within the narrower business of philosophy—e.g., when we model expected utility by appealing to possible world-states or when we distinguish between the extensions and intensions of predicates.

In tendering a metaphysical explanation of why and how things could be otherwise, it is commonplace for metaphysicians to resort to quantification over "ways things could have been" or, in more familiar jargon, *possibilities*. Possibilities, unlike cats and canoes, can obtain or fail to obtain. These entities do not seem to be ordinary concrete objects. A common assumption is, then, that possibilities are abstract entities of some kind. On some views, they are propositions, so talk about possibilities obtaining is therefore talk about propositions being true or false. On other views, they are properties, so this talk is analyzed in terms of instantiation.

A metaphysical explanation of modality isn't a haphazard undertaking. Modal reasoning involves careful attention to the logic of possibility and necessity and the complexity of the modal concepts we deploy in our thought and talk. Among systematic treatments of modality, the most influential are those that take the notion of a *possible world* as a theoretical starting point. Intuitively, a possible world is a maximal possibility or a total way things could be. Non-maximal possibilities—e.g., that Obama is president—are non-total ways things could be. Using the apparatus of possible worlds, we can give a fairly straightforward analysis of the notions of necessity and possibility: a proposition is *necessarily true* if and only if it is true at all possible worlds, while a proposition is *possibly true* if and only if it is true at some possible worlds. In turn, contingent truths are those propositions that hold at some but not all possible worlds. The theoretical benefits of possible worlds extend far beyond these simple analyses. They have been used to model and investigate the logic of modal reasoning and to provide a semantics for modal expressions.

The analytic fecundity of possible worlds has prompted many platonists to admit such entities as ontological commitments. Platonist options on this front are remarkably diverse, since possible worlds have been identified with various species of abstracta including properties, propositions, sets, and have also been held to be *sui generis* entities in their own right.[31] Despite widespread disagreement about their precise nature, platonist views of possible worlds provide a powerful, unifying explanation of many features of modality. In Chapter 7, we will consider the modal realism of David Lewis, which takes possible worlds to be concrete entities of the same ontological category as the actual world. But, setting aside that radical alternative, there is ample reason to think possible worlds are well motivated posits that serve as a kind of "philosopher's paradise" when it comes to explaining, not just modality, but any notions connected to modality. In comparison, modalist views that hope to account for modality by admitting only primitive modal operators are demonstrably weaker in their expressive and explanatory resources. So, unless one opts for Lewis' modal realism, those who explain modal notions via possible worlds seem saddled with abstract entities.[32]

§1.5.3 *Other arguments from metaphysical explanation*

The preceding arguments hold our best explanations of resemblance and modality to mandate a commitment to abstract entities of some sort. Other arguments from metaphysical explanation draw upon equally important notions. For example, facts about value and goodness are regularly modelled and explained within a metaphysical framework that admits properties, while leading theories of knowledge and justification typically help themselves to a parallel commitment to propositions. Perhaps most strikingly, many platonists claim that a satisfactory explanation of validity and other logical notions requires a commitment to abstract entities. This is because a standard logical framework holds facts about the validity of formulae and arguments to be explained by appeal to facts about what is true in (intended) models, where models are held to be complex structures, built up out of sets, propositions, or some other abstracta. For those who hold logical notions like validity to require some underlying metaphysical explanation, the default explanatory package is a thoroughgoing platonism. Nominalists will, of course, resist this contention and likely claim that no metaphysical explanation is required for logical facts regarding validity. Instead, such facts about logical structure are to be treated as an explanatory ground floor; they admit of no further explanation and require no ontological commitments from the world.

Several other arguments from metaphysical explanation concern notions in the conceptual neighbourhood of modality and resemblance like causation and lawhood. For example, arguments regarding the laws of nature hold that our best account of physical laws requires a commitment to abstract properties. The particulars of this argument vary depending upon one's preferred view of laws, but, on one influential view, there is a special second-order relation of *nomic necessitation* that holds between properties.[33] Roughly put, laws of nature are facts of the form that, necessarily, anything that is F is also G, where such facts concern properties standing in the relevant necessitation relation. Although such views of laws face serious challenge, the fate of the argument from laws of nature does not hang on the success of this specific view. Alternative proposals—e.g., dispositionalist views about laws—also make crucial appeal to properties in explaining nomic facts. So, for many who hope to explain the nomic structure of the world, platonism is a mandatory commitment.

Platonists swayed by one or more arguments from metaphysical explanation hold abstract entities to be crucial for our extra-scientific explanatory projects.

Nominalist views that eschew abstracta will therefore seem explanatorily impoverished. So, if one takes these explanatory projects seriously, there is considerable pressure to acquiesce to platonism. Alternatively, nominalists must show that, in these and other cases, platonist explanations are problematic or, at the very least, inferior to nominalist alternatives.

Summary

This chapter provided a survey of arguments for platonism. Although our critical interrogation of these arguments was fairly limited, some general morals can still be drawn. Among semantic arguments, the strongest are explanatory ones in favour of propositions or properties. And, while alethic arguments can be developed in various ways, the Quinean argument has a fair claim to being the strongest, especially when paired with ontological naturalism. The resulting package of views delivers some version of the indispensability argument. For those who reject ontological naturalism, arguments from metaphysical explanation are the most promising route to platonism, though which are the strongest is an open question. Ultimately, the extent to which nominalists can face down this battery of arguments depends upon whether nominalists' ideological and ontological resources are a match for the explanatory power of abstract entities.

Recommended reading

On explanatory semantic arguments, see Church (1950, 1951) and Jubien (1989). Historical concerns about the One over Many argument are numerous, but see Fine (1980) on interpretive issues. On alethic arguments for platonism, see Swoyer (2008), Armstrong (1978), Hale (1987), and Hoffman and Rosenkrantz (2003). The canonical version of Quine's conception of ontology is set out in Quine (1948), but see Burgess (2008) and Chihara (2008) on Quine's views regarding abstract entities. On Fregean alethic arguments, see Wright (1983), Rosen (1993), and MacBride (2003). On truthmaker theory and nominalism, see Armstrong (1997) and Melia (2005).

On the history of the indispensability argument, see Liggins (2008), Putnam (2012), and Bueno (2013). Book-length treatments of the argument include Colyvan (2003), who endorses it, and Leng (2010), who sides against it. On the enhanced indispensability argument, see Baker (2009). On the nature of mathematical explanation and our best scientific theories, see Colyvan (2006), Baker (2009), Daly and Langford (2009), and Pincock (2011). On platonism's explanatory role in analyzing resemblance, modality, and laws, see Armstrong (1978), Hoffman and Rosenkrantz (2003), Swoyer (1996), Carmichael (2010), and Tooley (2009). On the general role of abstract entities in metaphysical explanation, see Kraut (2010) and Nolan (2015).

Notes

1. According to most nominalists, the antecedent of this counterfactual conditional is necessarily false. An influential view takes this and any other counterpossible to be vacuously true, but this is in serious tension with our apparent ability to be right or wrong about what would hold if this or that (metaphysically necessary or impossible) theory were true or false. For example, although it is necessarily true that there are no Leibnizian monads, the conditional "If there were Leibnizian monads, they would be simple substances" is true, but, in contrast, the conditional, "If there were Leibnizian monads, they would be football-shaped," is false. Throughout, we will follow Nolan (1997a) in taking the truth of counterpossibles to be a non-trivial matter.
2. I know of no contemporary proponent of direct semantic arguments in anything like their full generality. The closest relatives are what we might call *intentional arguments*, which take the intentionality or "directedness" of our thoughts to require the existence of their subject matter. On the requirement that thoughts have objects, see Meinong (1960) and Bricker (2006).
3. On Frege's Context Principle, see Frege (1884), Wright (1983), and Dummett (1956, 1991: 225)
4. An example: we might be tempted to hold the meaningfulness of sentences of the form "a is F" to require the existence of the referent of "a," but this proposal delivers bizarre (or at least contentious) results once we consider that "is F" might be a predicate like "is imaginary" or "is fictitious."
5. Platonists might try to exploit this loophole by taking a vast swath of seemingly distinct entities to be one and the same thing. In one familiar guise, this approach takes a single entity—e.g., the empty set—to be the referent of all non-referring terms like "Vulcan" or "Wittgenstein's tallest grandson."
6. Another objection accuses the direct semantic argument of assuming an implausible "semantic idealism," according to which facts about what exists

metaphysically depend on mind-dependent facts about meaningfulness. Such a view would seem to require that we are capable of thinking or speaking entities into existence, but, strictly speaking, no such view is required. The proponent of the direct semantic argument need only assume that semantic facts are necessarily *constrained* by ontological facts, where the existence of entities is a precondition for our thought and talk about them.

7 *De re* attitudes, unlike the *de dicto* attitudes we bear to propositions, have entities other than propositions as their objects as, for example, in cases of desiring or fearing a specific object. On the *de re/de dicto* distinction, see Quine (1956) and Kaplan (1968).

8 There is some disagreement about whether propositions bear the relation *is true at* to times or worlds rather than having it *simpliciter*. On this debate, see Richard (1981) and Schaffer (2012).

9 On sentences and their relation to propositions, see Church (1950).

10 Not all views holds propositions to be eternal, necessarily existing, or mind-independent; however, such views are likely to reject the platitudes in question. For discussion, see King et al. (2014).

11 One might hope to somehow identify properties with predicates. But, as Armstrong (1978: 11–24) shows, no such view is plausible. (See also van Cleve (1994).) Along with requiring bizarre modal ties between predicates and the entities to which they apply, such a view is explanatorily vacuous. No metaphysical explanation of why an apple is red plausibly draws upon the fact that speakers apply the predicate "red" to it. Note, also, that if predicates are types rather than tokens, so-called "predicate nominalism" is of little help to nominalists, since types would be abstract entities.

12 Some views take propositions and properties to belong to the same ontological category. On such a view, monadic "one-place" properties like *being human* have one "argument place," binary or "two-place" properties like *is taller than* (more usually called "relations") have two or more, propositions are "zero-place" properties without any argument places. They are not "true of" some entities, but rather true *simpliciter*. See, e.g., Zalta (1983).

13 This sentiment is not universal. As we'll see, ardent supporters of a spatiotemporal criterion of abstractness might endorse somewhat peculiar verdicts, according to which immanent universals, impure sets, or tropes are concrete. As noted earlier, I assume that properties are abstract entities, whether or not they are universals, sets, or tropes.

14 Tropes are usually held to be necessarily connected to their bearers. So, for example, the *wisdom of Xanthippe* could not be had by Socrates nor

could Socrates' own wisdom trope be had by Xanthippe. There is some disagreement about what unites tropes under a common kind, but, on many views, tropes of the same kind—e.g., *wisdom* tropes—are duplicates of one another.

15 Sets are sometimes called "classes" so, confusingly enough, this view is sometimes called "class nominalism." (And, even within set theory, some collections like "proper classes"—collections "too big" to be sets—are non-sets.) Note, also, that some versions of trope theory identify properties with sets of tropes. Such views straddle the divide between trope and set-theoretic views.

16 Set-theoretic views face notable challenges when held to be the semantic values of predicates. Suppose, for example, we identify the property *being human* with the set of all humans and the property *being bipedal* with the set of all bipedal entities. If, as a matter of coincidence, these sets are "coextensive"—i.e., share all the same actual members—the property of *being human* would be identical with the property of *being bipedal*. The standard strategy for avoiding this problem is to individuate properties *intensionally* by identifying them with, not just sets of actual entities, but with sets of both actual and merely possible entities. On such a view, *being human* is the set of all possible humans, which is distinct from the set of all possible bipedal entities—e.g., Yoda belongs to the latter but not the former. This raises metaphysical concerns about the status of merely possible entities. (See Chapter 6.) It also leaves unaddressed similar challenges regarding necessarily coextensive (alternatively, cointensive) properties such as *being triangular* and *being trilateral*. The apparent distinctness of such properties spurs some to support a "hyperintensional" conception of properties, which allows for distinct yet cointensive properties. This issue is a serious concern within the metaphysics of properties, but, in what follows, I will largely assume the adequacy of the intensional view. On concerns about necessarily coextensive properties, see Lewis (1986) and Stalnaker (1984). On hyperintensional views, see Eddon (2011) and Nolan (2014).

17 With the exception of the empty or "null" set (written, "∅"), all sets have members. Given the axiom of extensionality—one of many axioms that governs the nature and variety of sets—the members of a set determine whether it is identical with or distinct from other sets. If some sets share all the same members, they are identical. And, if some sets have different members, they are distinct. Moreover, with the exception of certain

paradox-inducing cases, for any given entities, there is a set that has all and only those entities as its members.
18 On "ostrich nominalism," see Devitt (1980) and van Cleve (1994).
19 As Quine (1951: 14) puts it, "As a subdivision of ideology there is the question of what ideas are fundamental or primitive for a theory, and what ones derivative."
20 Quine (1976b) defends eliminativism about modality. On modalism, see Melia (1992a). Note that a defender of possible worlds is not a modalist in the relevant sense. The modalist eschews quantification over possible worlds of any kind, using only primitive modal operators to express modal claims
21 It's tempting to express this relation as one of necessitation, but doing so squares poorly with Quine's hostility to modal notions. Here, the specifics of this feature of the Quinean construal of ontological commitment can be left open. See Bricker (2014) for discussion.
22 Bound variables occur within the "scope" of quantifiers (e.g., in sentences like "There is an x and x barks" or "$\exists x Fx$"). Free variables occur in open sentences, which include variables not within the scope of any quantifier (e.g., in the English sentence "x is a dog" or "Fx").
23 This view is most famously associated with Alexius Meinong. For discussion, see Meinong (1960), Parsons (1980), Priest (2005), and Lewis (1990).
24 Quine (1948) dismisses the view on the basis of worries about the individuation of possibilia and impossibilia. These arguments have been by and large rebutted by Meinongians like Parsons (1980) and Priest (2005); however, several serious issues remain (e.g., how exactly to reconcile Meinongianism with classical logic and how to properly characterize the distinction between what exists and what there is).
25 See Russell (1905) and Quine (1948). Note that this view, as typically formulated, requires that all names be dispensed with in terms of general predicates like "is the tallest human" or that we admit what seem to be intuitively "cooked-up" predicates like "pegasizes." On Quine's implementation of the Theory of Descriptions and predicates like "pegasizes," see Hylton (2001, 2003).
26 On Quine's hostility to intensional notions like modality, see Quine (1976b).
27 On arguments for platonism that seek to show certain ordinarily acceptable claims require quantification over properties, see Jackson (1977) and Hoffman and Rosenkrantz (2003).

28 This sentiment owes largely to Malament (1982), but see Balaguer (1998) for a dissenting opinion. Cf. Dorr (2010).
29 Cf. Quine (1969) and Goodman (1972).
30 There are a few options in this regard (e.g., a three-place relation between entities and numbers, a three-place comparative relation between entities, or a four-place relation between pairs of entities). A primitive two-place predicate of "resemblances" is, however, inadequate for capturing any remotely interesting resemblance structure.
31 This menu of options divides further, since possible worlds have been identified with both complex collection of properties and with simple "world properties"—intuitively, total ways the world could be. (Cf. Stalnaker (1984) and Forrest (1986a).) In a similar vein, some platonists hold possible worlds to be maximal consistent sets of propositions. Still other platonists hold that propositions are sets of possible worlds, which are themselves entities of some different sort.
32 Along with abductive arguments for positing abstract entities to explain modality, some alethic arguments seek to show that the truth of claims that quantify over possibilities requires a commitment to abstract entities. See, e.g., Hoffman and Rosenkrantz (2003).
33 On this conception of laws, see Armstrong (1983) and Dretske (1977).

2

THE ABSTRACT–CONCRETE DISTINCTION

2.1 **The standard view**
2.2 **Analyzing abstractness**
2.3 **Primitivism**
2.4 **Eliminativism**

This chapter investigates the distinction between the abstract and the concrete, which is of fundamental importance for the nominalist–platonist debate. For, as we saw in the previous chapter, platonism requires both the ontological thesis that entities like numbers exist as well as the categoreal thesis that such entities are abstract rather than concrete. As we'll see, however, the nature of the abstract–concrete distinction is a contentious matter. Not only is there disagreement about its significance and about which entities fall on which side, ontological disagreements over the existence of properties, propositions, and other entities quickly complicates any theory about the nature of abstract entities.

No chapter-long survey can do justice to every way in which the distinction has been conceived, but, for our purposes, it will be useful to begin by introducing what we can call *the standard view*. This view of the general features of the abstract–concrete distinction has a fair claim to the status of orthodoxy. After presenting it in detail, we will examine three stances one might take regarding the abstract–concrete distinction: (i) reductionism, according to which the distinction is properly analyzed in terms of facts about location, causation, or facts of some other sort; (ii) primitivism, which holds the distinction to resist reductive analysis and so takes it as a theoretical primitive, admitting of no further explanation; and (iii) eliminativism, which rejects the abstract–concrete distinction altogether and denies it is theoretically worthwhile. Roughly speaking, reductionism and primitivism offer different ways to further refine the standard view, while eliminativism holds the standard view to be badly mistaken. After examining each of these stances, I'll argue that primitivism, when paired with an austere rather than expansive ontology of abstract entities, makes for the most plausible form of platonism.

§2.1 The standard view

The standard view incorporates various widespread assumptions about the abstract–concrete distinction. These assumptions can be and have been challenged, but, even so, the standard view remains a natural starting point for theorizing about the abstract–concrete distinction. It consists, in the first place, of six theses, each partially characterizing the abstract–concrete distinction:

(i) *Exhaustiveness.* The abstract–concrete distinction is exhaustive. It applies to absolutely all entities and guarantees that each entity is either abstract or concrete.

(ii) *Exclusivity.* The abstract–concrete distinction is exclusive. No entity belongs to the category *abstract entity* and to the category *concrete entity*. When paired with Exhaustiveness, Exclusivity partitions all entities into the two categories of *abstract entity* and *concrete entity*.

(iii) *Absoluteness.* Absolute distinctions divide entities into categories where membership in these categories is not a matter of degree. According to Absoluteness, entities cannot be "more or less" abstract or "more or less" concrete. Abstractness and concreteness are all or nothing affairs. Unlike quantitative properties like *mass* or *length*, they do not admit of degrees.

(iv) *Non-Relationality.* Non-relational distinctions divide entities based upon their monadic properties rather than the relations they stand in. According to Non-Relationality, abstractness and concreteness are monadic properties, not relations like *being abstract at* or *being concrete at* that entities bear to worlds, times, or locations. Entities are therefore abstract (or concrete) *simpliciter*, not merely relative to some index.

(v) <u>Spatiotemporal Constancy.</u> Spatiotemporally constant distinctions hold that the category to which entities belong does not vary across regions of spacetime. According to Spatiotemporal Constancy, if an entity is abstract (or concrete) at some spatiotemporal region, there is no spatiotemporal region at which it is concrete (or abstract). Granted certain assumptions about the relationship between spacetime and our loose talk about "space" and "time," Spatiotemporal Constancy entails Spatial Constancy, according to which the abstractness (or concreteness) of an entity cannot vary across spatial locations, as well as Temporal Constancy, according to which abstractness (or concreteness) cannot vary across times.

(vi) <u>Modal Constancy.</u> While Spatiotemporal Constancy rules out entities changing from abstract to concrete (and *vice versa*) across spatiotemporal regions, Modal Constancy rules out entities changing categories across possible worlds. According to Modal Constancy, the abstract–concrete distinction divides entities in a non-contingent way. So, if an entity is actually abstract, it could not have been concrete (and *vice versa*). In addition, if an entity necessarily exists, then it is either necessarily abstract or necessarily concrete. And, if an entity only contingently exists, then, if it is possibly abstract, it is not possibly concrete (and *vice versa*).

The formal features of the standard view suggest that the abstract–concrete distinction is a remarkably well-behaved divide in reality, separating entities into two exhaustive, disjoint ontological categories. It is perhaps unsurprising, then, that each of these six theses has been challenged at some point or other. Those who deny Exhaustiveness, posit entities that are neither abstract nor concrete. Others, who reject Absoluteness or Non-Relationality, take abstractness to come in degrees or to be a relation entities bear to different worlds or times. Still others reject Spatiotemporal and Modal Constancy and allege that entities can vary in their concreteness or abstractness across regions or worlds.[1] More often than not, these challenges issue from a commitment to fully developed metaphysical theories that simply end up in conflict with the standard view. Indeed, it is somewhat rare for opponents of the standard view to take the features just set out to be, at first glance, implausible, inconsistent, or otherwise objectionable. Accordingly, most who are not in the grip of a theory that runs contrary to the standard view are usually content to accept (i)–(vi). And, since the impetus for most challenges to (i)–(vi) depend upon the details of complex alternatives, we cannot do justice to these challenges here. We will, however, note certain of them in passing below.

The standard view does not consist solely in these six theses above. After all, (i)–(vi) say almost nothing about which entities fall on either side of the divide in question. So, like any other theory, a proper characterization of the standard view also comes with a cluster of less formal theses and remarks that clarify the distinction and its attendant conception of abstractness. These informal theses and remarks come in three kinds: examples, disambiguations, and generalizations.

Examples. Fully characterizing the standard view requires that we provide examples of those entities properly counted as abstract. In this regard, we are best served to point to properties, propositions, sets, and other mathematical entities as paradigm cases. Conversely, we can offer tables, tuques, and toboggans as examples of paradigmatic concrete entities.

Disambiguations. The abstract–concrete distinction must be explicitly distinguished from closely related distinctions with which it might be conflated. The abstract–concrete distinction is not, for example, merely the distinction between particular entities (e.g., the Eiffel Tower, Obama) and general entities (e.g., universals like *redness* and *humanity*) nor is it the distinction between non-sets like Socrates and sets like {Socrates}. For, while these distinctions align with the abstract–concrete distinction in some ways, they come apart in other cases, especially since the category of *abstract entity* includes entities in addition to sets and universals.

Generalizations. Our characterization of the standard view can be developed by pointing to some standard generalizations about the nature of abstract entities. These rough generalizations typically extrapolate from our paradigm cases like the number seven or the Pythagorean theorem. And, as we've already seen, it is commonplace to single out abstracta as entities without locations or without causal powers, or as entities to which we have special cognitive access.

Taken together, the preceding theses and informal remarks suffice to characterize the standard view in a way that allows the uninitiated to grasp the abstract–concrete distinction. And, for certain philosophical tasks, these remarks do seem adequate for clarifying our talk of abstract and concrete entities. Unfortunately, this somewhat lax practice has led to the proliferation of questionable arguments involving abstract entities. These arguments turn on an uncritical acceptance of generalizations which some philosophers have been too quick to assume as premises to argue from rather than as controversial theses to argue for. And, given the considerable divide between, say, austere and expansive platonism, this is a source of no small disagreement.

Since our present concern is the fate of nominalism and platonism, we require a considerably greater level of theoretical precision than the above characterization of the abstract–concrete distinction. So, in the next section, we will assess the plausibility of various generalizations about the nature of abstract entities. (We will also face tough questions about the proper method for assessing these generalizations.) We will ask, for example, whether abstracta uniformly lack spatiotemporal locations, causal powers, and so on. Often, these generalizations are put forward as either necessary or sufficient conditions for being an abstract entity. It is fortunate, then, that our investigation into these generalizations can be usefully paired with a closely related task: evaluating potential reductive analyses of the abstract–concrete distinction. These reductive analyses aim to explain the abstract–concrete distinction in informative, non-circular terms by appealing to distinctions or facts concerning, say, causation or location. Traditionally, these analyses take the form of a necessitated biconditional that specifies jointly necessary and sufficient conditions for an entity to be abstract. (In what follows, we will use "$=_{df}$" to mark those analyses offering jointly necessary and sufficient conditions.) So, in investigating these potential analyses, we will also examine whether there are any useful generalizations about the nature of abstract entities.

According to reductionists, the abstract–concrete distinction admits of analysis or "reduction" to notions independent from "abstract" and "concrete." But what are the requirements for a successful reduction? One requirement is, of course, that the proposed analysis make no explicit or implicit appeal to the notions of abstractness or concreteness. Failure on this front is grounds for immediate disqualification, since analyses that violate this constraint are circular: they fail to analyze their target notion in genuinely independent terms. Along with being non-circular and so genuinely informative, a successful reductive analysis must meet two other criteria. It must be finitely stateable, not merely an infinitely long list of all abstract entities. It must also be extensionally adequate, counting all and only abstract entities as abstract. Note also that we will be somewhat flexible in our formulation of potential analyses. For, given Exclusiveness and Exhaustiveness, it makes no difference whether we proceed by analyzing abstractness and then define concreteness in terms of it or begin instead with concreteness and proceed to define abstractness. We will therefore indulge in somewhat loose talk about analyzing "the distinction," where this can be taken as shorthand for analyzing either of our two interdefinable target notions.

Methodologically, the prospects for and value of reductive analyses are controversial. Crucially, the project undertaken here is not aimed at conceptual autobiography or the analysis of our own particular psychological representations. Rather, it takes aim at the notions of *abstractness* and *concreteness* insofar as they figure into our best metaphysical theories in much the same way that notions like *species* and *planet* figure into scientific ones. So understood, the project of reductive analysis aims to explain the features of the world that are targeted by these concepts. Accordingly, the pursuit of a reductive analysis of the abstract–concrete distinction is worthwhile for a few reasons. If successful, it supplies us with some independent guidance about which entities are abstract. For example, if abstractness admits of analysis in causal terms, then we can settle open questions about the abstractness of entities by considering causal facts. It also ensures that the notion of *abstractness* (or, alternatively, *concreteness*) need not be adopted as a primitive bit of theoretical ideology in formulating platonist theories. As we'll discuss in Chapter 3, this affords platonists a certain kind of ideological simplification of their preferred theory. Finally, in asking whether abstractness admits of explanation in more fundamental terms, we can make progress in determining which notions play a substantive role in fundamental metaphysics. For, by investigating potential analyses that invoke causation, location, and other sorts of facts, we can make inroads into broader questions about which facts have a fair claim to being metaphysically fundamental.

§2.2 Analyzing abstractness

Within the tradition of analytic metaphysics stemming from Frege, Moore, and Russell, analyses of abstractness receive fairly little attention until the 1980s. Up to that point, conflicting characterizations are commonplace. For example, Goodman and Quine (1947) tie the notion of abstractness to the notion of spatiotemporal location, but, after Benacerraf (1973), discussions about abstracta regularly focus on causal notions in characterizing the abstract–concrete distinction.

Lewis (1986: 81–86) usefully surveys the many ways in which philosophers have conceived of the abstract–concrete distinction. There, he suggests that talk about the abstract and the concrete is a theoretical hodge-podge, picking out certain features on some uses and importantly different features on others. Ultimately, Lewis' discussion suggests a deflationary view on which there is no uniquely fundamental distinction in the neighbourhood of the abstract–concrete distinction. At best, there are a few roughly overlapping distinctions (e.g., the distinctions between the general and particular, between sets and non-sets, and so on), but none of these have a claim to being the abstract–concrete distinction.

What should we make of Lewis' claim that the abstract–concrete distinction is a mere hodge-podge of different distinctions? Here, the boring answer is the right one: it depends. Specifically, it depends on what, if any, theoretical role is assigned to the abstract–concrete distinction. As we'll see throughout this chapter, different views of the distinction deliver importantly different views about its significance. To see what, if any, theoretical role the distinction might play, it will be useful to first examine some of the accounts of the distinction that Lewis discusses along with some potential analyses he leaves undiscussed.

Following Lewis' terminology, let's call these accounts of the abstract–concrete distinction "Ways." Most of these are rightly viewed as proposals for reductively analyzing the abstract–concrete distinction. That said, not all Ways are aimed at offering a reductive analysis. (Note, too, that I've relabelled some instances of what Lewis calls the Way of Negation and introduced a few Ways that Lewis omits.) For instance, the Way of Example is simply a label for the perfectly legitimate heuristic of introducing the abstract–concrete distinction by citing examples. It is neither put forward as a reductive analysis nor does it offer anything like necessary and sufficient conditions for being abstract. It is, instead, part of any suitable characterization of the abstract–concrete distinction, but, when left unsupplemented, it cannot underwrite the use of the distinction for any serious theoretical purpose. Our interest will therefore be in Ways that go beyond the Way of Example in trying to spell out what exactly abstractness consists in.

One of these is what Lewis (1986: 84) calls the Way of Abstraction, according to which abstract entities "result from somehow subtracting specificity, so that an incomplete description of the original concrete entity would be a complete description of the abstraction." So described, the Way of Abstraction admits of several very different interpretations. The least plausible of these takes abstract entities to be "abstractions" akin to "abstract ideas" and therefore much like our ideas of redness or sphericality that we cognitively "subtract" from experiences. Interpreted this way, the Way of

Abstraction implausibly requires that all abstract entities are mind-dependent mental entities and therefore runs contrary to any standard conception of platonism.

A more plausible interpretation of the Way of Abstraction takes abstract entities to be the referents of terms introduced using what are sometimes called "abstraction principles." These principles seek to implicitly define terms referring to abstracta by specifying the truth-conditions of identity claims about abstracta in terms of concrete entities. On this view, abstract entities are not somehow brought into existence by a mental act of "subtracting specificity," but our success in referring to them and, in turn, our epistemic access to them owes to the relevant abstraction principles. In using such principles, a standard ambition is to implicitly define abstract objects—most notably, numbers—in terms of nothing more than certain relational predicates among concrete entities (e.g., "are in one-to-one correspondence"). One such proposal holds that we can define putative abstracta like directions in terms of a relational predicate "is parallel with" that is true of certain lines.[2] Speaking loosely, such a view introduces an operator, "is the direction of" and then defines an expression like "the direction of line b" by noting that directions of lines are identical if and only if they are parallel. In this way, abstraction principles are what allow us to define and, in turn, refer to alleged abstract entities like the *number* of planets or the *directions* of lines.

There is a venerable platonist tradition that relies upon abstraction principles in providing an epistemology of mathematics and other abstract entities; however, it is unclear whether such a view might plausibly explain the abstract–concrete distinction itself. It is also rather unclear how notions like "incompleteness" or "subtracting specificity" might be of much help in this regard. Finally, there is no guarantee that abstract entities are all and only those entities that admit of contextual definition along these lines. So, while we are under no obligation to reject the use of abstraction principles and we will return to views in this neighbourhood in subsequent chapters, we can set aside the Way of Abstraction here. In its place, we will turn to reductionist proposals that invoke criteria like location, causation, and necessity to analyze abstractness.

§2.2.1 *Location*

Numbers do not have locations in spacetime. In fact, the claim that "The number thirty-six is in Halifax" is a category mistake, if anything is. It is no less odd to claim that propositions are located. It seems plausible, then, that like numbers and propositions, all abstract entities might be "outside" of spacetime. In marked contrast, concrete entities do have locations within spacetime. It is therefore tempting to view the difference between the abstract and the concrete as simply a matter of spatiotemporal location. So, according to the Way of Location, what is to be abstract is just to be something that lacks any spatiotemporal location:

Way of Location: x is an abstract entity $=_{df} x$ has no spatiotemporal location.

This formulation of the Way of Location draws exclusively upon the notion of *spatiotemporal* location. This notion, obviously enough, depends upon a prior commitment to spacetime or spatiotemporal relations as well as the assumption that things have spatiotemporal location rather than, say, separate spatial or temporal locations. This assumption squares with our best physical theories, which standardly dispense with a pre-relativistic distinction between space and time. And, while some entities like Cartesian souls have been alleged to possess temporal but not spatial locations, views that require a fundamental distinction between spatial and temporal location fit poorly with our best physical theories. Here, we will focus exclusively on *spatiotemporal* location and set aside views that take abstractness to consist in, say, merely a lack of temporal location. We will also ignore variations on the Way of Location like the one offered in Quine (1948), which holds abstractness to consist, not in a lack of spatiotemporal location, but, even less plausibly, a lack of spatiotemporal *extension*.[3]

We can also set aside a worry regarding spacetime regions. Since spatiotemporal regions are locations rather than *located* entities, the Way of Location seems to deliver the peculiar verdict that spacetime points and the regions built out of them are abstract entities. (Interestingly, Carnap (1950) seems to endorse precisely this verdict.) But, given their causal role and their commonalities with other physical posits, there is reason to view spatial regions as no less concrete than the objects occupying them. Fortunately, this problem for the Way of Location is easy enough to remedy. We can simply stipulate that, on the relevant sense of "location," spatiotemporal locations are trivially self-located and so properly counted among concrete entities.

Presented with the Way of Location, it might seem a fairly simple matter to determine whether it aptly characterizes the abstract–concrete distinction. Unfortunately, assessing this proposal comes with a cluster of methodological problems. Chief among these problems is that, on certain views about properties, some apparently abstract entities are, in fact, located within spacetime. Recall, as we noted in Chapter 1, that some hold the theoretical role associated with properties to be occupied by universals, while others assign tropes or sets to this role. Views about universals divide in two when it comes to whether universals are located. *Platonic* views claim that universals are *ante rem* or "transcendent" entities without locations in space or time. *Aristotelian* views claim that universals are *in re* or "immanent" entities, existing wherever they are instantiated.[4] So, for the Aristotelian, the universal *being a moose* is located throughout spacetime, wherever moose are located. A parallel disagreement arises over the location of impure sets. Some hold them to be located wherever their members are located, while others deny impure sets have locations.[5] Finally, trope theorists typically hold that at least some tropes are located in spacetime.

If there are Aristotelian universals, located impure sets, or tropes and such entities are abstract, this would be enough to show that the Way of Location is extensionally inadequate. There is, however, disagreement about whether there are such entities and there is potential disagreement about whether such entities are properly counted among the abstract. Notice, also, that expansive platonism clashes rather badly with the Way of Location, since created or conventional abstract entities like recipes, dances, and nations seem to be located in time. It is peculiar, for example, to think that the recipe for duck confit pre-dates the existence of ducks or that the tango existed during the Big Bang. For those who reject these allegedly located abstracta and posit only *ante rem* entities like transcendent universals, the Way of Location will seem fairly plausible. That said, when assessing analyses, the fact that an analysis misclassifies competing metaphysical posits—even those one rejects—is of uncertain bearing on its adequacy. Should, for example, the proponent of *ante rem* universals be forced to abandon the Way of Location on the grounds that, if *there were tropes* rather than universals, it would give the wrong verdict? More generally, should we reject potential analyses on the basis of conceptually possible counterexamples even while we might deny that these counterexamples are genuine metaphysical possibilities? If so, the conceptual possibility of located impure sets and Aristotelian universals is a good reason for anyone to reject the Way of Location. If not, one could, in principle, tailor her ontology to match her preferred analysis and set aside the sorts of counterexamples just noted.

The methodological issue just raised is a deep one with broad consequences. Since we won't try to settle it here, this all but guarantees that no counterexample to the Way of Location will be unanimously accepted. Despite this, there remains good reason to reject the view that abstractness is properly analyzed in terms of location and to hold that matters of abstractness and concreteness are separable from concerns about location. Suppose, for example, there is a realm of fundamental physical entities from which spatiotemporal reality is itself generated or, instead, that there are non-spatial Cartesian minds in a timeless world. While these are exotic posits, there is no temptation to deem them abstract rather than concrete. So, along with the more tendentious cases just noted, they strongly suggest that a lack of location is neither a necessary nor sufficient condition for abstractness. We are therefore best served to look elsewhere for an analysis of abstractness.

§2.2.2 *Causation*

Properties, propositions, and mathematical entities seem to be neither created nor destroyed. They also seem to have no active causal role in the world, given that they lack physical quantities like mass and perceptible features like colour. Nor, as Armstrong (1978: 128) memorably remarks, do they seem to "exert some sort of steady unchanging pressure." Abstract entities therefore seem to be outside of the causal order of the world in some important sense. In stark contrast, the fleeting nature of concrete reality suggests that all concrete entities play at least some part in the causal order of the world. They come into being, pass away, exert forces, hold doors open, and flood basements.

According to the Way of Causation, abstract entities are distinguished precisely by their conspicuous absence from the causal order of the world:

Way of Causation: x is an abstract entity $=_{df}$ x is causally inactive.

Where the Way of Location draws upon the notion of location, the Way of Causation appeals to the far murkier notion of causation. Not only is there a vast list of competing views about the nature of causation, the more general question of whether causation deserves a place in our best theory of the world remains a live issue. For those sympathetic to the Russellian sentiment that talk of causation is a "relic of a bygone age," there is no reason to think causation is well suited for explicating the abstract–concrete distinction. And, for those who part company with Russell, the diversity of views about causation still makes it difficult to specify the nature of abstract entities' causal impotence, since doing so requires choosing a background metaphysics of causation for explaining the relevant notion of "causal inactivity." The wealth of controversy that comes with the Way of Causation might scare off some, but, even after we assume that the notion of "causal inactivity" is well understood, there remain serious challenges for the Way of Causation.

An initial challenge denies that causal inactivity is a necessary condition for being abstract. This is because entities like propositions and properties are claimed to have a causal role in the world. It might seem, for example, that it is in virtue of believing the proposition that the mug is full, that you reach for your coffee and that, similarly, it is in virtue of instantiating *being hot* and *being fragile* that the mug is dropped and shatters. When we describe the role of propositions and properties in this way, proponents of this challenge are tempted to think that abstracta *do* figure into the causal order of the world, contrary to the Way of Causation.

The standard response to this challenge holds that, although abstract entities figure into *metaphysical* explanations, their role is not a causal one. While your mental states caused you to reach for the mug, the relationship between your mental state and the proposition *that the mug is full* is not causal in nature. Similarly, while objects like the mug have causal powers that depend upon the properties they instantiate, the instantiation relation is not a causal relation either. Properly understood, these relations provide metaphysical rather than causal explanations. So, while the mug was dropped partly because it instantiates the property of *being hot*, the genuinely causal "action" involves only concrete reality.

There is something plausible in the above response. At the same time, its success depends upon adequately explicating the nature of non-causal relations like *instantiation* that objects bear to properties. This is no small part of the broader platonist project. If it can be accomplished, there is no reason to think that abstract entities are causally active just because they figure into metaphysical explanations. It also suggests that the role of properties and propositions in metaphysical explanations is markedly different from, say, the role of elbows and potholes in more familiar causal explanations. In this vein, Frege says of "thoughts," which, again, are just propositions (or close metaphysical cousins): "How different the process of handing over a hammer is from the communication of a thought. The hammer passes from one control to another, it is gripped, it undergoes pressure and on account of this its density, the disposition of its parts, is changed in places. There is nothing of all this with a thought."

Let us grant, then, that abstract entities like properties and propositions can figure into metaphysical explanations without thereby entering into causal relations. Even so, there are other abstract entities that do seem to stand in certain causal relations. Consider, for example, an impure set like {Socrates}, which seems to have come into and then gone out of existence precisely when Socrates himself came into and went out of existence. Since coming into and going out of existence is typically held to be a causal process, there is *prima facie* evidence for thinking that impure sets must play some part in the causal order of the world by being created or destroyed.[6] A similar concern arises for views on which the *relata* of the *causation* relation are held to be events, which are in turn identified with impure sets—e.g., sets of spacetime points *a la* Lewis (1986c) or sets of properties, times, and individuals *a la* Kim (1970). On such views, the event of my dropping the mug is an impure set of some sort and stands in the causation relation to the event of the mug shattering. On such views, sets are implicated in the causal order of the world by virtue of being identified with events. What, then, should defenders of the Way of Causation say in addressing these apparent counterexamples?

The best hope for sustaining the Way of Causation without riding roughshod over our judgments about abstractness is to insist that, on the relevant understanding of causation, impure sets and events remain causally inactive. According to this proposal, only the concrete entities like spacetime regions or individuals that are the *members* of impure sets are causally active. And, while this squares with our rough intuitions, it is either plainly circular or comes with the considerable baggage. For example, we cannot hold that entities are causally active in virtue of standing in the causation relation, since, on some views, it has set-theoretic entities as its relata. We therefore require some analysis or explanation that does not illegitimately presuppose the abstract–concrete distinction that we set out to analyze. Whether this can be accomplished is unclear, but it strongly suggests that nothing like the Way of Causation will be satisfactory unless paired with a full-fledged theory of causal activity and perhaps causation itself.

Like the Way of Location, the Way of Causation conflicts quite badly with expansive versions of platonism. After all, our ordinary talk about the abstract entities posited by expansive platonists suggests such entities are created and therefore causally active. It seems that John Le Carré created George Smiley, that Smiley inspired many imitators, and that George Smiley is the product of Le Carré's experiences in MI6. Similar examples abound.

Moreover, we seem to ascribe causal roles to putative abstract entities like GDPs, sonatas, and gang signs. So, while the Way of Causation is in tension with austere platonism, it is in outright opposition to expansive versions of platonism. Expansive platonists therefore have no reason to accept the Way of Causation as an account of abstractness.

Along with worries about causally active abstract entities, the Way of Causation faces concerns about causally inactive concreta. Suppose, for example, that there could be entities of the sort that Peter Forrest (1982: 458) calls *epiphenomenalons*—"particles that than which no more useless can be conceived of"—that are neither created nor destroyed and stand in no causal relations to other entities (including other epiphenomenalons). Although there is no reason to think the actual world includes such creatures, they have a fair claim to being possible and so presumably inhabit some merely possible worlds. Intuitively, these causally inactive entities are concrete, but this intuitive verdict disagrees badly with the Way of Causation. Consider, too, the similar fate of a lonely Cartesian soul, existing eternally in a world with no other minds and incapable of causal interaction. Given this lonely soul's profound causal isolation, the Way of Causation seems to errantly classify it as abstract rather than concrete. This, again, suggests that causal inactivity is not a sufficient condition for being abstract. So, even if austere versions of platonism can dodge the counterexamples above, causal inactivity does not appear to be a sufficient condition for being abstract

In Chapter 4, we'll further explore the connection between causation and abstract entities. But, given the challenges just noted, the Way of Causation seems a poor candidate for supplying us with a reductive analysis of abstractness.

§2.2.3 Necessity

Numbers, propositions, and properties are perhaps the least contentious examples of necessary existents. According to most platonists, it is impossible that these entities fail to exist. In fact, nominalists typically concede that, if abstract entities of these kinds *were to exist*, they would exist necessarily. Since familiar concrete entities like islands and igloos are contingent existents, one might suspect that a modal distinction between necessary and contingent existents would provide an analysis of the abstract–concrete distinction. Taking our cue from Lewis' terminological convention, we can call the resulting analysis the Way of Necessity:

Way of Necessity: x is an abstract entity $=_{df}$ x necessarily exists.

Counterexamples quickly threaten the Way of Necessity. But, before examining them, it is worth pointing out that the necessary existence of abstract entities like numbers and propositions is, when explained at all, typically explained by appeal to their apparent causal inactivity. This explanation, which assumes the causal inactivity of the relevant abstracta, runs roughly as follows. If abstract entities can be neither created nor destroyed, then their existence cannot be contingent upon any concrete matters. So, unless the existence of abstract entities is a brute and contingent fact resisting explanation, abstract entities necessarily exist. And, since the existence of abstracta like numbers is not plausibly held to be an inexplicable brute fact, such entities must be necessary existents.

This argument depends upon two highly contentious claims: (i) that abstract entities are, in fact, causally inactive; and (ii) that the existence of abstract entities like numbers cannot be a brute fact. Whether or not we reject one of these premises, many platonists are independently committed to denying that all abstract entities exist necessarily. For, as noted above, many hold that impure sets are contingent existents—e.g., {Socrates} exists only in worlds where Socrates does. Additionally, since in re universals are located where and only where they are instantiated, such views typically hold that properties like *mass* exist in only some worlds, namely those worlds where *mass* is instantiated. And, as we'll discuss in Chapter 6, some austere versions of platonism hold that non-qualitative "haecceities" like *being Napoleon* exist in only some possible worlds—namely, ones with Napoleon.

These examples suggest that necessary existence is not a necessary condition for abstractness. Still other examples suggest that necessary existence is not a sufficient condition either. After all, the Abrahamic God is a commonly posited necessary existent and, despite its exceptional metaphysical features, there is no compelling reason to believe such an entity is abstract solely on account of its necessary existence. Such a being would, for example, have formidable causal powers and stand in a variety of spatial and temporal relations to the concrete world in virtue of creating it. Moreover, whether or not one accepts theism, it is clear that our concept of necessary existence and abstractness can come apart. Suppose, for example, that the radical view attributed to Spinoza is correct and that all truths are necessarily true. Even so, there is no good reason to infer, on the basis of this surprising modal fact, that you and your favourite mug are abstract rather than concrete.

The ambition of the Way of Necessity—to distinguish the abstract from the concrete on the basis of necessary existence—is a mistaken one. But, it usefully draws out a contentious assumption common to many inquiries into abstract entities: that abstract entities must be either necessary or contingent existents. As noted above, there is a lengthy tradition of holding abstract entities to lack locations in spacetime. In holding abstract entities to lack spatiotemporal location, we rule out views on which they are omnipresent or eternal since, on such views, abstracta are simply located across all regions. And, if abstract entities like numbers lack locations in spacetime, those who posit such entities owe some account of why they are rightly held to exist at this or that possible world. While we'll revisit this issue in Chapter 6, a live option that has largely gone unconsidered is that, in parallel to the denial that numbers exist eternally, one might similarly deny that abstract entities exist necessarily or contingently. On such a view, abstract entities are neither necessary nor contingent existents. Instead, they are "outside" modal reality just as they are "outside" spatiotemporal reality. Admitting entities with such a peculiar modal status is no small thing, but to whatever extent abstract entities might be singled out in modal terms, it is more likely to be for occupying a peculiar modal status of this kind rather than for being necessary existents.[7]

§2.2.4 Complexity

Neither facts about location, causation, nor necessity deliver a reductive analysis of abstractness. Our best bet is therefore to explore somewhat less familiar strategies for demarcating the abstract from the concrete. The first place we can look is to facts regarding the complexity (or lack thereof) of abstract entities. For, while concrete objects can have other concrete objects as parts, it is not obvious that abstract entities like numbers, properties, and propositions can also have parts. So, in our hunt for a reductive analysis in terms of complexity, we can now ask whether the complexity or structure of abstract entities might distinguish them from concrete entities.

In this regard, one initial conjecture would hold that all abstract entities are "simple" entities that lack parts.[8] It looks, however, like this conjecture isn't especially plausible. On several theories, properties have other properties as parts. For universal theorists, a commitment to what are usually called "structural universals" is commonplace. It holds that a hydrocarbon universal like *being methane* has *being carbon* and *being hydrogen* as parts. Analogous views about propositions are similarly common and hold propositions like that pigs fly is true to have as parts both other propositions like that pigs fly as well as the properties and objects they are about.[9]

Although it is fairly common to hold that some abstract entities have other entities as parts, this talk about parthood and complexity is a delicate matter. Taken one way, talk of parthood and complexity is understood mereologically, where the relevant parthood relation obeys the axioms of classical extensional mereology. Such a view takes parthood to be reflexive, transitive, and anti-symmetric. Taken another way, parthood and complexity is non-mereological in nature, where non-mereological "constituency" relations violate these or other constraints. (Among other things, non-mereological composition allows for distinct entities composed from the very same constituents.) Typically, most views of structural universals hold such entities to be non-mereologically complex, since, for example, different hydrocarbon universals seem to be built out of *being carbon* and *being hydrogen*. Similarly, the propositions that Steve kissed Jane and that Jane kissed Steve are distinct, despite having the very same constituents.

Once we distinguish between mereological and non-mereological complexity, the space of possible options for analyzing abstractness expands considerably. We might hold, for example, that abstract entities are mereologically simple yet non-mereologically complex. But, regardless of the kind of complexity we have in mind, there is good reason to think at least some abstract entities are complex. Along with the above examples, it is plausible that, whether or not sets have their *members* as non-mereological parts, they do have their *subsets* as mereological parts.[10] Moreover, there is no good reason to believe that a lack of complexity is a sufficient condition for being abstract. Fundamental physical objects, lacking mereological or non-mereological parts, are a perennial metaphysical posit, but such "atoms" are not therefore abstract in virtue of lacking parts.

If abstract entities are not distinguished by their lack of complexity, perhaps there is a specific kind of complexity they fail to exhibit. A natural thought here is that, unlike concrete entities, it might be impossible for there to be abstract entities that are infinitely complex or "gunky," where gunky entities have parts all of which have further proper parts. In contrast to familiar structural universals, the possibility of gunky abstract entities is fairly exotic. But, while such posits are unfamiliar, it is unclear why gunky abstract entities should be thought impossible. For example, one might argue that the existence of infinitely complex abstract entities like gunky propositions, gunky properties, or gunky impure sets follows from the existence of gunky concrete objects—e.g., if such objects are parts of propositions or sets. Similarly, a fan of gunky structural universals might argue that the possibility of gunky concrete objects presupposes the possibility of gunky universals that they instantiate. Regardless, there seems to be nothing incoherent about infinitely complex abstract entities. As a result, we are left without any promising analysis of the abstract–concrete distinction that turns on matters of complexity or parthood.

§2.2.5 Indiscernibility and duplication

Regardless of whether one holds properties to be universals, tropes, or sets, distinctions between different kinds of properties—e.g., between mental and physical properties or between moral and non-moral properties—are commonplace. One strategy for analyzing the abstract–concrete distinction is to draw upon the most general distinctions among properties in hopes of singling out abstract entities from concrete ones. To see whether this strategy might succeed, we can begin by introducing two foundational distinctions among properties:

(i) *Qualitative and non-qualitative.* Imagine a possible world in which there are only two perfect iron spheres floating five feet from one another. These spheres, A and B, are exactly alike with respect to their physical features: they have the same mass, shape, colour, and so on. In general, A and B share all their qualitative properties such as *being made of iron* and *being five feet from a sphere*. The only properties they do not share are non-qualitative properties like *being identical to A* and *being distinct from B*. Intuitively, these and other non-qualitative properties like *being the daughter of Socrates* are tied to specific individuals. And, while it is controversial how to draw the distinction between qualitative and non-qualitative properties, once we help ourselves to it, it is uncontroversial that A and B are qualitatively indiscernible from one another. They differ only with respect to their non-qualitative properties.

(ii) *Intrinsic and extrinsic properties.* Imagine a possible world in which, along with A and B from above, there is a speck of dust three feet from A and four feet from B. In such a world, A and B are no longer qualitatively indiscernible: they differ in their *extrinsic* properties, since only A has *being three feet from dust*. Despite this, A and B share all the same *intrinsic* properties. They are therefore perfect duplicates, where duplicate entities are just those entities that share all the same intrinsic qualitative properties. As above, it is controversial how, if at all, we can analyze the notion of an intrinsic property (and, in turn, an extrinsic property). But, roughly speaking, an entity's intrinsic properties are those properties it has in virtue of how it is rather than how other objects are or how it is related to other objects. So, for example, properties like *being ten feet from a duck* and *being the tallest giraffe* are extrinsic; their instantiation depends upon, not only their bearer, but also upon other entities (e.g., ducks and other giraffes). In contrast, *being an electron*, *being made of iron*, and *being conscious* are plausibly viewed as intrinsic; they seem to be features their bearers have independently of other objects.

If we assume that the above distinctions partition the entire space of properties, there are four kinds of properties: qualitative intrinsic properties (e.g., *mass*, *being an electron*), qualitative extrinsic properties (e.g., *being five feet from an electron*, *being the largest sphere*), non-qualitative intrinsic properties (e.g., *being Napoleon*), and non-qualitative extrinsic properties (e.g., *being five feet from Napoleon*).

Given this fourfold division, it is worth asking whether there is any distinctive restriction on the properties that abstract or concrete entities can instantiate. At first glance, it looks as though concrete objects instantiate all four kinds of properties. It is not obvious that this is true of abstract entities. Extrinsic properties are metaphysically cheap and, since numbers and propositions are entities we can speak about and that lack locations, they bear extrinsic properties like *being expressed by a sentence of English*, *being thought about for many years*, and *taking up less space than the Spruce Goose*. So, if there is an interesting limitation on the properties of abstract entities, it will concern the intrinsic properties they might instantiate.

Given what we said about complexity above, there is some reason to believe that abstract entities do have qualitative intrinsic properties. These seem to include categoreal and complexity properties like *being abstract* and *being mereologically simple (or complex)*. They also seem to have various non-qualitative intrinsic properties—e.g., the number seven has the property *being identical to the number seven*. So, while abstract entities lack qualitative physical properties like *mass* and *charge* borne by concrete entities, they do seem to have qualitative and non-qualitative intrinsic properties. As such, the general distinctions between intrinsic and extrinsic properties and between qualitative and non-qualitative properties provide no easy way to distinguish the abstract and the concrete.

Abstract entities like properties lack paradigmatic physical intrinsic properties like *mass*. Despite this, there is reason to think platonists are still obliged to attribute distinctive "intrinsic natures" unique to each property or proposition. Consider, for example, the standard platonist view according to which an object has its mass in virtue of instantiating the property of *mass* (or various *mass* determinates). On such a view, there must be some feature of the property *mass* that makes it uniquely able to explain why object resists acceleration and distinguish it from other properties like *charge*. Put differently: there must be some intrinsic and presumably qualitative features of *mass* that accounts for why it makes its particular contribution to the nature of its bearers rather than the contribution made by *charge*. To explain how each property plays its distinctive explanatory role, platonists seem required to ascribe a special intrinsic nature to each property. Similar remarks apply to propositions, given the distinctive connections they bear to specific mental states and to states of the world.

Accounting for the intrinsic nature of properties is another requirement for a successful platonist metaphysics. If, however, properties each have a distinctive intrinsic nature, this suggests that properties are, of necessity, importantly different from one another. The same verdict does not hold for concrete entities, since concrete entities can coexist with qualitatively indiscernible doppelgangers—see, e.g., the case of our spheres, A and B, described above. Some have taken this contrast between properties and concreta as a potential route for analyzing the abstract–concrete distinction.

According to the Way of Indiscernibility, it is possible that, for any concrete entity, there is some entity qualitatively indiscernible from it. (See, e.g., Baldwin (1996: 233).) In contrast, it seems impossible that there be entities distinct from but qualitatively indiscernible with properties like *redness* and *mass*, since each property must have a distinctive intrinsic nature that accounts for its metaphysical contribution. Put more explicitly:

Way of Indiscernibility: x is an abstract entity $=_{df}$ there can be no entity distinct from but qualitatively indiscernible with x.

Is this a plausible analysis of the abstract–concrete distinction? Not for those who endorse the Principle of the Identity of Indiscernibles (PII), according to which qualitative indiscernibility suffices for identity. For, as Lewis (1986) notes, the truth of PII, conjoined with the Way of Indiscernibility, delivers the bizarre result that absolutely everything is concrete. And, although the conceivability and concomitant possibility of worlds with indiscernible spheres like A and B is usually thought to undermine PII, there are other reasons to reject the Way of Indiscernibility. As Lewis also points out, impure sets that have qualitatively indiscernible members are plausibly thought to be abstract but qualitatively indiscernible. More generally, the Way of Indiscernibility might be suitable for distinguishing universals from particulars, but, since there is no good reason to believe that other abstracta like numbers cannot be qualitatively indiscernible from one another, it cannot capture the broader abstract–concrete distinction.

If the Way of Indiscernibility is motivated by the apparent insight that abstract entities have distinctive *intrinsic* natures, it is also needlessly strong. For, if entities have distinctive intrinsic natures, they cannot even be duplicates of one another, much less qualitatively indiscernible. A weaker proposal that still captures the guiding idea would run as follows:

> **Way of Duplication**: x is an abstract entity $=_{df}$ there can be no entity that is distinct from but also a duplicate of x.

The Way of Duplication entails that each abstract entity has a unique intrinsic nature. And, since perfect duplication concerns only qualitative properties, these unique intrinsic natures would have to be qualitative in character. (Recall that entities can be duplicates even while differing in non-qualitative properties like *being identical to B*.) The Way of Duplication therefore requires an enormous diversity of qualitative intrinsic natures, one unique to each abstract entity. Since these qualitative properties are not just properties like *mass, charge*, or even more general properties like *being mereologically simple*, what might they be? Since such properties are so unlike any familiar qualitative properties, it is simply unclear how we might get an independent grip on their metaphysical status.

The intrinsic nature of abstract entities is a pressing concern for platonists. Should they hold that each entity has a unique property exclusive to it alone? Or are the intrinsic natures of abstracta unique permutations of some infinite stock of progressively higher-order properties? Whatever platonists ought to think in this regard, it seems that the costs of the Way of Duplication are prohibitive. And, since this proposal enjoys little independent motivation, no analysis of the abstract–concrete distinction along these lines seems especially promising.

§2.2.6 Fundamentality

According to *existence* monism, there is only one entity: the cosmos. Of course, since there are many things, existence monism is false, but a more plausible monistic thesis, defended in Schaffer (2010), holds instead that there is only one *fundamental* concrete entity: the cosmos. According to this *priority monism*, all other concrete entities—e.g., people and particles—are *derivative* entities: they are metaphysically dependent, either immediately or through a chain of intermediate entities, upon the cosmos.

Most philosophers endorse the competing view, *priority pluralism*, and posit many fundamental entities like particles or spacetime regions. But, for either priority thesis, the relation of metaphysical dependence that holds among entities is crucial for describing the metaphysical structure of the world. For some, this relation of metaphysical dependence is a primitive one, resisting further analysis. For others, there is no univocal relation of metaphysical dependence. Instead, talk of metaphysical dependence can be unpacked in terms of supervenience, realization, and other relations. Between these views are numerous alternatives, but, however one conceives of metaphysical dependence, it worth briefly considering whether abstractness and concreteness admit of analysis in terms of metaphysical dependence.

Since almost everyone believes that at least some concrete entities depend upon other concrete entities (e.g., you seem to depend upon fundamental particles), there is no reason to think that all dependent entities are therefore abstract. A more plausible thought therefore holds abstract entities to be the *least fundamental* and *most derivative* entities. Although propositions and properties might seem less fundamental than their concrete subject matters or bearers, the fact that some abstract entities metaphysically depend upon other abstract entities confounds this initial suggestion. Consider, for example, the hierarchy of pure sets: a vast iterative structure of entities, each of which ultimately depends upon the empty set. In addition, structural universals seem to be complex abstract entities that depend upon their constituent universals. So, even if abstract entities are among the most derivative entities, not all abstract entities enjoy this lofty status, since some are more fundamental than others. An alternative analysis might claim, instead, that abstract entities all fall below a certain "threshold" of metaphysical fundamentality. Echoing Plato's metaphor of the Divided Line, such a view would take the abstract–concrete distinction to be a special sort of line in the ultimate ranking of more or less fundamental entities. And, while nothing rules out the possibility of such a view, the fact that we have no clear means for specifying this threshold suggests that no analysis of this sort is likely to avoid implicit circularity or outright obscurity.

Despite their failure, the analyses just considered are noteworthy for the common assumption that abstract entities are derivative rather than fundamental. A historically influential strand of platonism runs opposite to this assumption, asserting the metaphysical priority of the abstract over the concrete. On what we might call *priority platonism*, abstract entities are the only fundamental entities, so concrete entities depend for their existence upon abstract reality.[11] For priority platonists, it is the fundamentality of abstract entities that singles them out from the concrete. But, for the reasons noted above and because of its questionable plausibility, there is still no viable way to informatively mark the threshold of fundamentality that carves the joint between the abstract and the concrete.

Metaphysical dependence seems to be of little help in singling out abstract entities, but we might fare better if we focus on the relative fundamentality of *properties*. If we assume a sparse conception of properties, according to which there is an elite stock of fundamental or "perfectly natural" properties like *mass* and *charge*, it is plausible that only fundamental concrete entities like particles will instantiate fundamental properties. And, since all derivative concrete entities are built up from these fundamental concrete entities, it is plausible that all concrete entities will have fundamental concrete entities as parts. We might therefore attempt to distinguish abstract entities on account of their having no parts that instantiate fundamental properties.[12]

Way of Fundamentality: x is an abstract entity $=_{df} x$ has no parts that instantiate fundamental properties.

The Way of Fundamentality tethers the abstract–concrete distinction to the elite class of fundamental properties. If such a view is to be extensionally adequate, it therefore requires certain contentious metaphysical assumptions—e.g., that there are, in fact, fundamental properties. And, along with this commitment to fundamental properties, it rules out any view on which abstract entities have concrete entities as (mereological) parts.[13] It similarly rules out the possibility of fundamental second-order properties—i.e., fundamental properties that are instantiated by properties, propositions, or numbers. (In defence of fundamental properties of properties, see Eddon (2013).) In several cases, this seems to be a mistaken verdict, given that properties like *being abstract* or *being a property* are plausibly viewed as fundamental.

Granted its rich stock of background assumptions, the Way of Fundamentality might prove to be extensionally adequate. But, like some other analyses we've considered, this is only due to a carefully tailored ontology and some tendentious metaphysical assumptions. In light of this recurring pattern, it is tempting to draw a general conclusion about proposals for analyzing the abstract–concrete distinction: no single account fits all metaphysical views. It is, then, high time to consider a different methodological option: primitivism, which would have us give up on the fraught project of providing a non-tendentious analysis of abstractness. And, as we'll see, primitivism opens up explanatory options unavailable to reductionists.

§2.3 Primitivism

No reductive analysis of the abstract–concrete distinction avoids serious challenge. And, as we've seen, many of these challenges turn on the existence of abstract entities like impure sets, in re universals, or created abstracta that certain versions of platonism reject. Such challenges can, in principle, be addressed by pruning back one's ontological commitments in order to avoid apparent counterexample. (Generally speaking, the narrower the range of abstract entities one admits, the more likely a reductive analysis is to avoid counterexample.) It looks, though, like no reductive analysis will be acceptable to absolutely all platonists. On its own, this shouldn't be especially surprising. Neutrality is hard to come by in constructing theories and it is especially rare in metaphysics where almost all theoretical commitments are up for grabs. This leaves the defender of the standard view with two natural routes to pursue.

The first route disavows any hope of neutrality and seeks only to provide a reductive analysis that squares with one's preferred stock of abstract entities. In effect, it tests its adequacy only against its distinctive ontological commitments and leaves aside other conceptual possibilities. The second route abandons the project of reductively analyzing the distinction and instead treats the distinction as theoretically primitive, resisting independent explanation. Properly understood, primitivism in this and other forms isn't a thesis *per se*, but, rather, a certain theoretical stance towards a cluster of notions. It involves, among other things, refraining from defining a piece of ideology, while taking it to be graspable and fair game for the purposes of serious theorizing.

This section considers the prospects for this second route with an eye towards its costs and benefits. As I'll suggest, there is reason to believe that primitivism might ultimately be preferable to reductionism and not merely because it allows for a broader church than carefully but controversially tailored reductionist views.

As we saw in the previous chapter, primitive ideology comes in a variety of forms. Some ideological primitives are operators like the box and diamond of modal logic, but, for the Quinean who rejects properties, ideology is most familiar in the form of predicates. And, while some predicates within a theory will admit of analysis in terms of one another, primitive predicates are those predicates for which no non-circular analysis is possible. They are the conceptual bedrock of a theory. They cannot be explained in any simpler terms.

Theories fare better when they adopt the right theoretical primitives. A judicious choice of primitives allows for ideological simplification by positing fewer primitives while still explaining a broad range of phenomena. Primitive ideology also places constraints on the explanations that a theory can provide. Suppose, for example, a theory takes "is F" as a primitive piece of predicational ideology. Proponents of this theory are now in a position to explain facts about certain entities by appeal to the fact that some entity (or entities) is (or are) F. At the same time, this choice of primitives forecloses the prospects for further explaining the fact that something is F. Since "is F" is primitive, there is no more that can be said in our explanatory efforts to further explicate the fact that something is F. So understood, being an F is theoretical bedrock. (Of course, one could say more about the various roles "is F" plays in one's preferred theory, but this is not to explain what it means for something to be F in simpler or independent terms.)

As we'll discuss in the next chapter, ideological parsimony, which consists in the minimizing of primitive ideological commitments, is a valuable thing, but simplicity is by no means the only virtue of theories. Theories must provide explanations. And, where we cannot have ideological parsimony, we ought to have explanatory power. So, in taking abstractness as primitive ideology, platonists find themselves in an interesting position. This is because they can sustain or extend the explanatory power of theories by drawing upon the primitive predicate "is abstract." Among other things, they can use the primitive ideology of abstractness to explain the striking and often puzzling metaphysical features of abstracta. They can, for instance, explain the fact that abstract entities exist outside of spacetime by taking this feature to be a typical or essential feature of abstracta. Such explanations make direct appeal to the fact that certain entities are abstract. The resulting methodological gambit therefore takes seriously the commitment to abstractness as a primitive notion that should be put to serious explanatory work.

In contrast, reductionists seem unable to use abstractness as the same kind of explanatory wedge. For, on reductionist views, to be abstract is to be, say, without spatiotemporal location, without causal powers, or to have some other sort of feature. But, if to be abstract is just to be, say, without causal powers, we will have no explanatory success in explaining why abstracta lack location by pointing to their lack of causal powers or their lack of intrinsic natures. (As we saw above, there are potential exceptions here—e.g., the argument from a lack of location to necessary existence.) So, although reductionism offers ideological parsimony, primitivism about the notion of abstractness promises an increase in explanatory power, since abstractness can underwrite otherwise unavailable metaphysical explanations.

To illustrate the explanatory power of primitivist platonism, let's assume, for the moment, an austere platonist ontology, admitting *ante rem* universals, propositions, and numbers but neither impure sets nor created abstracta. According to this austere form of platonism, abstract entities are without spatiotemporal location or causal powers. And, while such a view is naturally motivated by the strongest arguments set out in Chapter 1, its success crucially depends on several auxiliary assumptions. Two of these assumptions are of particular significance: (Necessity) that these entities exist necessarily and (Publicity) that these entities are "cognitively public"—i.e., they are expressible by our predicates and sentences, serve as objects of our thoughts, and are cognitively accessible in some distinctive way. Were (Necessity) not to hold, the systematic explanations of truth, meaning, and modality platonists proffer would be untenable. And, were (Publicity) not to hold, there would be no way to make sense of how properties and propositions can play the explanatory roles assigned to them.

(Necessity) and (Publicity) are striking facts about entities. Each seems to cry out for some metaphysical explanation. Above, we briefly considered how certain reductionist views like the Way of Causation might try to explain (Necessity). And, while we'll consider epistemological issues regarding abstract entities in Chapter 4, no reductionist proposal seems to supply us with an explanation of (Publicity). One cannot, for example, explain the cognitive publicity of abstract entities merely by noting that they are causally inert or that they are without spatiotemporal location.

Reductionists are therefore in an awkward position if the notion of abstractness cannot be used to explain these and other features of abstracta. They are left, it seems, with three options: (i) deny (Necessity) and (Publicity) and, in doing so, radically hinder the explanatory power of platonism; (ii) deny that facts like (Necessity) and (Publicity) admit of any explanation whatsoever and, in doing so, call into question the worth of platonist metaphysical explanations; or (iii) attempt to explain facts like (Necessity) and (Publicity) by appeal to independently motivated theses regarding, say, location, causation, and necessity—e.g., in the way that the Way of Causation tries to explain the necessary existence of abstracta entities.

Options (i) and (ii) would be a boondoggle for platonists, since the case for platonism turns on the explanatory credentials of abstract entities. Option (iii) is therefore the best bet for reductionists, but no familiar form of reductionism offers a plausible way to successfully explain the distinctive features of abstract entities.

Primitivism does not face the just-noted problem. Although it requires additional ideology, it is a view on which facts like (Necessity) and (Publicity) are explained precisely by the abstractness of properties, propositions, and numbers. So, when asked why abstract entities exist necessarily or are cognitively public, the primitivist has a swift and direct answer: *because they are abstract*. Moreover, any other generalizations about abstract entities upheld by the austere platonist—e.g., that they are without causal powers or spatiotemporal locations—can be explained in the same way.

For those who like talk of essences in metaphysics, there is a natural way to parse the proposal at hand: primitivism holds abstract entities to be of a distinctive metaphysical kind and holds the essence of this metaphysical kind to explain the features of those things it includes. So, just as the essence of *humanity* explains our rationality and risibility, *abstractness* explains metaphysically peculiar features like (Necessity) and (Publicity). And, since abstractness is a theoretical primitive, the primitivist need not and cannot say more to explain the features in question. A primitive notion of abstractness therefore provides platonists with a principled account of the distinction between the abstract and the concrete and the structure of this distinction. For, given the essence of abstractness, reality must divide up, exclusively and exhaustively, into those things that are abstract and those that are concrete.

Opponents of this primitivist gambit are likely to find something fishy about explanatory appeals to a primitive notion of abstractness, but it is unclear how they can successfully press the case against primitivism. One way to sharpen up this complaint would be to argue that abstractness serves as an unduly powerful primitive. Like a "God of the gaps," perhaps abstractness, when alleged to explain (Necessity) and (Publicity), is claimed to account for such a broad range of facts, that it no longer constitutes a genuine explanation. Against such concerns, the primitivist should simply deny the charge; she should maintain that abstractness is a primitive notion. Moreover, it is one ideally suited for explaining the cluster of features distinctive to abstract entities.

A better way to press this complaint is to allege that abstractness is somehow unintelligible or ungraspable and therefore unsuitable for playing a part in the relevant metaphysical explanations. But this charge is also unconvincing. The means for introducing a primitive notion of abstractness are perfectly familiar. Some structural features have been outlined, some examples have been given, and, like other licit theoretical notions, it seems easy enough to grasp despite some tough cases.

Ultimately, the strongest challenge to primitivism is the Ockhamite one noted earlier: that, other things being equal, it would be better to avoid taking on novel primitives. But, if the explanatory merits of primitive abstractness are close to what has been claimed above, things aren't equal. Primitive abstractness is simply the best available choice when it comes time to fix upon our basic metaphysical notions.

Those who accept platonist views that admit impure sets and other abstracta that are contingent or spatiotemporally located will have a different concern about the primitivist strategy just laid out. If primitive abstractness suffices to explain distinctive features of properties, propositions, and numbers, then abstractness presumably necessitates that the relevant features are had by *all* abstract entities. So, for primitivism to be explanatorily useful in the way outlined, abstract entities must be a metaphysically homogenous lot: uniformly necessary, non-causal, and non-contingent. If, however, primitivism is coupled with an expansive platonism or even a relatively austere one that admits impure sets, then either impure sets must share the features in question or abstractness cannot, on its own, explain these features in the first place. If, for example, abstractness is held to explain the necessary existence of numbers, this would seem to require that all abstract entities are necessary existents. The same goes for features like causal inertness, lack of location, and special cognitive accessibility. So, unless we are willing to revise our views about the contingent existence of impure sets and perhaps other abstracta, only especially austere versions of platonism can reap the explanatory benefits that come with primitivism.

Is there anything platonists can do to preserve the explanatory benefits of primitive abstractness while opting for a more diverse portfolio of abstracta? One option is to accept *generic* metaphysical explanations, which hold true of *kinds* even while admitting of some exceptions. Consider, for example, an attempt to explain the fact that you and I are rational by noting that we are human. In doing so, our generic explanation seems satisfactory, despite the fact that not all humans are rational. Similar generic explanations are commonplace both within and outside of the sciences as when we explain that Daisy laid an egg in virtue of being a duck, despite the fact that at least half of all ducks cannot lay eggs. By analogy, the platonist might appeal to abstractness to provide an explanation of, say, the necessary existence of numbers, but need not commit herself to a universally quantified claim asserting that absolutely all abstracta are necessary existents. Instead, she would merely require that, generically speaking, abstracta are necessary existents in much the way that ducks lay eggs or that humans are rational, and so on.

The prospects for accepting generic explanations in metaphysics are uncertain, but, given their value in our general explanatory practices, there's reason for suitably austere platonists to be optimistic. Impure sets might therefore be admitted alongside other austere abstract entities without surrendering primitive abstractness as a tool for explaining the necessary existence, cognitive publicity, and other features of abstracta. (Alternatively, austere platonists might hold that, perhaps somewhat surprisingly, {Socrates} can exist without Socrates.) At the same time, expansive platonists are in trouble: if there are very many abstract entities without the features allegedly explained by abstractness, the merits of proposed generic metaphysical explanations look increasingly shaky. There is, I suspect, little reason to think that exception-riddled generics remain admissible when it comes to metaphysics. And, if such generic explanations are ruled inadmissible, primitivist austere platonism looks to be in a far more stable position that its expansive rivals.

The primitive ideology of abstractness is a powerful explanatory device within certain platonist theories. This makes primitivism a natural way to build upon the standard view in articulating a metaphysics of the abstract realm. In the next section, we will consider a third, more radical option: eliminativism, which aims to dispense with the abstract–concrete distinction altogether.

§2.4 Eliminativism

Primitivists and reductionists agree that the abstract–concrete distinction has a place within our best metaphysical theories. In contrast, eliminativists deny that our best metaphysical theories include the abstract–concrete distinction or talk of entities being abstract or concrete. For the eliminativist, abstractness and concreteness are notions that either fail to apply to any entities or, on certain versions of eliminativism, are downright meaningless. So, while eliminativists might retain ontological commitment to entities like numbers and neighbours, these entities are neither abstract nor concrete, since the categoreal structure of the world includes no such division.

Arguments in favour of eliminativism come in a few different forms. The most direct line of argument proceeds by pointing to disagreements over where the abstract–concrete distinction falls—e.g., whether entities like possible worlds or musical works are abstract. This sort of naked appeal to disagreement will, however, fall short of undermining the abstract–concrete distinction. Comparable disagreement prevails in almost any metaphysical domain (e.g., regarding the necessary and contingent, the mental and physical, and the fundamental and derivative). So, just as pervasive ontological disagreement provides no reason to jettison the distinction between existence and nonexistence, disagreements about which entities are abstract provide us with no good reason to jettison abstractness altogether. There is, after all, widespread agreement about paradigm cases (e.g., numbers and propositions). And, even while there are few exceptionless generalizations available, we still have some viable heuristics for evaluating claims of abstractness by asking after features like mind-independence, causal activity, and location.

A better argument for eliminativism turns on careful consideration of the theoretical role of the abstract–concrete distinction and points back to Lewis' concerns mentioned in Section 2.2. To see how this argument proceeds, consider the following passage from Sider (2013: 287):

> The abstract/concrete distinction behind this objection is a relic of a certain theory. According to this theory, reality divides into two realms—abstract and concrete—in a way that is significant on various fronts. Epistemic: we know about the abstract a priori. Modal: facts about the abstract are necessary. Causal: the abstract is causally inert. Spatial: abstract entities are not in space and time. But this is just a theory, nothing more. It's not sacrosanct; nothing supports it other than tradition; and it should stand aside if it obstructs an attractive simplification of ideology.

Sider's recommendation that we dispense with the abstract–concrete distinction comes in the midst of his defence of a bold metaphysical thesis: that ordinary objects like you and your favourite mug are actually sets of mereological simples. This proposal stands in opposition to orthodoxy about both the nature of ordinary objects and any familiar construal of the abstract–concrete distinction. But, in addressing the tension between his proposal and the standard view, Sider suggests that violating orthodoxy is no vice at all, provided that, when doing so, we accrue theoretical or explanatory benefits.[14]

The plausibility of Sider's response depends on how much theoretical freight the abstract–concrete distinction hauls. And, for certain metaphysical theories like radical idealisms or theistic monisms, Sider is exactly right: retaining the distinction is pointless since it plays no worthwhile theoretical role. Generally speaking, if you make no appeal to a distinction or concept anywhere in the deployment of your preferred theory, you are under no obligation to accommodate its alleged significance (much less take it as a primitive). So, for those who make no use of the abstract–concrete distinction, Sider's case for eliminativism is straightforward: it plays no part in our best theories, so there is no reason to believe it is a part of the world's categoreal structure.

With this in mind, the eliminativist can accept the existence of numbers, properties, and propositions. And, if so inclined, the eliminativist can also grant that these entities have noteworthy features like, say, causal inactivity. But, the eliminativist will part from primitivists and reductionists by denying that appeal to abstractness or concreteness aptly describes the metaphysical status of these entities. There is, for the eliminativist, no interesting aspect of categoreal structure that answers to the abstract–concrete distinction and therefore no genuine subject matter at issue between nominalists and platonists.

Presented with Sider's challenge, a tempting but wrongheaded response denies the eliminability of the distinction because of its place in our ordinary conceptual repertoire. While the nature of the distinction has no good claim to being "common knowledge," this response alleges that the distinction is still familiar or intuitive enough to be counted as a non-negotiable extension of our ordinary worldview. Any conservative metaphysical theory ought therefore account for it. Put differently: the abstract–concrete distinction is a corollary of our everyday metaphysical theory, so intellectual conservatism warrants retaining it.

The force of this challenge depends on the weight one assigns our commonsense conception of the world in metaphysical theorizing and on whether it is plausible to think that the abstract–concrete distinction has a role in any modest extension of this conception. While we need not settle the former issue, the latter contention is implausible. Investigations into commonsense notions surrounding the abstract–concrete distinction are unlikely to bear philosophical or explanatory fruit. Ordinary discourse about numbers, properties, and meanings is fraught with incoherence and a nightmarish pile-up of use–mention errors.

A more plausible stance for facing down eliminativism is the one implicit in Sider's remarks. The significance of the abstract–concrete distinction is entirely dependent upon its explanatory and theoretical value for our philosophical projects. So, if the distinction matters, it is only because it can be put to work in providing an account of metaphysical, epistemological, or semantic phenomena. Questions about the abstract–concrete distinction are therefore of interest, not because they track some shared, inchoate intuitions of the folk, but because they demarcate explanatory projects and theoretical roles undertaken by the abstract realm and its inhabitants. So, while the abstract–concrete distinction is part and parcel of a historically influential tradition of providing metaphysical explanations of truth, meaning, objectivity, and other notions, it is a plausible commitment only to the extent these explanations are credible.

Ultimately, the fate of eliminativism turns on whether the abstract–concrete distinction has theoretical work to do. And, as we saw in the previous section, there are primitivist versions of platonism on which the distinction plays an absolutely central role in metaphysical explanations. On this view, it is abstractness itself that explains why some entities are outside of spacetime, exist necessarily, or are cognitively accessible yet imperceptible. (Presumably, these are the versions of platonism that Sider has in mind when he alludes to "a certain theory" about abstract entities in his quote above.)

Primitivist versions of platonism can therefore resist the eliminativist challenge that entreats us to dispense with the abstract–concrete distinction. In contrast, reductionists once again find themselves in a more precarious position. Although reductionism about a distinction or a concept does not entail that the distinction or concept plays no theoretical role, reductionists cannot use the notion of abstractness to explain the distinctive features of putative abstract entities. Instead, reductionism holds that other, presumably more fundamental distinctions concerning, say, location, causation, and modality explain our talk about the abstract–concrete distinction. And, since the fate of the abstract–concrete distinction turns on the work we assign to it, any reduction in its workload threatens its job security. For, if we can ultimately dispense with talk of abstract and concrete entities in terms of located and unlocated or causal and acausal entities, it is far from clear why we ought to retain an additional distinction between the abstract and the concrete.

For primitivists who accept an austere version of platonism, abstract entities share a cluster of standard features like necessary existence, lack of spatiotemporal location, causal inactivity, and special cognitive accessibility. This clustering of features is, in turn, explained by the fact that such entities are of a common metaphysical kind. If, however, abstract entities are a heterogeneous lot as expansive versions of platonism contend, the prospects for using primitive abstractness to explain such features dims quickly. And, if the domain of abstract entities includes entities such as artworks and recipes alongside numbers and properties, it seems to be a diverse assemblage of entities, insufficiently unified to uphold any robust generalizations. The primitivist's response to Sider's challenge is therefore more stable when packaged with an austere rather than expansive conception of abstract reality.

Sider's eliminativist challenge can be met by only some platonists. And, as we've now seen, it points towards a theoretical instability in reductionism and in expansive versions of platonism. For those who would hope to defend such positions, a substantial explanatory role must be carved out for abstractness. Unless that can be done, the best platonist option is to combine austerity and primitivism. The resulting view admits only abstract entities like numbers, properties, and propositions that exist outside of spacetime. (Depending upon the prospects for generic metaphysical explanations, this list might include impure sets as well.) In doing so, it takes sides on the debate over properties by identifying them with either sets or with *ante rem* universals. We will therefore largely set aside trope theory and *in re* universals in what follows, though each deserves serious consideration.[15] It also takes abstractness as a piece of primitive ideology, which accounts for the remarkable features of abstracta like their necessary existence, cognitive accessibility, and so on. So, for austere primitivist platonists, the abstract–concrete distinction is an explanatory lynchpin at the heart of a sprawling metaphysical framework.

Throughout the remainder of this book, this austere primitivist view will be our primary focus. And, while reductionists and expansive platonists are well within their rights to object, unless they can provide a compelling answer to Sider's challenge, there is no good reason to prefer such views to an eliminativism that does without the distinction. If that's right, this means that the pursuit of reductionist proposals for analyzing the distinction is of far less significance than showing that the abstract–concrete distinction plays a substantive metaphysical role. The latter should therefore be a primary concern for would-be reductionists.

§2.4.1 Nominalists on the distinction

Before concluding our discussion of the abstract–concrete distinction, let us briefly consider how nominalists ought to view the debate between primitivism, reductionism, and eliminativism. In particular, how should nominalists conceive of the distinction?

At first glance, it looks as though the nominalist can tidily dispense with the ideology of the abstract–concrete distinction and, in doing so, secure a simplification in ideology unavailable to some platonists. Notice, however, that nominalism is standardly formulated in a way that makes direct appeal to either abstractness or concreteness. It might seem, then, that even nominalists require some account of the abstract–concrete distinction. But, unlike platonists, nominalists make no *substantive* appeal to the abstract–concrete distinction in providing metaphysical explanations. They do not use it to explain the features of concrete entities nor do they use abstractness to account for facts about, say, resemblance, causation, or laws. At most, talk of abstractness arises when nominalists specify the kinds of entities they do or do not admit into their ontologies. But, this "negative use" of abstractness does not, by itself, require nominalists to retain the notion of abstractness within their official theoretical ideology. For, if a merely negative use of some theoretical notion requires that we include that notion into our ideology, almost any theory would seem required to take on a radically bloated ideology, since they will reject a vast range of potential commitments. In general, then, negative uses of concepts and distinctions—i.e., uses aimed merely at rejecting certain commitments—have a peculiar theoretical status insofar as they are not plausibly held to require additional ideological commitments. Applied to the present case, nominalists can therefore state their denial that there are abstract entities or, conversely, the claim that everything is concrete without having to choose between reductionism or primitivism. And, while this is something of a minor puzzle for those interested in metaphysical ideology, nominalists seem to be in a position similar to eliminativists. Provided they can discharge their explanatory obligations, they likely enjoy a gain in ideological simplicity by dispensing with any primitive notion of abstractness. Platonists will, of course, argue that the benefit of this modest ideological simplification is dwarfed by the gains in explanatory power that come with abstract entities. To see which way the balance of evidences ultimately falls will, however, require a far more comprehensive cost-counting. And, over the next few chapters, we will consider a series of nominalist arguments aimed at showing that the theoretical virtues of nominalism outweigh those of platonism.

Summary

After introducing the standard view of the abstract–concrete distinction, this chapter presented several accounts of the distinction between abstract and concrete entities. Reductionist proposals for analyzing the distinction in terms of location, causation, and other features were surveyed and, in most cases, shown to be inadequate or highly contentious. We then considered primitivism, which admits abstractness as a basic piece of theoretical ideology. After exploring how primitivists might put the theoretically primitive notion of abstractness to theoretical use, we evaluated the case for eliminativism, which seeks to do away with the abstract–concrete distinction altogether. We tentatively concluded that primitivism, coupled with an austere view of abstract entities, is likely the best option for platonists. Such a view, which posits mathematical entities, propositions, and *ante rem* properties, will therefore be the version of platonism we will focus upon in much of what follows.

Recommended reading

On competing conceptions of the abstract–concrete distinction, see Lewis (1986), Burgess and Rosen (1997), Katz (1998), Lowe (1995), Hoffman and Rosenkrantz (2003), and Rosen (2014). For various challenges to the standard view, see Williamson (1998), Linsky and Zalta (1994), and Cowling (2014a). On causation and abstract entities, see Cheyne (2001). On location and abstract entities, see Hale (1988) and Effingham (2015). On the intrinsic nature of properties and complexity of abstracta, see Hawley (2010), Nolan (forthcoming), Cowling (forthcoming), Rodriguez-Pereyra (forthcoming). On the qualitative/non-qualitative distinction, see Lewis (1986) and Cowling (2015a). On the intrinsic/extrinsic distinction, see Marshall (2012, 2013). On fundamentality and metaphysical dependence, see Schaffer (2009) and Wilson (2014). For discussion of theism and abstract entities, see Leftow (1990), van Inwagen (2009), and Gould (2014).

Notes

1 Here's a brief sample of some challenges to theses (i)–(vi):

- *Against Exhaustiveness.* According to Williamson (2002), some entities—e.g., merely possible entities like the Sino-Canadian suspension bridge—fall in between the abstract and the concrete. Note that while Parsons (1990: 339) introduces the notion of a "quasi-concrete" entity—i.e., something that can be instantiated or realized by concreta—he takes such entities to be abstract. Cf. Katz (1998: 141).
- *Against Absoluteness.* Cowling (2014a) argues that modal realists ought to view abstractness as relative to possible worlds in parallel to the indexical treatment of actuality defended in Lewis (1986). Dummett (1991: 239) remarks that abstractness "resembles a scale upon which objects of varying sorts occupy a range of positions."
- *Against Modal Rigidity.* With Williamson (2002), Linsky and Zalta (1994) hold that the concreteness of entities is a contingent and temporally variable matter. On such a view, although you are actually and presently a concrete entity, there are worlds or times at which you are non-concrete.

2 The relevant abstraction principle for introducing directions relies upon a relational predicate, P, (read: "is parallel with") and "$d(x)$", a term-forming operator that refers to the direction of a line and the assumption that, for any lines a and b, $d(a)=d(b) \leftrightarrow P(a,b)$. Read: "the direction of a is the direction of b if and only if a is parallel to b."

3 By focusing on spatiotemporal location, we also bracket complications regarding *non*-spatiotemporal locations—e.g., within property-theoretic "spaces" or within exotic possible worlds unified by non-spatiotemporal external relations. On location in non-spatiotemporal regions, see Hawthorne and Sider (2002), Arntzenius and Dorr (2012), and Cowling (2014b). On non-spatiotemporal possible worlds, see Bricker (1996).

4 This distinction among theories of universals has a storied but contentious history. For a canonical treatment of contemporary property theories, see Armstrong (1978). On the divide between Aristotle and Plato regarding universals, see Fine (1993) and Penner (1987). Throughout this book, I mostly avoid calling properties "Platonic" to ward off potential confusion.

5 On whether impure sets are located, see Katz (1998: 117) and Lewis (1991: 32).

6 Similar concerns extend to non-qualitative haecceities like *being Socrates* and singular propositions—i.e., propositions about specific individuals such as *that Socrates flies*. On the modal ties between the abstract and the concrete, see Chapter 6.
7 The platonist who takes abstract entities to be "outside" modal reality is likely to hold that truths about such entities are *amodal*—i.e., neither necessary nor contingently true. See Cowling (2011) for a defence of amodalism regarding truths about modal reality and possible worlds.
8 Strictly speaking, entities have themselves as *improper* parts, but we will typically use "part" to mean *proper* part.
9 On constituency relations between propositions and their subject matter—in particular, those of Russell and Frege—see Hylton (2003).
10 See Lewis (1991, 1993b).
11 This name is somewhat less misleading than Pythagoreanism, if only because Pythagoreanism is ambiguous between this view and what we might call *existence platonism*—the thesis that all that exists is abstract.
12 Bricker (2008) suggests the Way of Fundamentality as one of five ways of understanding "concrete." As he puts it: "concrete entities have an intrinsic qualitative nature in virtue of instantiating, or having parts that instantiate, perfectly natural properties."
13 How such a view ought to treat mereological sums of arbitrary concrete and abstract entities—e.g., an objection composed of propositions and turkeys—is unclear. That said, the status of arbitrary sums drawn from either side of the abstract–concrete distinction is an open question and a thorn in the side of the standard view *qua* challenge to exclusiveness or exhaustiveness.
14 In responding to a suggestion in Quine (1976a) that all entities are reducible to sets, Paseau (2009: 45) voices the kind of conservatism Sider has in mind. Paseau says: "There is an entrenched semantic constraint that the interpretation of mathematical kind terms such as 'set' and 'number' cannot overlap with that of concrete kind terms such as 'person' and 'chair.' . . . The systematization that takes persons to be sets strays too far from *our* beliefs . . . ."
15 On tropes and their connection to the abstract–concrete distinction, see Campbell (1990: 3–5). Note also that certain trope theories—e.g., the natural class trope nominalism of Ehring (2011)—are packaged with a commitment to both tropes and sets.

3

PARADOX, PARSIMONY, AND INFINITE REGRESSES

3.1 Paradox
3.2 Parsimony
3.3 Infinite regresses

The previous two chapters set out the thesis of platonism and the case in its favour. The next four chapters examine the case against platonism. Roughly speaking, they proceed in order of increasing force (though, of course, there is ample room for disagreement in this regard). The present chapter briefly surveys three kinds of arguments sometimes alleged to make problems for platonism. These arguments divide into the following categories: (i) *arguments from paradox*, which hold that the paradoxes generated by platonism require that we reject abstract entities; (ii) *razor arguments*, which appeal to the theoretical virtue of parsimony in defending nominalism; and (iii) *regress arguments*, which hold that objectionable explanatory or metaphysical regresses result from a commitment to platonism.

These arguments can be put forward individually in mounting a case against platonism, but, more usually, they are offered as supplementary considerations that, in concert with other arguments, show nominalism to be preferable to platonism. For example, after avowing nominalism on the basis of an ultimate "philosophical intuition," Goodman and Quine (1947: 105) add that the case for nominalism is "fortified" by worries about paradoxes. Similar remarks are often made about Ockham's razor serving as a kind of tiebreaker in favour of nominalism.

The belief that paradoxes, razors, and regresses help tip the scales against platonism is not uncommon. So, given their potential role as tiebreakers in the nominalist–platonist debate, our interest in these arguments is not limited to whether one of them might, on its own, undercut platonism. We will therefore be equally concerned with the merits of these arguments as standalone challenges to platonism and as supplemental considerations to be drawn upon in making the case against abstract entities. As we'll see, however, these arguments only challenge certain versions of platonism and, even in those cases, provide little reason to dispense with abstract entities altogether. Those who claim to be nominalists because of Russell-style paradoxes, Ockham's razor, or Bradleyan regresses are therefore likely to be nominalists for no good reason.

§3.1 Paradox

Viewed one way, platonism is a theoretical umbrella, subsuming a range of sub-theories about different kinds of abstract entities like sets, properties, and propositions. Ideally, these sub-theories would be perfectly integrated with one another or, at the very least, mutually consistent. And, while platonists can accept or reject various sub-theories, one criterion of adequacy is that these sub-theories yield neither contradictions nor paradoxes of any worrisome sort. With this in mind, the argument from paradox contends that platonism ought to be rejected precisely because of the paradoxes it generates. The simplest version of this argument holds that paradoxes arise from one or more platonist sub-theories like set theory, property theory, or proposition theory and, since such theories are a part of the best version of platonism, we ought to reject platonism altogether.

That some platonist theories give rise to paradox is beyond dispute. Indeed, even those who know only a little about set theory know that naïve set theory—roughly, any set theory according to which any given predicate corresponds to a set—yields contradictions. Here's a quick reconstruction of a Russell-style paradox for naïve set theory:

> Suppose, for any predicate F, there is some set that has as its members all and only those things that satisfy F. Further suppose that some sets have themselves as members as in the case of the set of non-Canadians, which is, by virtue of being a set, a non-Canadian. Now, consider the set corresponding to the predicate "is non-self-membered" (i.e., does not have itself as a member). If this set is a member of itself, then it cannot be a member of itself. If, however, it is not a member of itself, then it must be a member of itself. But no set can be both a member of itself and a non-member of itself.

The contradiction underlying Russell's paradox thwarted early efforts to provide a set-theoretic foundation for mathematics. It also spawned a litany of proposals for recasting set theory in order to avoid this and other closely related paradoxes. Some of these proposals abandon naïve set theory by placing constraints on the formation of sets and the predicates that suffice to define sets. Perhaps most famously, "limitation of size" approaches deny that certain predicates or collections have or correspond to sets. In its most familiar form, this pairs with the "iterative conception" of sets that underwrites the now-orthodox Zermelo–Fraenkel set theory (hereafter, ZF). On the resulting view, set formation is cumulative and governed by axioms that foreclose the possibility of Russell-style paradoxes, allowing for the formation of sets only from the subsets of earlier "levels" of the set theoretic hierarchy. An alternative approach, building upon early efforts by Russell, rejects naïve set theory by placing type-theoretic constraints on predicates, where predicates can apply only to certain "types" of sets or entities. (Note that this sense of "type" has no connection to the one mentioned earlier.) The resulting typed language rules out troublemaking predicates like "is non-self-membered" as non-grammatical and so not meaningfully applied to the sets that would produce contradictions. Still other approaches like Quine (1937) opt for even more dramatic revisions to naïve set theory.

Settling on the proper response to the paradoxes of naïve set theory is well beyond the scope of this discussion (and the expertise of this author). There is, however, no compelling reason to believe that naïve set theory is part of the best versions of platonism even if set theory in some form is. Consequently, there is no reason to think that paradox is endemic to any available set theory that might be usefully employed in mathematics or metaphysics. This first version of the argument from paradox is therefore unsound.

It is important to note, however, that the structure of the above paradox is not unique to set theory. An analogous paradox arises in naïve property theory, according to which any given predicate corresponds to a property:

Some properties instantiate themselves, while other properties do not. For example, the property *being a property* instantiates itself, while the property *being a barn light* does not. Suppose that predicates express properties, so the predicate "is a property that does not instantiate itself" expresses the property P. Does P instantiate P? Put differently: does the property of *being a property that does not instantiate itself* instantiate itself or not? If P does not instantiate P, then it does. Conversely, if P does instantiate itself, then it does not. P therefore instantiates itself if and only if it is not the case that P instantiates itself. But no property can both instantiate itself and not instantiate itself.

The property-theoretic version of the Russell-style paradox is no less serious than the set-theoretic one. Since sets and properties are each standard commitments of platonism, each paradox requires some resolution. This is no less true if one posits only sets and takes them to play the role of properties (or vice versa).[1] So, regardless of one's preferred version of platonism, a solution to these Russell-style paradoxes is required.

Proposed solutions to the property-theoretic paradox commonly draw upon extant set-theoretic strategies for avoiding contradiction. And, since there is an abundance of competing proposals for revising set theory in order to avoid Russell's paradox, parallel proposals provide a variety of paradox-free property theories. It is therefore implausible to claim that no version of property theory is able to escape paradox. Additionally, those who would opt for a sparse conception of properties that denies each predicate expresses or corresponds to a property can also deny that predicates like "is self-instantiated" express genuine properties. So, despite their historical influence and importance, naïve set and property theories have no plausible claim to being a part of our best platonist theories. The availability of superior alternatives therefore undermines any argument from paradox that would try to draw upon these worries regarding naïve set or property theories.

A stronger version of the argument from paradox pursues a different route. This second argument, hinted at in Goodman and Quine's brief remarks, claims that any theories descended from naïve set theory or naïve property theory are objectionable. They say:

> What seems to be the most natural principle for abstracting classes or properties leads to paradoxes. Escape from these paradoxes can apparently be effected only by recourse to alternative rules whose artificiality and arbitrariness arouse suspicion that we are lost in a world of make-believe.
> Goodman and Quine (1947: 105)

In keeping with this remark, a revised argument from paradox holds that any theories descended from naïve set theory or naïve property theory will avoid paradox only by *ad hoc* revisions. But, since *ad hoc* revisions are theoretically vicious, any theories that descend from naïve set or property ought to be rejected as speciously motivated.

This argument isn't much better than the previous version of the argument from paradox. After all, it would require showing that absolutely all strategies for addressing Russell's paradox within set theory are merely *ad hoc* manoeuvres that avoid paradox in an unprincipled way. Against this claim, platonists can plausibly assert that the iterative conception of sets is intuitive, well-motivated, and, when put forward as a theory of collections, no more *ad hoc* than naïve set theory itself. So, while naïve set theory is intuitively appealing—in part, because of its unrestricted character—it is implausible that any descendent like ZF is objectionable solely in virtue of its efforts to avoid paradox. To be sure, ZF and other alternatives to naïve set theory do owe some rationale that motivates their preferred axioms, but this charge of *ad hoccery* is too weak to trouble platonists who would posit sets, properties, or propositions.

Ultimately, the strongest version of the argument from paradox is based, not on paradoxes internal to a particular version of set theory or property theory, but on paradoxes that result from the interaction among platonist sub-theories. According to this version of the argument from paradox, even if we can dodge paradox in our best sub-theories, "interactional" paradoxes—paradoxes arising from the interaction between theories about different species of abstracta—inevitably result when we conjoin these sub-theories. Put metaphorically: although we can get abstract entities to behave themselves when quarantined, they will inevitably generate paradoxes once released into the wild of abstract reality. Interactional paradoxes might therefore involve sets and properties, properties and propositions, or, as in the following paradox presented in Russell (1903: 527), propositions and sets (or, in Russell's terminology, "classes"):

> Let us state this new contradiction more fully. If *m* be a class of propositions, the proposition "every *m* is true" may or may not be itself an *m*. But there is a one–one relation of this proposition to *m*; if *n* be different from *m*, "every *n* is true" is not the same proposition as "every *m* is true." Consider now the whole class of propositions of the form "every *m* is true," and having the property of not being members of their respective *m*'s. Let this class be *w*, and let *p* be the proposition "every *w* is true." If *p* is a *w*, it must possess the

defining property of *w*; but this property demands that *p* should not be a *w*. On the other hand, if *p* be not a *w*, then *p* does possess the defining property of *w*, and therefore is a *w*. Thus the contradiction appears unavoidable.

This paradox, which is considerably more ornate than those set out above, suggests that once we help ourselves to the dual resources of set theory and proposition theory, paradoxes invariably sprout up. Potential solutions to this interactional paradox are numerous. Some rely on principles internal to set theory and proposition theory that restrict the generation of such entities. Others restrict the unfettered interaction between these theories. We might, for example, wheel out a type-theoretic solution that precludes certain propositions being members of sets (or sets of a specific type) in order to rule out the existence of the troublemaking propositions—e.g., about whether the members of a given set are true. Such proposals will, however, seem somewhat peculiar when compared to proposals aimed at repairing set theory or property theory in isolation. This is because, by virtue of their interactional nature, these proposals require platonists to jointly revise theories about sets, properties, and propositions that are typically put forward in a manner largely independent of one another.[2]

One familiar interactional paradox owes to David Kaplan. Unlike previously considered paradoxes, Kaplan's paradox makes crucial appeal to the Cantorian insight that the "power set" of a set—i.e., the set of all a set's subsets—is greater (in cardinality) than the set itself. Like the Russellian paradox just presented, Kaplan's paradox draws upon sets and propositions, but, unlike the Russellian paradox, Kaplan's paradox also involves the additional category of possible worlds. And, while later chapters will examine the status of such entities, orthodoxy takes possible worlds to be no more or less abstract than sets, properties, and propositions. Following Kaplan (1995), the paradox runs roughly as follows:

> Suppose we believe in sets and possible worlds. Further suppose that sets of possible worlds are either identical with or correspond to propositions. Assume the cardinality of the set of possible worlds is κ, so there are 2^κ propositions. Now consider some agent capable of thinking or uttering propositions. For any proposition, that agent could think or utter that proposition at a given time. If so, there is some possible world where that agent thinks or utters that proposition at that time. But, if so, there are at least 2^κ possible worlds, which is contrary to our initial assumption that there are exactly κ-many possible worlds.

As with the Russellian paradoxes, proposed solutions are numerous and quickly multiply on account of the different kinds of abstract entities involved. Some, like Lewis (1986: 104–105), deny that agents can, in fact, think or utter all (indeed, most) propositions and so reject the premise that there is a unique possible world wherein each unique proposition is thought or uttered. More commonly, a type-theoretic solution is proposed according to which quantification over all propositions is forgone. In its place, type-restricted quantification allows us to quantify over propositions of various types or orders, but never over absolutely all propositions regardless of type or order. In this way, we cannot quantify over both ordinary propositions and those propositions about the stock of propositions. Regardless of one's preferred response, a resolution to these and other paradoxes comes at some sort of cost—e.g., contentious constraints on what is expressible within type theories—or the potential charge of theoretical *ad hoccery*.

Unfortunately for nominalists, there seems to be nothing exceptional about interactional paradoxes or at least nothing that can sustain a convincing argument from paradox. To see why, notice that our best version of platonism is not merely the conjunction of our best set theory, best property theory, and best proposition theory, but, rather, the carefully considered combination of each of these theories. The formulation of our best global platonist theory therefore requires due attention to the internal standards of adequacy governing these sub-theories and to the requirement of mutual coherence and consistency. Once properly understood, attention to interactional paradoxes is a sign of fruitful cross-pollination. It signals a natural effort to reconcile platonist theories that issue from specific domains like mathematics, semantics, and logic. This is not to deny that interactional paradoxes are serious or that they require plausible solutions. Clearly, they do. But, as it stands, there is no reason to believe them less tractable than familiar paradoxes arising within separate sub-theories. And, since there is no compelling reason to think interactional paradoxes are by their very nature inherently insuperable, they are more plausibly viewed as a part of the broader platonist project of articulating a comprehensive theory of the abstract realm rather than as a symptom of a decaying platonist research programme.

Given the failure of the argument from paradox, nominalists are best served to throttle back their dialectical ambitions. Nominalists might, for example, attempt to show that, although the argument from paradox can't sink platonism on its own, it remains one of several reasons jointly supporting nominalism. Perhaps this is because, other things being equal, it would be good to avoid the challenge of addressing the paradoxes that attend platonism and only nominalism allows us to do so. (Naturally, platonists will take pains to deny that matters are, in fact, equal.) If correct, this conditional conclusion would allow the nominalist to assert, with Goodman and Quine, that the paradoxes arising from platonism are indeed an additional vice that helps "fortify" the case for nominalism.

At first glance, this may seem plausible enough. For, if resolving paradoxes is work we can avoid, theories that allow us to do so should be welcome options. The challenge, however, comes in spelling out precisely what is gained by opting out of the project of resolving the paradoxes associated with platonism. Obviously enough, someone who doesn't believe in sets is not obligated to address set-theoretical paradoxes, but, given their common structure, the Russellian paradox that afflicts naïve set and naïve property theory is plausibly viewed as the same kind of paradox. For this reason, the task of resolving of Russell's paradox for sets is not entirely avoided unless we dispense with (at least) both sets and properties. If that's right, we would accomplish nothing by dispensing with sets while retaining a commitment to properties.

So, is it plausible that, by rejecting abstract entities, we thereby avoid the burden of resolving the kind of paradoxes associated with platonism? According to some platonists, this will seem badly mistaken, since the very same kinds of paradoxes arise for nominalism, but under a very different guise. Support for this response naturally draws upon views like that of Priest (1995), who takes several of the paradoxes considered above to share a common core with paradoxes like the Liar and the Knower. And, since these and other paradoxes are no less pressing for nominalists, trying to dodge them by dispensing with abstracta affords no real advantage. Those who surrender the theoretical benefits of abstract entities in hopes of avoiding paradox therefore do so only in a futile effort to avoid an almost unavoidable problem. As such, anyone who endorses nominalism in order to avoid set-theoretic paradoxes owes both a full inventory of paradoxes and a careful account of how to disentangle the elements of paradox that are distinctive to platonism. Absent such an account, there is insufficient reason to view nominalism as a panacea for those feeling unduly burdened by paradox.

Regardless of how we formulate it, the argument from paradox shouldn't be a pressing concern for the platonist. The underlying thought—that abstract reality is, by its very nature, a source of paradox—is a strange one and made even stranger when we recall the host of paradoxes grounded in concrete reality (e.g., those regarding motion, space, and time). It is also worth noting that, as the history of our engagement with paradoxes shows, the resources of set theory provide us with some of the best tools for finding our way through and around paradoxes of motion and others. There is, then, no reason to think that pointing to paradoxes within set, property, and proposition theories strengthens the case against platonism. Again, this does not mean that these paradoxes pose no threat to specific platonist sub-theories; proponents of such theories plainly owe some resolution to the paradoxes their preferred theories generate. It is just that paradoxes are the price of doing philosophical business: everyone, whether nominalist or platonist, is required to pay them eventually.

§3.2 Parsimony

Parsimony, when viewed as the minimizing of theoretical commitments, is commonly claimed to be a theoretical virtue. So, like fertility, explanatory power, conservativeness, and certain other features of theories, it is thought to make theories that possess it preferable to otherwise equally good rivals. And, while some hold parsimony to be merely a *pragmatic* virtue—i.e., a feature that makes the use of a theory *practically* preferable to rival theories—many of us hold that parsimony is also an *epistemic* virtue: a feature that makes belief in a theory better *justified* than belief in otherwise equally good rivals.

The idea that parsimony or simplicity serves as a legitimate guide to theory choice is commonly glossed as a commitment to Ockham's razor, the methodological injunction to avoid positing entities beyond necessity. And, while the historical pedigree and many disambiguations of Ockham's razor give rise to a raft of complications, we can follow this rough usage and take "razor arguments" to be those arguments that defend a theory by appealing to the epistemic virtue of parsimony.

Once taken as an epistemic virtue, parsimony provides useful guidance in the assessment of theories and proves to be of deep methodological significance. In debates within the philosophy of science over the truth of our best physical theories, virtues like parsimony are commonly claimed to tip the scales in favour of scientific realism, since the approximate truth of our best scientific theories provides an especially simple explanation of their empirical success. In a similar vein, parsimony is sometimes held to undermine arguments for external world scepticism. For, while elaborate sceptical hypotheses might seem consistent with our evidence, some reject scepticism by pointing to the relative simplicity of pedestrian hypotheses when compared to bizarre sceptical alternatives. In these and other areas, parsimony plays a key role in deciding among competing theories. But why should we think simple theories are, other things being equal, better justified? Put differently: why accept Ockham's razor as a guide to the truth? As Benacerraf and Putnam (1964: 35) put it:

> It is hard enough to believe that the natural world is so nicely arranged that what is simplest, etc., by *our* lights is always the same as what is *true* (or, at least, *generally* the same as what is true); why should one believe that the universe of sets . . . is so nicely arranged that there is a pre-established harmony between *our* feelings of simplicity, etc., and *truth*? (Italics from original.)

A boldly contrarian reply simply denies that appeals to parsimony are meritorious and claims, instead, that they provide no epistemic reasons. But, for those of us who take appeals to parsimony and other super-empirical virtues seriously, the challenge of defending the epistemic standing of parsimony is a pressing concern. One option is to posit some sort of *a priori* connection between simplicity and truth; however, it is far from clear what such a connection might look like. Indeed, it is a striking fact that so many dismiss such a connection even upon sustained reflection. A second, historically influential option is to appeal to a divine being whose very nature accounts for why "less is more." But, along with a contentious commitment to theism, this strategy seems no more plausible than a vaguely Leibnizian insistence to the contrary—namely, that we should think the world is *maximally* rather than minimally populated. A third, more promising strategy appeals to some form of methodological naturalism, which holds our best epistemic practices to be those undertaken in a manner consonant with the natural sciences. (For discussion, see Rosen (2001).) And, since one finds regular appeal to theoretical virtues like simplicity, fertility, and conservativeness in scientific theorizing, the methodological naturalist contends that such appeals are sound epistemic policy in other areas of inquiry—most notably, metaphysics.

Defending parsimony along methodological naturalist lines requires that we substantiate its use in the sciences and that our employment of Ockham's razor in metaphysics squares with its use in science. And, given the value of parsimony in addressing challenges from scientific anti-realists and external world sceptics, there is reason to hope a sound defence of razor arguments can be supplied, along these or some other lines. For, without licence to defer to theoretical virtues, there is little hope for useful inquiry in metaphysics or elsewhere in philosophy. It is hard to overstate the extent to which this under-discussed issue matters for metaphysics and philosophy more generally. But, here and in what follows, we will swim with the methodological tide and continue under the assumption that simplicity and other theoretical virtues are epistemic rather than merely pragmatic.

We now face the challenge of fixing upon what counts as parsimony within our theories. This is no small task, since talk of parsimony regularly overlaps with talk of simplicity, elegance, concision, and other features; however, two general kinds of parsimony are especially significant. We've also encountered these notions in preceding chapters, since they each concern a different aspect of theoretical structure. The first kind, *ontological parsimony*, concerns ontological commitments—roughly, the entities that must exist for a theory to be true. The second kind, *ideological parsimony*, concerns the primitive concepts, in the form of predicates and operators, needed to express a theory.

Granted the distinction between these sorts of parsimony, the simplest razor argument against platonism begins by noting that platonists accept ontological commitments—e.g., numbers and properties—in excess of those admitted by nominalists. So, in light of Ockham's razor, it concludes that we are justified in believing nominalism rather than platonism.

In assessing this argument, it is crucial to note that, like any plausible razor argument, it presupposes that the competing theories are "otherwise equal"—i.e., evenly matched in their explanatory adequacy. This is because the application of Ockham's razor licenses belief in one theory over its rival *only* if the competing theories are already in general parity with one another. This qualification rules out the implausible view that parsimony somehow licenses a belief in theories that, while ontologically modest, are manifestly inadequate in other respects—e.g., by being explanatorily vacuous or wildly non-conservative. So, when properly wielded, Ockham's razor affords parsimony only a tie-breaking role in theory choice. Parsimony cannot, on its own, justify belief in theories that are otherwise defective.

The status of parsimony as a tie-breaking consideration importantly constrains its role in the nominalist–platonist debate. Most notably, it requires that any razor argument like the one above be paired with a compelling case for holding nominalism and platonism to be roughly equal in the first place. This is no small thing, considering that few parties to the nominalist–platonist debate are willing to concede the explanatory merits of their rivals. Platonists will regularly claim, for example, that nominalism is explanatorily impoverished, while many nominalists will have a dim view of the platonist's proposed metaphysical explanations. Since so few parties are willing to grant that nominalism and platonism are otherwise equal, it is unclear, dialectically speaking, whether any argument of this kind could be effective. But, despite this potential dialectical impotence, it is still worth carefully considering how parsimony bears upon this debate if we grant that platonism and nominalism are close competitors.

Assuming that nominalism and platonism are on roughly equal footing, it still looks as though ontological parsimony, considered in isolation, is unable to establish the superiority of nominalism. As Melia (2008) points out, when faced with choosing between nominalism and, say, a Pythagorean view on which all apparently concrete entities are abstract, Ockham's razor licenses us to cut away properties and propositions, but leaves open whether the remaining posits are concrete or abstract. This is because auxiliary theoretical virtues play a crucial role in assessing the merits of competing theories. In this case, an especially key role is played by conservativeness—roughly, the virtue of preserving antecedent commitments over novel alternatives—which licenses our belief that persons, puddles, and piñatas are concrete rather than abstract. Only after we grant that conservativeness is a virtue, do we have warrant to "razor down" to a nominalist ontology rather than "razoring upward" to a Pythagorean view on which everything is abstract. And, while few are interested in defending Pythagoreanism in this (or any other) way, this point nicely illustrates that successful appeals to specific theoretical virtues are almost always intertwined with other theoretical virtues. For this reason, parsimony, in isolation, cannot break the tie in favour of nominalism.

Setting aside the complex interconnections among theoretical virtues, there is a general tension between ontological and ideological parsimony, which is especially clear in the nominalist–platonist debate. This is because razor arguments for nominalism almost always address themselves to matters of *ontological* parsimony, but platonist theories have a strong claim to exhibiting greater *ideological* parsimony than their nominalist rivals.

Following our discussion of Quine in Chapter 1, consider two competing views about predication and properties. On a representative platonist view, there is a single ideological primitive of *instantiation* and a vast plurality of abstract entities like universals, which are said to be instantiated by entities. On a Quinean nominalist view, there are no properties, but, instead, a wealth of ideological primitives—one for each primitive predicate. So, in explaining the fact that *a* is F, the platonist appeals to both ideology (the predicate "instantiates") and ontology (the property, F*ness*), while the nominalist appeals only to a primitive predicate, "is F." Once we factor ideological commitments into our evaluation of parsimony, any obvious advantage for nominalism disappears. We are left, instead, with the difficult question of how to assess these two theories' claims to parsimony, given their respective ideological and ontological commitments.[3]

There is no mechanical recipe for counting up the cost of ideological primitives and weighing them against ontological commitments (or *vice versa*). But we might be able to make headway by further distinguishing between two conceptions of parsimony: *quantitative parsimony*, which concerns only the *number* of commitments, and *qualitative parsimony*, which concerns the *number of kinds* of commitments. The most familiar conception of parsimony deployed in metaphysics is probably quantitative ontological parsimony, which holds that, in comparing otherwise equal theories, we are justified in believing whichever theory posits the fewest entities. And, while this sort of parsimony plays a key role in evaluating theories, we are ill-advised to ignore other conceptions of parsimony. For, as we've already seen, ontology and ideology play equally significant theoretical roles. Ideological commitments are therefore no less important than ontological commitments when it comes to weighing theoretical virtues.

Any epistemic priority claimed for qualitative over quantitative parsimony will be contentious, but the guiding idea behind the qualitative conception is that theories flout parsimony by proliferating *kinds* of commitments, not simply by positing more entities of a given kind. Marking a commitment to qualitative rather than quantitative ontological parsimony, Lewis (1973: 87) says, "I subscribe to the general view that qualitative parsimony is good in a philosophical or empirical hypothesis; but I recognize no presumption whatever in favour of quantitative parsimony." While Lewis' stance squares well with his commitment to a modal realist ontology of vastly many concrete worlds, the full-scale dismissal of quantitative ontological parsimony is difficult to square with ordinary and scientific reasoning. It is hard, for example, to believe that a theory positing two million particles of kind K_1 is more parsimonious than a theory positing three particles of kinds K_1, K_2, and K_3. Even so, Lewis is surely right about this much: there are plainly cases where qualitative parsimony does matter and we ought to avoid positing novel kinds of entities when additional entities of an already-posited kind suffice.

Investigating the status of qualitative and quantitative parsimony and how they crosscut the ontology–ideology divide is a task that looms large for those interested in the general evaluation of theories. Here, we are best served to ask how these competing conceptions of parsimony bear upon the nominalist–platonist debate. More specifically: is there a conception of parsimony that could underwrite a successful razor argument against platonism?

For platonists, prioritizing qualitative ontological parsimony over quantitative ontological parsimony helps defuse worries about the explosive ontology of set theory. Since set theory is almost unrivalled in the sheer vastness of the number of entities it admits, it offends profoundly against quantitative ontological parsimony with each particular abstract entity offending against Ockham's razor. But, since sets are all entities of a common kind, a qualitative conception of ontological parsimony counts the entire hierarchy of sets to be no more or less worrisome than a lone singleton. The same goes for other equally vast theories that posit properties or propositions. Unfortunately for nominalists, it is difficult to believe that the quantitative should be uniformly or decisively prioritized over the qualitative. It would, for example, be a bizarrely flat-footed methodology that takes each set, property, or proposition to weigh against the general merits of platonism. So, although platonism does forgo some measure of qualitative ontological parsimony, given the metaphysical distinction between abstract and concrete entities, this is a very modest advantage when compared to the decidedly pro-nominalist verdict supported by quantitative ontological parsimony.

Razor arguments for nominalism are in far worse shape once we turn to ideological parsimony. Generally speaking, minimal ontologies require correspondingly richer ideologies to match the explanatory power of rival theories. For example, presentists require primitive temporal operators, since, unlike eternalists, they reject ontological commitment to non-present times. In a similar vein, modalists require primitive modal operators, since, unlike non-modalists, they reject ontological commitment to possible worlds. If we focus on the case of properties, we can see that Quinean nominalists seem to require a vast stock of primitive predicates in order to make do without the platonist's ontology of properties. For this reason, the ideological commitments of nominalism typically far outstrip those of platonism, which might even get by with only the single primitive of instantiation. So, regardless of whether we attend to qualitative or quantitative parsimony, the ideological cost of nominalism is likely greater than that of platonism.

Any narrow conception of parsimony is likely to favour one of nominalism or platonism. Roughly speaking, ontological parsimony cuts against platonism, while ideological parsimony cuts against nominalism. But, in each case, much depends upon whether we prioritize qualitative or quantitative conceptions of parsimony. A successful razor argument against platonism would therefore have to show, first, that we ought to prioritize a specific conception of parsimony and, second, that the relevant conception counts against positing abstract entities. It looks, however, like there is no compelling reason to uniformly prioritize ontological over ideological parsimony or qualitative over quantitative parsimony. Ontology and ideology are each necessary for articulating our best theories and theoretical bloat of either sort is vicious.

Since we have no compelling reason to uniquely prize a specific conception of parsimony, viable razor arguments must look to the cumulative ontological and ideological commitments of theories to assess their "total costs." But, once again, there is no mechanical recipe for adding up and comparing differing ontological and ideological commitments. For, while there may be reason to believe these commitments admit of rough comparison and evaluation, it would be bizarre to claim that, say, three entities are equal to exactly one primitive predicate. There is therefore no clear answer about whether nominalism is more or less parsimonious than platonism. Consequently, no razor argument provides good reason to uphold nominalism and disavow abstracta.

§3.3 Infinite regresses

The history of the nominalist–platonist debate is peppered with regress arguments. The most influential of these is Plato's Third Man argument, which targets the theory of forms or universals on the basis of two crucial assumptions: (A) that any entity having a feature like *being beautiful* or *being human* has that feature in virtue of instantiating a universal like *beauty* or *humanity* which is distinct from it; and (B) that universals have the features they confer upon the entities that instantiate them. Given (B), a universal like *beauty* must itself be beautiful. But, (A) requires that, if *beauty* is beautiful, it is so in virtue of instantiating a universal, *beauty**, which is distinct from *beauty*. And, if *beauty* is beautiful in virtue of instantiating *beauty**, then, given (A), *beauty** must itself instantiate yet another universal, *beauty***. Repeated applications of (A) and (B) seem to yield an infinite regress of universals, *beauty*, *beauty**, *beauty***, and so on *ad infinitum*.

There is little to like about theories that yield this kind of infinite regress. Not only do such theories seem to fail in their explanatory ambitions, their failure comes at a steep ontological price. This price prompts many to reject theories that exhibit this sort of infinite regress or, at the very least, to take the presence of such regresses as a serious theoretical vice. For, intuitively, no halfway decent theory should generate an infinite regress of the very kind of claims that it initially set out to explain. And, as we just saw, the Third Man suggests that any fact about the beauty of a given entity requires an ascending hierarchy of universals, each specially related to *beauty* and bearing still other beauty-conferring universals. Platonist theories that generate the regress in question are therefore rightly deemed unacceptable.

For contemporary platonists, the Third Man is far from troubling. Many platonists reject (A), allowing for some true predications that do not require corresponding universals—e.g., predications that involve primitive predicates like "instantiates." Other platonists reject the ban against universals instantiating themselves, noting, for instance, that *being a property* is plausibly thought to instantiate itself. In addition, few platonists accept the especially troublesome assumption, (B), since there is little reason to believe that universals like *mass* and *charge* must themselves be massive or charged.

Since the Third Man regress is fairly easy to avoid, it is no longer the regress argument of greatest concern to platonists. That honour goes to Bradley's regress, an argument attributed to the British idealist, F.H. Bradley. Although its historical particulars and canonical formulation are contentious, this section will focus on a version of the argument that targets the existence of structured entities—roughly, any entities built up out of relations among entities. (This reconstruction owes much to Maurin (2012).) This version of Bradley's regress aims to show that no adequate metaphysical explanation can be given for the existence of structured entities.[4] And, since all but the most radical monistic theories admit structured entities whether abstract or concrete, Bradley's regress promises widespread metaphysical consequences.

Although Bradley's regress seeks to undermine a commitment to structured entities, this conclusion is compatible with both nominalism and platonism. We might, for example, retreat to a metaphysics that includes either unstructured concrete entities or unstructured abstract ones. Despite this, Bradley's regress is held to generate especially thorny problems for platonism. In general, it threatens any view that posits relations as a means for explaining the unity of entities. It therefore takes aim at platonist views that rely upon instantiation to explain the unity of properties with their bearers. It is, for example, the tie of instantiation between Alcibiades and *beauty* that is held to explain, at least in part, the fact that Alcibiades is beautiful. Other variations on Bradley's regress target different kinds of structured abstract entities and a closely related argument concerns the "unity of the proposition," which seeks to show that there is no plausible account of how propositions are built up out of their constituents. So, while Bradley's regress is not a general argument against abstract entities *per se*, it is a direct threat to the coherence of platonist views which aim to explain the existence or unity of structured entities by invoking relations of some kind.

Here, our best bet for examining Bradley's regress is to begin with a fairly generic formulation of the argument. In presenting it, we will help ourselves to the convenient assumption that talk about facts, taken the right way, is nominalistically acceptable. In assuming this, we grant that nominalists can help themselves to talk about facts like the fact that Alcibiades is beautiful without requiring the existence of some additional entity over and above Alcibiades. In contrast, we will reserve talk of "states of affairs" for explicit reference to entities—sometimes called "facts"—that some platonists hold to be abstract entities over and above mere concrete objects.

Suppose a and b are entities, R is a relation, and that a bears R to b or, for short, $R[ab]$. Further suppose that a, b, and R could all coexist without $R[ab]$. (E.g., you and I could coexist with *being taller than*, since you and I might be the same height while someone else is taller than either of us.) Since the mere existence of a, b, and R cannot explain why $R[ab]$ obtains, some explanation of why it does is still needed. Here's a natural suggestion: $R[ab]$ is explained by the fact that a, b, and R are all related in some special way. Suppose, then, that there is a relation R^* that explains why $R[ab]$ obtains. $R^*[Rab]$ will therefore explain $R[ab]$. But what explains why $R^*[Rab]$ obtains? If we appeal to yet another relation in order to explain $R^*[Rab]$, we will once again need to posit an additional relation, R^{**}, that holds among R^*, R, a, and b. In this way, $R^{**}[R^*Rab]$ will explain $R^*[Rab]$. But, if continued indefinitely, this strategy for explaining why $R[ab]$ obtains saddles us with an infinite regress of R-relations. To be sure, each of these relations will play an explanatory role, but an additional relation will always be needed to provide some further explanation. No explanation of why $R[ab]$ obtains will therefore prove satisfactory if it draws upon such a regress of relations. Bradley's regress therefore generates not only an infinite rug of facts and relations; it requires us to push the explanatory bump infinitely far from where we started.

This schematic presentation of Bradley's regress can be filled out in more detailed ways. If we take facts to be abstract states of affairs, the regress seems to show that the unity of states of affairs cannot be explained.

Other formulations of Bradley's regress focus on the distinctive notion of *metaphysical dependence* rather than the broader notion of explanation invoked above. (See, e.g., Cameron (2008).) To see how such arguments go, suppose that *fundamental* facts are those facts that obtain in virtue of no other facts. Let us then say that a fact is *well-founded* if and only if it obtains in virtue of some fundamental fact or in virtue of some fact that ultimately obtains in virtue of some fundamental fact. According to *Well-Foundedness*, all facts are either well-founded or fundamental. Now, assume that the fact *that a is F* obtains. If we assume, as seems plausible, that this fact, which must somehow connect together the entities, *a* and F, is not itself fundamental, then, necessarily, there is some fundamental fact upon which it ultimately depends. But, given the Bradleyan regress of candidate facts on which such a fact might depend—e.g., R[aF], R*[RaF], and so on—there seems to be no non-arbitrarily distinguished fact that might serve as the fundamental fact that ultimately grounds the fact *that a is F*. This Bradleyan regress therefore seems to show that Well-Foundedness is false, since not all facts are well-founded.

Well-Foundedness enjoys broad support, so this fundamentality-driven version of Bradley's regress is no less important than the one regarding explanation; however, we will focus on the explanatory version of Bradley's regress here. In doing so, we avoid deciding against views on which the world is not well-founded, but exhibits infinite metaphysical descent. This also squares with our focus on the explanatory ambitions of platonism, which underwrite the strongest arguments for platonism surveyed in Chapter 1. And, with those credentials at stake, Bradley's regress threatens to undercut platonism. We can therefore turn our attention to an assortment of platonist responses to the regress argument, which urges us to reject properties, relations, and any other abstracta that might deliver worries about explaining unity.

Platonist strategies for addressing Bradley's regress are diverse, but, if we squint hard enough, we can lump them into three categories. (Here, we set aside Bradley's preferred response, existence monism, which holds there to be only a single entity.) The first of these seeks to downplay the threat of the regress, claiming it to be either benign or, in some cases, even theoretically beneficial. Typically, this sort of anodyne response begins by noting that various infinite regresses like the endless sequences of natural numbers or the indefinite iterability of the "is true" predicate are far from vicious and are, in fact, beneficial features of their respective mathematical and semantic theories. Proponents of the anodyne response—most notably, Russell

(1903: 99–100)—then allege that Bradley's regress is closer in character to these benign regresses than it is to vicious ones like, say, the Third Man.

The success of the anodyne response is hard to assess. There are, of course, a host of infinite regresses that arise for various theories and many of them are in no way worrisome. That said, the high bar of the anodyne response requires that we show absolutely all regress arguments in the neighbourhood of Bradley's regress to be unproblematic. This task would require either assimilating each of these potential regresses to obviously benign regresses or, instead, providing some adequate solution to them. With this in mind, it is striking that the version of the Bradleyan regress above involves a notion like explanation that seems markedly different from regresses regarding natural numbers or the iterability of "is true," where no explanatory considerations come into play. This is reason to be suspicious that at least some regress arguments akin to Bradley's are not benign in nature. As such, the anodyne response is plausible only to the extent that some solution is available for addressing explanatory regresses. If that's right, the anodyne response still owes a full-fledged solution to at least some versions of the regress argument. It therefore seems to collapse into either of the two remaining responses, which seek to solve rather than stomach the regress. There is reason, then, to think that Russell and others like Armstrong (1997: 118–119) who pursue this anodyne response are mistaken in downplaying the threat of Bradleyan regress arguments by singling out potentially benign readings. If Bradley's regress is, in all its variations, merely a regress of equivalences between claims like R[ab] and R*[Rab], proponents of the anodyne response are right to claim that the regresses at issue are benign. But, since, on at least some versions of the regress argument, the relevant relations play a crucial role in explanations of unity and are not mere claims of equivalences, at least some versions of Bradley's regress remain problematic.

A second strategy treats Bradley's regress with utmost seriousness and seeks to address it by positing additional or distinctive ontological commitments tailored to block the regress. Intuitively, this family of solutions shares a common belief that some sort of "metaphysical widget" suffices to thwart the looming regress. The leading member of this family of responses holds that tropes, unlike universals, are uniquely suited to explain the unity between properties and their bearers. This is because tropes have especially rich essences that tether each trope to its bearer as a matter of necessity. Specifically, if a trope is instantiated by a given individual, it could not be instantiated by any other individual. So, for example, the redness had by the fire truck outside my window could not be the redness of any other entity and that very redness trope could not have existed without being had by that very fire truck. Consequently, if that redness trope exists, then it must be had by that fire truck and so the mere existence of the trope is alleged to explain the unity of the trope with the fire truck. Roughly speaking, this strategy enriches the "essence" of tropes in such a way that the unity of properties with their bearers is to be explained by the individual nature of the property itself. A related strategy holds, following the terminology of Frege, that properties are "unsaturated" insofar as they must *essentially* be unified with objects and so, by their very nature, are properly united with entities into facts.

A third strategy for resolving Bradley's regress eschews additional ontology or enriched essences. Instead, it opts for an expanded commitment to primitive ideology. According to this ideology-driven response, the culprit behind Bradley's regress is the mistaken reification of relations like instantiation and identity, and, in particular, the view that these relations are entities "out there in the world" that must be added into the ontology of a theory. To remedy this mistake, the ideology-driven response holds that a relational predicate like "instantiates" is a primitive bit of ideology and not a predicate that picks out any relational ontology. Loose talk surrounding "instantiation" (and other putative relations) is therefore liable to mislead, for, on this view, "instantiation" is a primitive, metaphysically special "non-relational tie" between entities. So, when facing instances of Bradley's regress that revolve around talk of instantiation and facts, the platonist who admits the primitive ideology of instantiation can tender a fairly straightforward resolution.[5] She simply denies that facts about instantiation—e.g., that *a instantiates* F—admit of any further metaphysical explanation. Such facts are, instead, a kind of metaphysical ground floor. And, if we seek to explain the fact that R[ab], when R is a relation other than instantiation, this response holds that the proper metaphysical explanation is unproblematic: it is simply a matter of *a* and *b* instantiating the relation, R.

There remains no received view about the correct resolution of Bradley's regress. The above-noted options provide a rough sense of the leading responses, but our ultimate concern here is whether the regress might underwrite an argument for nominalism. On this front, we can begin by noting that Bradley's regress leaves untouched any heterodox versions of platonism that avoid relations or structured abstract entities altogether. But, since most varieties of platonism traffic in relations, the only versions of platonism left untroubled by Bradley's regress are among the least appealing.

If we set aside peculiar versions of platonism that disavow relations, defenders of abstract entities have three options: (i) they can claim, in keeping with the anodyne response, that all relevant regresses are benign; (ii) they can claim, in keeping with the metaphysical widget response, that certain special abstract entities like tropes provide an explanation of what unifies complex entities; or (iii) they can hold that ideology rather than ontology unifies complex entities and thereby addresses Bradley's regress.

Although I am sceptical about the use of metaphysical widgets like tropes in responding to Bradley's regress, we can leave open whether such entities might be up to the job. This is because, in assessing its merits as an anti-platonist argument, we can get away with focusing exclusively on the ideology-driven response. For, as I will now suggest, nominalists must concede this is a tenable solution to Bradley's regress or face a *tu quoque* that would undermine any nominalist metaphysics that dispenses with properties.

To see why there is no stable ground from which nominalists can launch Bradley's regress, notice that the nominalist requires a stock of primitive ideology at least as rich as the platonist who admits primitive instantiation. Viewed one way, the ideology-driven response to Bradley's regress is just the general strategy of Quine's ostrich nominalism applied to the special case of *instantiation*. So, if there is something objectionable about the use of primitive ideology in rebutting Bradley's regress, there is something similarly objectionable about the nominalist's even more widespread reliance on ideology rather than ontology. Upon pain of inconsistency, nominalists are therefore in no position to find fault with platonists who draw upon primitive ideology like *instantiation* to address Bradley's regress.

The only way nominalists might succeed in using Bradley's regress to challenge platonism would be to show that, while appeals to ideology are in *general* acceptable, the platonists' particular appropriation of a primitive "instantiation" predicate is somehow theoretically vicious. To this end, nominalists might claim that the platonist's theory of instantiation is objectionably *ad hoc*. After all, it invokes primitive ideology solely to resolve Bradley's regress but still endorses a broader platonist view rather than a stock of primitive predicates. Unfortunately, this charge of *ad hoccery* isn't very convincing. If any relation or predicate deserves special treatment in a metaphysical theory, it is instantiation, which tethers entities to properties and relations, and plays a pervasive explanatory role. Furthermore, platonists have a natural rejoinder to nominalists that charge them with an *ad hoc* appeal to ideology. Unlike the nominalists, they have secured ideological parsimony by admitting a single primitive of "instantiation" as well as a qualitatively parsimonious ontology of properties. Now, as we saw in our survey of razor arguments above, the ultimate force of this rejoinder is far from clear. But, despite this, we have successfully located a key theoretical tradeoff that divides nominalists and platonists: platonists must stomach the charge of *ad hoccery* in taking instantiation as a unique primitive predicate, while nominalists must flout ideological parsimony in providing their uniform treatment of predicates.

Ultimately, the value of Bradley's regress as an argument for nominalism is settled by the tenability of the ideology-driven response. If the response is adequate, platonists can address Bradley's regress. If the response is inadequate, nominalism is in trouble as well. So, if Bradley's regress is bad news for platonism, it is even worse news for nominalism. Bradley's regress therefore provides no convincing case for the superiority of nominalism over platonism.

Summary

This chapter examined arguments from paradox, razor arguments, and infinite regress arguments. In doing so, we found no argument that shows platonism to be untenable and no compelling reason to think nominalism is superior to platonism. Arguments from paradox turn on implausible assumptions about whether paradox is endemic to the abstract realm. Razor arguments are unconvincing once we distinguish among varieties of parsimony and mark their complex relations to nominalism and platonism. Finally, worries about infinite regresses—in particular, Bradley's regress—can be addressed by using resources that nominalists themselves rely upon. So, if one hopes to motivate nominalism, something other than impressionistic appeals to paradox, parsimony, and infinite regresses is needed.

Recommended reading

Quine (1962) provides an overview of some of the paradoxes above. On Russell's paradox and its precursors, see Hallett (1986), Klement (2010a, 2010b), Chihara (1973). On modality and its connection to relevant paradoxes, see Uzquiano (2015). On the relationships among paradoxes, see Priest (1995). For a canonical presentation of ZF, see Fraenkel et al. (1973).

On theoretical virtues and the question of their pragmatic and epistemic status, see Kuhn (1977) and Harman (1997). On the connection between theoretical virtues and rationality, see McMullin (1976). On inference to the best explanation and its connection to realism, see Lipton (2004) and Psillos (1999). See Vogel (1990) for discussion of abductive responses to external world scepticism. On Ockham's razor and the nature of simplicity, see Sober (1975) and Burgess (1998). On fertility, see Nolan (1999) and, on conservativeness, Rosen (2001: 70, 84–87) and Lewis (1986: 235). For discussion of parsimony in metaphysics, see Lewis (1986), Nolan (1997b), Melia (2008), and Cowling (2013).

Bradley (1897) and Russell (1903) set the stage for subsequent discussion of Bradley's regress. On the Russell–Bradley exchange, see Candlish (2007). Recent discussions of Bradley's regress and variations thereof include Maurin (2012), Cameron (2008), Simons (2010), and MacBride (2011). On infinite regresses in metaphysics, see Bliss (2013), Nolan (2001), and Schaffer (2003).

Notes

1 On options for reconciling or reducing sets and properties, see Lewis (1983) and Jubien (1989). Comparable problems arise for those who would posit similar abstract entities like *sui generis* propositional functions. On propositional functions, see Russell (1903: 82–88).
2 There are, of course, exceptions in this regard. See Fine (1977) and Bealer (1982).
3 There are other nominalist options in this regard, which seek out other ontological and ideological packages. For example, the resemblance nominalism of Rodriguez-Pereyra (2002) dispenses with a plurality of primitive predicates in favour of a single predicate of *resemblance* but, at the same time, takes on ontological commitment to sets and concrete possible worlds.
4 Perhaps the clearest formulation Bradley provides of a regress argument is the following: "But how the relation can stand to the qualities is, on the other side, unintelligible. If it is nothing to the qualities, then they are not related at all; and, if so, as we saw, they have ceased to be qualities, and their relation is a nonentity. But if it is to be something to them, then clearly we shall now require a *new* connecting relation. For the relation hardly can be the mere adjective of one or both of its terms; or, at least, as such it seems indefensible. And, being something itself, if it does not itself bear a relation to the terms, in what intelligible way will it succeed in being anything to them? But here again we are hurried off into the eddy of a hopeless process, since we are forced to go on finding new relations without end. The links are united by a link, and this bond of union is a link which also has two ends;

and these require each a fresh link to connect them with the old. The problem is to find how the relation can stand to its qualities; and this problem is insoluble." (1897: 32–33)

5 On "non-relational ties," see Strawson (1959: 167–173) and Maurin (2012). Loux (1998: 30–36) also points out that denying the existence of an instantiation relation potentially allows for a principled resolution to the paradox involving "non-self-instantiating properties."

4

CAUSAL CONCERNS

4.1 Epistemic access
4.2 Ensuring epistemic access
4.3 Semantic access
4.4 Cognitive access
4.5 Eleaticism

§4.1 Epistemic access

You bear causal relations to a diverse range of entities. In some cases, these causal relations are fairly direct as when the ground presses against your feet or light stimulates your retina. In other cases, these causal relations are far less direct. Distant particles exert miniscule gravitational forces on you and long-dead evolutionary ancestors beget still more of your ancestors. But, while our causal interactions with concrete reality are complex and varied, many platonists deny that we ever causally interact with abstract reality. Moreover, this lack of causal interaction is no accident. According to these platonists, abstract entities simply aren't the kind of entities that can be pushed, poked, or prodded. They are, by their very nature, causally inactive.

This chapter surveys arguments against platonism that turn on the non-causal nature of abstract entities. As we saw in Chapter 2, there is no consensus about whether abstract entities are causally inactive. Nor is there consensus about what it means to be causally inactive. But, despite disagreement on this front, the prevalent assumption that abstract entities are causally inactive warrants taking these arguments seriously. And, if it does turn out that "causal arguments"—i.e., arguments premised upon the causal inactivity of abstract entities—are sound, this shows that platonists must either grant the causal activity of abstract entities or disavow them altogether.

Our survey of causal arguments begins with an argument most famously presented by Paul Benacerraf. This argument revolves around our epistemic access to causally inactive entities and, in particular, mathematical objects. After considering Benacerraf's version of what we will call the epistemic access argument as well as several variations, we will briefly examine a very different kind of causal argument based upon a commitment to Eleaticism, which claims causal activity to be a metaphysical prerequisite for existence.

Epistemic access arguments proceed from the plausible observation that causal relations structure our cognitive and epistemic life. Perception—one kind of causal back and forth between agents and the world—furnishes us with much of our knowledge. Other processes like testimony and memory are also causal in nature. And, just as knowledge of our immediate surroundings depends upon our causal interactions with the environment, knowledge of the distant past owes to lengthy and complex causal chains that tie together myriad perceptual and testimonial interactions. It is difficult to imagine how someone might acquire knowledge or justified beliefs about some subject matter in the complete absence of causal connections to it. Where there are no perceptual episodes, no chains of testimony linking agents, no causal ties whatsoever, we seem to be necessarily ignorant. This suggests a kind of "causal constraint," which holds, very roughly, that we can have no epistemic access to subject matters from which we are causally isolated.

This causal constraint on our knowledge underwrites the epistemic access argument against platonism. Suppose that abstract entities are causally inactive and that, as platonists contend, our knowledge of mathematics is knowledge about abstract entities. If so, the causal constraint rules out the possibility of mathematical knowledge. But, of course, we do have mathematical knowledge, so something has to give. And, since we have better reason to believe the causal constraint than to believe platonism, we ought to reject platonism and deny that mathematical truths are truths about an abstract realm of mathematical entities.

This first pass at capturing the epistemic access argument—we'll consider Benacerraf's particular version below—requires some immediate clarifications. The first thing to note is that the epistemic access argument is not a sceptical argument that seeks to show we lack mathematical knowledge. Unlike sceptical arguments, it explicitly affirms that we possess mathematical knowledge. In fact, the plausibility of the initial assumption that we possess this knowledge is what makes this argument so worrisome for platonists. This is because the causal constraint, when paired with platonism, seems to make our possession of this knowledge profoundly mysterious. So, even if platonism supplies a handy face-value interpretation of our thought and talk about mathematical entities, the epistemic access argument threatens to show that it still involves an untenable view of mathematical knowledge.

The second point to note is that not just any causal interaction will serve to quell worries regarding epistemic access. For, while causal relations underwrite perception and other processes that afford us knowledge of the world, the mere presence of causal interactions does not, on its own, account for the possibility of knowledge. So, even if abstract entities exert "some sort of steady, unchanging pressure" as Armstrong considers, this would not guarantee an improvement in our epistemic situation. For, unless there is some clear way in which this "unchanging pressure" might facilitate justified beliefs about abstracta—e.g., by allowing us to perceive mathematical entities—platonists still have no means of accounting for our epistemic access. Arguing that abstract entities are, in some trivial way, causally active is therefore insufficient for showing that we can have knowledge of them. So, even if one posits some sort of causal interplay between the abstract and the concrete, the epistemic access argument remains intact unless this interplay is of the right epistemic kind.

A third point to note is that, while the epistemic access argument usually targets mathematical entities, there is no reason to think that it cannot be extended to apply to all abstract entities, provided such entities are causally inert or bear no epistemically significant causal relations to us. But, rather than qualify remarks to include propositions and properties in what follows, we will retain our focus on the mathematical case throughout the next few sections. We will, however, return to concerns about our epistemic access to propositions and properties in Section 4.4. For convenience's sake, we will also omit the just-noted qualification regarding causal inactivity and take talk of "causally inactivity" to be inactivity with respect to any causal interactions that might underwrite knowledge or justified belief.

With these clarifications in hand, we can turn to the canonical formulation of the epistemic access argument. As presented (though not endorsed) in Benacerraf (1973), this argument is a dilemma for theories of mathematical knowledge. The first horn sets out the above problem for the standard platonist interpretation of mathematics. As Benacerraf suggests, the platonist account of mathematical entities "places them beyond the reach of the better understood means of human cognition (e.g., sense perception and the like)" and, in doing so, "appears to violate the requirement that our account of mathematical truth be susceptible to integration into our overall account of knowledge." This violation owes to a causal constraint on our overall account of knowledge that Benacceraf (1973: 671) puts as follows: "I favor a causal account of knowledge on which for X to know that S is true requires some causal relation to obtain between X and the referents of the names, predicates, and quantifiers of S."

The second horn of Benacerraf's dilemma presents a problem for nominalist interpretations of mathematical discourse that likely require a non-standard semantics. This problem arises because, in dispensing with abstract entities, nominalists and others forgo the face-value construal of mathematical talk available to platonists. While such views avoid certain epistemological woes, they require that we break the semantic analogy between mathematical expressions like "the number seven" and comparable non-mathematical expressions like "the Dean of Students." The resulting interpretation of mathematical thought and talk therefore requires an awkward and disunified treatment of our mathematical and ordinary discourse, despite ample evidence for the semantic homogeneity of mathematical and non-mathematical language. As Benacerraf (1973: 666) says:

> Perhaps the applicability of this [homogeneity] requirement to the present case amounts only to a plea that the semantical apparatus of mathematics be seen as part and parcel of that of the natural language in which it is done, and thus that whatever semantical account we are inclined to give of names or, more generally of singular terms predicates, and quantifiers in the mother tongue include those parts of the mother tongue which we classify as mathematese.

In response to this dilemma, Benacerraf points out that, regardless of one's preferred interpretation of mathematics, we face an explanatory challenge in interpreting mathematical claims or making sense of how we might know them. And, if platonists cannot plausibly account for our mathematical knowledge, the second horn and its non-standard semantics seem all but unavoidable. For this reason, the first horn of Benacerraf's dilemma has received considerably greater attention with particular concern for the fate of the causal constraint on knowledge.

The causal constraint on knowledge enjoys some intuitive appeal. Not only is the nature of our epistemic access to the world worrisomely tentative at times, the standard view of the abstract–concrete distinction invites serious concerns about how we extend our epistemic reach across this metaphysical divide. The causal constraint has also been suggested as a way to repair proposed analyses of knowledge in the face of Gettier-style counterexamples. But, in light of its rather sweeping epistemic consequences—most notably, its threat to a platonist view of mathematical knowledge—even those like Goldman (1967), who considers it as a response to Gettier cases, deny it holds in full generality. For Benacerraf (1973: 672), however, the causal constraint is most naturally motivated by a general commitment to empiricism, since the proposed constraint "follows closely the lines that have been proposed by empiricists but with the crucial modification introduced by the explicitly causal condition." This line of defence is, of course, of little interest to anti-empiricists. So, regardless of its intuitive appeal, the causal constraint remains difficult to establish and, given its tension with platonist theories of mathematical knowledge, a final assessment of its plausibility raises some thorny methodological questions about where the burden of proof lies.

The causal constraint also faces a range of putative counterexamples that are independent of concerns about mathematical knowledge. We seem, for example, to have justified beliefs and knowledge about entities outside of our lightcone, about presently unsynthesized chemical elements, and about general laws or theories that involve entities we cannot causally interact with (e.g., physical laws that subsume instances beyond our causal influence). In weighing these sorts of apparent counterexamples, Benacerraf (1973: 672) says only the following:

> Other cases of knowledge can be explained as being based on inferences based on cases such as these, although there must evidently be interdependencies. This is meant to include our knowledge of general laws and theories, and, through them, our knowledge of the future and much of the past . . . .. The connection between what must be the case if *p* is true and the causes of *X*'s belief can vary widely. But there is always some connection, and the connection relates the grounds of *X*'s belief to the subject matter of *p*.

Benacerraf's response hints that causal connections do, in fact, underwrite our knowledge of what some have claimed to be counterexamples the causal constraint. And, for those who hope to uphold the causal constraint, a natural option is to posit some heretofore unacknowledged causal mechanism that plays a key epistemic role in these and other cases. Some have tried to make good on this strategy and apply it to the case of platonism by arguing that numbers do actually play a causal role in explanations, given the ineliminability of mathematical facts in any physical story about perception. (See, e.g., Steiner (1975: 114).) It is difficult, however, to see how appeals to mathematical facts in our best scientific accounts of perception actually address the epistemic access problem, since the issue is not about whether mathematics proves explanatorily useful for various scientific purposes. It is instead a puzzle about what causal relations put us in epistemic rapport with the mathematical. So, against this suggestion, Hart (1977: 125–126) memorably remarks:

> it is a crime against the intellect to try to mask the problem of naturalizing the epistemology of mathematics with philosophical razzle-dazzle. Superficial worries about the intellectual hygiene of causal theories of knowledge are irrelevant to and misleading for this problem, for the problem is not so much about causality as about the very possibility of natural knowledge of abstract objects.

Hart's remark takes issue with strategies that would circumvent the epistemic access problem by positing irrelevant causal connections to sidestep counterexamples rather than articulating a full-fledged platonist account of mathematical knowledge. But, setting aside counterexamples regarding unsynthesized elements and general laws, the most pressing objection to the causal constraint is still our evident mathematical knowledge. So, for platonists, there is considerable temptation to simply conclude that our knowledge of arithmetic immediately and conclusively refutes the causal constraint.[1]

Ultimately, the case for the causal constraint, in any form strong enough to threaten platonism, is too weak to show that knowledge of the abstract is unavailable to us. But, as subsequent commentators have pointed out, there are ways to build upon concerns about our knowledge of causally inert entities that do generate serious problems for would-be platonists. In this vein, the most influential reformulation of the epistemic access argument owes to Hartry Field.

Field's refinement of the epistemic access argument issues a challenge to the platonist: explain the reliability of mathematical beliefs, given that their subject matter is a domain of causally inert entities. As Field (1989: 25) says: "The way to understand Benacerraf's challenge, I think, is not as a challenge to our ability to *justify* our mathematical beliefs, but as a challenge to our ability to *explain the reliability* of these beliefs." If there is no way in which this challenge can be met, there is no way for platonists to explain mathematical knowledge. Field's reformulation is therefore a considerable hurdle for platonist views on which mathematics concerns a realm of abstract entities. Here, we can parse out Field's argument against platonism as follows:

Field's challenge

P1. Mathematicians possess reliable mathematical beliefs.

P2. If abstract mathematical entities exist, they would be causally inert and causally isolated from mathematicians.

P3. If mathematical platonism is true, the reliable connection between abstract mathematical entities and mathematicians' beliefs about mathematics must be, in principle, explicable.

P4. If abstract mathematical entities are causally inert and causally isolated from mathematicians, the reliable connection between abstract mathematical entities and mathematician's beliefs about mathematics cannot be explained.

C1. Therefore, mathematical platonism is not true.

P1 and P2 are general features of non-sceptical versions of mathematical platonism and make explicit the assumption that abstracta are causally inert. P3 is plausibly viewed as a constraint on any tenable epistemology of mathematics, since views that make the reliability of mathematical beliefs inexplicable make a mystery of mathematical knowledge. And, while Field (1989: 27) does not claim anything like certainty for P4, he remarks: "Like Benacerraf, I refrain from making any sweeping assertion about the impossibility of the required explanation. However, I am not all optimistic about the prospects of providing it." Field's pessimism is plausible enough. If mathematical reality consists of entities outside of the causal order, there is certainly no straightforward route for explaining our epistemic access to such a realm.

Crucially, the explanatory worry for platonism that Field raises here requires no general causal constraint on knowledge. Instead, it issues a modest demand that mathematical knowledge be integrated within our broader epistemology. In support of this demand, Field (1989: 26–27) notes that, were someone to claim to have true beliefs about events in a village in Nepal despite lacking any means for explaining the connection between these true beliefs and the events in question, we would be well within our rights to doubt, not only the truth of these beliefs, but also the relevant claim to knowledge about the village. So, if the reliability of mathematicians' beliefs about abstract mathematical entities resists explanation, platonism delivers a view on which our mathematical knowledge is inexplicable. Since mathematical platonism is therefore explanatorily impoverished, nominalism emerges as a preferable option even if it requires a non-standard interpretation of mathematics.[2]

Before assessing responses that seek to explain the reliable connection at issue, it is worth noting that some like Lewis (1986) take Field's challenge to be misconceived. According to Lewis, Field is correct that justified beliefs about contingent matters like populations and pool balls require some reliable connection between believers and subject matters. Justified beliefs about non-contingent subject matters are, however, an importantly different affair. The mathematical realm—except, perhaps, for impure sets—and the modal realm of non-actual possibilities are static and non-contingent. So, unlike concrete entities, these portions of reality could not have been otherwise. As such, no account can be given of the co-variation between beliefs and these non-contingent subject matters like mathematical reality, since the latter do not and and cannot vary. And, since we cannot explain the reliability of mathematicians' beliefs by pointing to some kind of systematic co-variation, our knowledge of non-contingent subject matters does not require the explicability of any such reliable connection. Mathematical knowledge, like knowledge of other non-contingent matters, is therefore importantly different from knowledge that must be underwritten by and subsequently explained in terms of reliable causal connections.

The necessity of mathematical truth does distinguish our mathematical knowledge from our more quotidian contingent knowledge. But, while this distinction is a significant one, it is important to note that Field's challenge does not presuppose that the nature of our epistemic access to abstract reality is perfectly analogous with our access to concrete reality. Field's challenge does not, for example, turn on showing that *were* mathematical reality different, mathematician's beliefs would also be different. Instead, Field's challenge requires that the reliability of these beliefs admit of explanation irrespective of the modal status of mathematical reality. So, although the non-contingent character of mathematics does suggest that our ordinary notion of a reliable connection—e.g., something like non-trivial modal co-variation—does not apply in the case of mathematics, this is no reason to believe that no explanation of reliability is needed. Put more simply: the peculiar modal status of mathematics does not exempt it from the demand that our knowledge be explicable. So, in spite of the non-contingent status of mathematical reality and mathematical truths, Field's explanatory demand stands as a reasonable one: platonists owe us some account of how we might know the abstract realm.

§4.2 Ensuring epistemic access

This section surveys some leading platonist responses to Field's challenge. These responses can be divided up in a few ways. Here, we can tentatively group them as follows: (i) *logical knowledge*—mathematical knowledge is explained through our knowledge of logic; (ii) *natural knowledge*—mathematical knowledge is explained through our knowledge of scientific theories; and (iii) *intuition*—mathematical knowledge is explained by appeal to a special epistemic capacity like mathematical intuition. Although these responses and others not considered here deserve considerably greater scrutiny than we can afford them, we will make do by outlining their central commitments and general structure. In so doing, we leave aside many important challenges and refinements but we still put ourselves in a position to assess the ultimate fate of epistemic access arguments. (Readers are strongly encouraged to consult the Recommended reading section for more extensive discussions.)

§4.2.1 Logical knowledge

Logicism, broadly conceived, takes mathematical facts to be logical facts and, in turn, mathematical knowledge to be logical knowledge. Since only the most radical sceptics will deny that we possess knowledge of logical truths, the reduction of the mathematical to logic would be good epistemic news for platonists. Moreover, our logical knowledge seems to have no distinctive subject matter. In fact, it is perfectly general, applying to absolutely all of reality and therefore seems to require no special epistemic contact with any specific entities. If logicists are right that mathematical knowledge is merely logical knowledge, our logical knowledge suffices for our mathematical knowledge. Better still, such a view requires no distinctive account of our epistemic access to some abstract portion of reality. As a result, this would place mathematical knowledge on far safer epistemic footing, since nominalists will also grant that we acquire logical knowledge in the absence of epistemic contact with the abstract realm.

The ambitions of logicism spurred key advances within the analytic tradition, but Frege's efforts to carry out the logicist project were confounded by Russell's paradox, which we touched on in the previous chapter. Subsequent efforts have raised difficult questions about the essential features of logicism. For, while different strategies for the reduction of mathematics have been offered, the extent to which the resources deployed are "properly logical" remains a bone of contention. In its current incarnation, a typical neo-logicist strategy seeks to derive the axioms of Peano arithmetic from second-order logic—roughly, logic admitting quantification into the predicate position—and an abstraction principle, usually called Hume's principle, which contextually defines the notion of a cardinal number using the relational predicate "is in one-to-one correspondence." Roughly put, Hume's principle says that the number of Fs equals the number of Gs if and only if the Fs and the Gs can be put in one-to-one correspondence.[3] Once given the contextual definition of terms like "the number of Fs" via Hume's principle, second-order logic allows us to derive arithmetic. As critics are quick to note, however, Hume's principle and second-order logic are only controversially viewed as belonging to logic proper, especially in light of their notable ontological consequences.

The prospects for logicism in its various incarnations hinge upon questions about the distinction between logic and the extra-logical. But, if our knowledge of mathematics can be shown to follow from logic alone, this would provide platonists with a way to explain our epistemic access to mathematical reality. At the same time, it leads to challenges for some familiar (though controversial) platitudes about logic—in particular, it would require that we surrender the thesis that logic is ontologically neutral and without any existential import. Since platonism requires ontological commitment to mathematical entities, the success of logicism would show that logic, properly conceived, places robust ontological demands upon reality by requiring the existence of infinitely many abstract entities.

An alternative to logicism shares in its commitment to the centrality of logical knowledge for explaining our knowledge of abstract mathematical entities. According to plenitudinism, our knowledge of mathematical reality is explained by our knowledge of the consistency of theories. On this plenitudinist or "full-blooded" version of platonism, we need not take sides on whether mathematics is properly reducible to logic. Instead, we need only endorse a radical view about the nature of the abstract realm, which takes all consistent mathematical theories to describe some portion of it.

Plenitudinism departs from familiar views of the abstract realm on which there is, say, a single set-theoretic hierarchy. Instead, the plenitudinist posits the existence of all (consistent) hierarchies and any other consistent mathematical structures. Each set-theoretic hierarchy therefore exists alongside countless others (and countless other kinds of mathematical theories) that obey different axioms. Once granted this especially fecund picture of mathematical reality, the plenitudinist claims that the epistemic challenge of accessing the abstract can be met. For, if any consistent mathematical theory is true of some part of mathematical reality, our knowledge that a theory is logically consistent guarantees knowledge of at least one portion of mathematical reality.

In keeping with Field's analogy that likened our knowledge of mathematical reality to that of a distant Nepalese village, a leading plenitudinist, Mark Balaguer (1998: 49) says:

> [I]f all possible Nepalese villages existed, then I could have knowledge of these villages, even without any access to them. To attain such knowledge, I would merely have to dream up a possible Nepalese village. For on the assumption that all possible Nepalese villages exist, it would follow that the village I have imagined exists and that my beliefs about this village correspond to the facts about it.

For the plenitudinist, the ontology of abstract reality is therefore sufficiently vast that, granted knowledge of which theories are consistent, we can lay claim to genuine knowledge of the abstract realm.

Plenitudinism is a powerful alternative to more familiar platonist theories, which admit only a single mathematical "universe" that obeys a unique set of axioms. It also does justice to the diversity of mathematical practice. Since a wide range of mathematical theories have been subjects of mathematical inquiry, there is comparatively little interest in discerning, say, which set of axioms correctly describe the one and only mathematical structure. Plenitudinism therefore avoids commitment to what some might allege is a brute fact about why only *some* consistent mathematical theories correctly describe mathematical reality.

Objections to plenitudinism typically take issue with its comparatively vast ontology or with its credentials as a solution to the epistemic access problem. Objections of the first sort are far from conclusive.[4] The most worrisome objection of the latter sort alleges that plenitudinism is itself unknowable. And, since it leaves our knowledge that abstract reality is plenitudinous more or less unexplained, it cannot adequately account for our pedestrian mathematical knowledge. But, as Balaguer argues, a committed externalist about justification can, at the same time, accept the plenitudinist account of mathematical knowledge even while she might leave open whether we are in a position to know that abstract reality is indeed plenitudinous. This makes the case against plenitudinism fairly tenuous. So, for platonists who are content to explain epistemic access while rejecting certain internalist views in epistemology, plenitudinism remains a viable option.

§4.2.2 Natural knowledge

Naturalistic responses to Field's challenge depart considerably from logicism and plenitudinism. To see why, consider the robust methodological naturalism set out in Quine (1981b: 72): "[Naturalism] sees natural science as an inquiry into reality, fallible and corrigible but not answerable to any supra-scientific tribunal, and not in need of any justification beyond observation and the hypothetico-deductive method." For some methodological naturalists, a commitment to this view of science's relation to philosophy requires that we reject Field's challenge as illegitimate. Since it seems to prioritize philosophical standards over the working standards of scientific practice, these methodological naturalists take Field's challenge as a demand that our best scientific theories answer to an extra-scientific epistemological standard. But, since our justification for believing our best scientific theories is precisely what justifies our knowledge of mathematics, no extra-scientific account of our justification for believing our best scientific theories and, in turn, mathematics is required. In other words, no "philosophically satisfactory" explanation of mathematical knowledge is needed, given that mathematicians are not actively concerned with providing one. Field's challenge is therefore properly dismissed as the kind of "first philosophy" at odds with methodological naturalism.

This dismissive stance is not mandatory, however. Other methodological naturalists might seek to uphold Field's challenge as naturalistically legitimate.[5] For, like other naturalistically acceptable philosophical projects, Field's challenge can be viewed as part of the general scientific enterprise of attempting to reconcile disparate parts of our total scientific worldview. In particular, it aims at reconciling our mathematical knowledge with our best scientific theories regarding our physical and psychological constitution. As Maddy (1990: 3) puts it: "Our current psychological theory gives the beginnings of a convincing portrait of ourselves as knowers, but it contains no chapter on how we might come to know about things so irrevocably remote from our cognitive machinery." So, when viewed as part of the naturalistic challenge of integrating various scientific disciplines, Field's challenge will still be a genuine concern in the eyes of at least some methodological naturalists.

Regardless of whether methodological naturalists take Field's challenge to be legitimate, it is important to note that their concern is not whether our mathematical beliefs are justified. For naturalists, the issue of whether we have justification for believing mathematical claims is easy to settle. By the standards of our best scientific theories, mathematical claims are justified, so we have compelling reason to think them so. Properly viewed, Field's challenge concerns whether we can explain the reliability of mathematicians' beliefs about *mathematical entities*, where such entities are claimed to be non-physical in nature. For the naturalist, the historical details regarding the development of mathematics will presumably be an ineliminable part of this story. But, as Burgess and Rosen (1997: 47) point out, these historical details do not, on their own, amount to a story about how abstract reality might be accessed by concrete entities like us. Moreover, if our justification for beliefs about mathematical entities really owes to their place within certain complex scientific theories, we will be hard-pressed to do justice to the obviousness of mathematical truths and the intuitive justification they seem to possess independently of our best scientific theories. But, again, accounting for these features is a task that many naturalists will refuse to take seriously, since it tacitly assumes that philosophical standards and extra-scientific considerations might take precedence over scientific standards. Naturalists are therefore in an odd position: they have no reason to doubt our mathematical beliefs are justified, but, given their methodological commitments, they seem to lack any philosophically satisfactory account of how we form these reliable beliefs about mathematical entities.

There is, I think, a plausible explanation for why naturalism offers no decisive resolution to Field's challenge. This is because naturalists seek to explain why mathematicians' beliefs are justified by appeal to our best scientific theories, but no part of this explanation requires a genuinely platonist interpretation of mathematics. For, while naturalism requires that we endorse the truth of mathematical claims, auxiliary metaphysical assumptions about the nature of mathematical entities fall outside the scope of our best scientific theories. And, since naturalism is concerned solely with the truth of mathematical claims, a plausible story about our epistemic access to abstract reality is no part of the scientific domains like mathematics and psychology that naturalists are pressed to reconcile with one another. Since mathematical truth matters to science but the precise nature of mathematical entities does not, the distinctive commitments of platonism have no significant place within our best scientific theories. Naturalists should therefore be content to leave open what exactly mathematical entities are like and whether their extra-mathematical features are those ascribed by platonist views. And, since Field's challenge specifically targets platonist views, there should be no real surprise that methodological naturalism provides little guidance as to how platonists ought to meet this challenge.

§4.2.3 Intuition

Field's challenge presupposes that familiar epistemic means like perception and memory can provide no explanation of our mathematical knowledge, given their causal nature. And, while this seems a reasonable conclusion, there is a long historical tradition that runs directly to the contrary. The Platonic doctrine of *anamnesis* set out in the *Meno* explains mathematical knowledge by way of our memory (and some fairly astonishing claims about our pre-corporeal existence). Much later and more plausibly, John Stuart Mill defended an empiricist view on which perception and induction supply us with mathematical knowledge, while, at the same time, eschewing the platonist's commitment to abstract ontology. More recently, Maddy (1993: 53) has argued that mathematical knowledge proceeds via perception but in a manner consistent with platonism. As Maddy puts it, "we can and do perceive sets and our ability to do so develops in much the same way as our ability to see physical objects." And, while our basic epistemic access to mathematical reality initially proceeds from our perception of sets, Maddy holds our perceptual knowledge is supplemented with a broader "two-tiered" epistemology that relies upon naturalistic considerations to justify belief in the axioms that govern the hierarchy of sets.

Maddy's proposal credits perception for our epistemic access to mathematical entities, but, in doing so, she endorses a metaphysics of sets at odds with any familiar view and with the causal inertness of abstracta. According to Maddy, impure sets are not only located within spacetime, but also causally active by virtue of being perceivable. So understood, Maddy's proposed version of "set-theoretic realism" is not, on most views, a theory about the epistemology of genuinely *abstract* entities.

In contrast, the orthodox platonism of Kurt Gödel seeks to sustain a familiar conception of abstract entities and accounts for our epistemic access to mathematical reality by positing "something like" perception: mathematical intuition. In perhaps the most quoted passage in contemporary philosophy of mathematics, Gödel (1964: 268) says the following:

> But despite their remoteness from sense experience we do have something like a perception also of the objects of set theory, as is seen from the fact that the axioms force themselves upon us as being true. I don't see any reason why we should have less confidence in this kind of perception, i.e., in mathematical intuition, than in sense perception, which induces us to build up physical theories and to expect that future sense perceptions will agree with them.... It should be noted that mathematical intuition need not be conceived of as a faculty giving an *immediate* knowledge of the objects concerned. Rather it seems that, as in the case of physical experience, we *form* our ideas also of those objects on the basis of something else which is immediately given. Only this something else here is *not*, or not primarily, the sensations. That something besides the sensations actually is immediately given follows (independently of mathematics) from the fact that even our ideas referring to physical objects contain constituents qualitatively different from sensations or mere combinations of sensations, e.g., the idea of object itself, whereas, on the other hand, by our thinking we cannot create any qualitatively new elements but only reproduce and combine those that are given.

This suggestive but abstruse passage suggests an epistemology of mathematics with mathematical intuition as its starting point. But, as commentators have noted, it's difficult to determine exactly how the Gödelian picture might (or is intended to) work. On one reading, Gödel accepts the existence of mathematical intuition—something distinct from but analogous to sense perception—that involves a causal or nearly causal interaction between agents and mathematical reality. And, while Gödel's striking talk of axioms "forcing themselves upon us" invites this sort of strong reading, Parsons (1995) plausibly argues that the Gödelian view is more subtle and far less straightforward. This is not to say that extreme views regarding mathematical intuition have gone undefended. Consider, for example, the view Penrose (1989: 554) describes:

> I imagine that whenever the mind perceives a mathematical idea, it makes contact with Plato's world of mathematical concepts.... When one "sees"

a mathematical truth, one's consciousness breaks through into this world of ideas, and makes direct contact with it . . . . Since each can make contact with Plato's world directly, they can more readily communicate with each other than one might have expected. The mental images that each one has, when making this Platonic contact, might be rather different in each case, but communication is possible because each is directly in contact with the *same* externally existing Platonic world!

Where Maddy's view places abstract entities within the physical world to render them perceptible, Penrose's view takes the opposite tack. We infiltrate the abstract realm through mathematical cognition and observe such entities directly. Somewhere in between these two options are views like Gödel's, which hold our mathematical judgments to be formed on the basis of our access to some basic elements "immediately given" in our experiences despite the fact we do not "immediately" perceive mathematicalia. For platonists who admit some faculty of mathematical intuition, such a faculty need not give us "immediate knowledge." Instead, mathematical knowledge is derived from our access in experience to "constituents qualitatively different from sensations" that are given via mathematical intuition. But, however we might try to unfurl the Gödelian tapestry, the underlying contention is that mathematical knowledge is explained by some special cognitive capacity that puts us in epistemic rapport with an objective mathematical reality.

The burdens of responding to Field's challenge by positing a kind of *sui generis* mathematical intuition are steep. Absent a full-fledged account of perception, intuition, and the contents of experience, responses in this vein require immodest psychological assumptions about the nature of mathematical cognition. Among other concerns, these responses also face the daunting challenge of explaining why exactly a special psychological faculty would be properly calibrated to form reliable beliefs about acausal abstract reality. And, while there is no need to rule out the very possibility of such faculties, there is no reason to believe that wishful thinking in psychology suffices to meet Field's challenge. More plausible are those modest views which take intuition to be a kind of general psychological or cognitive category, and hold our ordinary talk about *seemings* to capture some core idea of intuitive justification.[6] But, again, it is unclear how even these scaled-back proposals might account for a reliable connection between human minds and a causally isolated abstract realm. So, if we follow the platonist in taking mathematics to be about a realm of abstract entities, we are still left without any wholly satisfying response to Field's challenge.

§4.2.4 Taking stock

Our breakneck overview of platonist options suggests that Field's challenge resists any easy answer. In several cases, this is because the merits of the proposed responses turn on unsettled questions elsewhere—e.g., regarding the success of logicism or the evidence for a distinctive faculty of mathematical intuition. And, as suggested above, the connection between naturalism and Field's challenge is an even murkier affair with some naturalists inclined to dismiss the challenge altogether. Of the available responses, the most promising is likely plenitudinism, which vastly expands the ontology of mathematics to ensure that, in describing any consistent theory, we thereby describe at least some part of mathematical reality.

Presented with the above stock of options, the platonist might find herself pessimistic about the merits of these responses taken separately. But, as O'Leary-Hawthorne (1996) points out when assessing similar proposals for explaining modal knowledge, there is reason for a cautious optimism. Even if no view is of great promise on its own, our confidence that *one of these* approaches (or some other approach not surveyed here) will prove adequate might be notably higher. It would also be a mistake to think that hybrid views, which draw upon different components of several proposals, are without promise. So, although the absence of a swift and satisfying response is an unwelcome result for platonists, there are still enough live platonist options to rule out any decisive argument here for nominalism. At best, worries about our epistemic access to mathematical and abstract reality amount to a certain kind of explanatory burden that shifts to platonists, but this burden might be outweighed by the virtues platonism enjoys.

There is a prevailing tendency to treat the above worries about epistemic access and Field's challenge in isolation from other concerns about our interactions with and access to the abstract realm. In the next two sections, we will consider these other sorts of access and set out two additional kinds of "access problems." The first problem concerns our semantic access to abstract entities and therefore our capacity to think and speak about abstracta. The second problem concerns our cognitive access to abstracta. This second sort of access has received comparatively little attention, but it is crucial for platonist theories that invoke propositions and properties. As we'll see, concerns about cognitive access are pressing, but, given the right kind of platonism, they may prove to be the most readily resolvable and perhaps quite useful for tackling the epistemic and semantic access problems.

§4.3 Semantic access

The epistemic access problem threatens irremediable ignorance about mathematical reality. It does not, however, call into question our capacity to successfully think and speak about mathematical reality. So, even if the epistemic access problem cannot be overcome, we might nevertheless succeed in referring to mathematical entities and expressing their properties—for short, "talking about them"—despite our claims being false or unjustified. We might, for example, be badly mistaken about the state of abstract reality and be regularly misdescribing it. In stark contrast, the *semantic access problem* alleges that the divide between human agents and abstract reality leaves us incapable of even talking about mathematical and other abstract entities. And, since knowledge of entities typically requires access far more robust than mere semantic access, the semantic access problem threatens even broader consequences than its epistemic analogue. If it cannot be overcome, it rules out even those sceptical views that take us to be constantly mistaken in our claims about the state of the abstract realm.

In Chapter 1 we considered an argument for platonism premised upon our apparent success in thinking and speaking about abstract reality. Here, the semantic access problem requires that we grapple with views radically opposed to the assumptions that underpin the direct semantic argument we considered. Such views hold our apparent success in thinking and speaking about mathematical entities to be a spectacular failure, given our surprising inability to think and speak about the abstract realm. And, while there is no canonical formulation of the semantic access problem, one rough version runs much like Benacerraf's epistemic argument and proceeds from a causal constraint on reference. Roughly speaking, this causal constraint on reference holds that an individual is capable of referring to an entity only if that entity is causally connected with that individual. Assuming once again that mathematical entities are causally inactive, this constraint ensures that we are incapable of referring to mathematical entities. A parallel formulation focuses, not on the semantic relation of reference, but on different semantic relations such as the *expression* relation predicates bear to properties. These and other formulations of the semantic access problem draw upon causal constraints to call into question whether we can bear any familiar semantic relations like reference and expression to abstract entities.

Although a causal constraint on reference would rule out our ability to think or speak about mathematical entities, there is scant motivation for endorsing such a constraint. While the epistemic access problem arises because of the causal character of our ordinary epistemic means, any parallel theses about reference and causality are sure to be contentious. In hunting about for reasons to endorse such a constraint, some might look to views in semantics or metasemantics that hold causal facts to underwrite semantic relations like reference. In this regard, some might hope to draw upon the work of Saul Kripke and Hilary Putnam, which takes causal chains between speakers to play a crucial role in an anti-descriptivist semantics for proper names and other expressions. But, as Burgess and Rosen (1997: 49–51) note, these views fall well short of underwriting anything like a causal constraint on semantic access. Not only does the Kripkean view allow for the use of definite descriptions to fix the referents of terms referring to causally inert entities, Kripke (1980: 40) himself assumes that we have semantic access to mathematical entities. So, while the absence of a causal connection between speakers and their referents leaves our semantic access underexplained, we are still without compelling reason to believe that thought and talk about the causally inert is impossible. So, as with the epistemic access problem above, platonists seem within their rights to conclude that there is better reason to reject the causal constraint than deny that they can refer to, say, the number seven.

Now, even though a causal constraint on reference ought to be rejected, platonists still owe some explanation of our semantic access to abstract entities just as Field's challenge points to a parallel epistemic debt.[7] As Hodes (1984: 127) notes: "Numbers are so pure, so unstained by the cement of the universe, that reference to them and their ilk seems quite *sui generis*." In particular, there is an explanatory hurdle in accounting for our capacity to refer to specific mathematical entities that platonists must clear. Jubien (1977: 135) presents the most worrisome version of this challenge as follows:

> The difficulty arises when we try to isolate or single out the entity or entities in question. If this could be done, then the entities could perhaps be linked by fiat to the expressions in question, and the interpretation would be at hand . . . .. Thus we can imagine that we are trying to isolate a particular object to serve as the interpretation of some constant term like "o". Although it is ultimately up to the platonist to say how this can be done, at the outset there seem to be only two possible ways: by ostension and by (unique) description.

Jubien's argument here does not target our general capacity to think or talk about mathematical entities. Instead, it raises the challenge of how we might uniquely pick out a specific mathematical entity like the number seven just as we might succeed in referring to a concrete object like Obama with our use of "Obama."

According to Jubien's challenge, our success in singling out a unique abstract entity requires an explanation of our referential success that no platonist can provide. Since mathematical entities are imperceptible, no ostension or demonstration of them can be given, so we cannot single out the number seven by pointing to it as we might in the case of Obama. There is also no way to single out and subsequently refer to a specific mathematical entity by fixing it as the reference of a name via a definite description. For example, we can introduce the term, "Choppy Jack," as a name that refers to the tallest lumberjack in the Yukon. If someone uniquely satisfies that description, that person would be the unique referent of "Choppy Jack." But, when we turn to the abstract realm, the immediate candidates are definite descriptions like "the sum of two and three" or "the least of the natural numbers." And, as Jubien points out, there are no definite descriptions we can use to introduce such names that do not already assume our capacity to single out specific mathematical entities like the natural numbers or relations like summation. This problem is clear enough when it comes to pure descriptions like "the square of nine," but it also afflicts mixed descriptions like "the number of planets," which invoke both abstract and concrete entities. Since our success in using these mixed descriptions presupposes our capacity to single out a specific numbering relation, such descriptions are no help in meeting Jubien's challenge. The introduction of names via definite descriptions therefore fails to provide an explanation of how we latch onto specific abstract entities and leaves unexplained our capacity to fix upon unique mathematical posits in our thought and talk.

Jubien's challenge grants us referential access to abstract reality but denies we can explain our ability to speak about specific abstract entities. One general line of platonist response is, then, to reject the terms of the challenge and deny that our thought and talk about the abstract actually requires unique reference to specific entities. According to structuralist proposals in the philosophy of mathematics and elsewhere, there is, in fact, no unique entity, the number seven. There are, instead, various entities that play "the number seven role" within certain structures—most notably, the natural number structure. On such views, mathematical claims are general claims about mathematical reality, asserting that any entities that occupy certain roles have certain features—e.g., any entity that occupies "the number seven role" within any natural number structure is not divisible by any entity occupying "the number four role" in that structure. We will discuss various strategies for implementing this structuralist idea in Chapter 7, though it is far from clear how these proposals might help with our present concerns. For, like other platonist views, they require us to use definite descriptions drawn from mathematical vocabulary like "divisor" and "number" to distinguish and refer to various structures.

For non-structuralists, an alternative line of response leans heavily on the fact that our apparently definite talk about concrete entities is itself shot through with vagueness. To claim that we succeed in uniquely referring to Obama through our use of "Obama" is to omit the raft of complications that come with the problem of the many and the plurality of physical objects that seem equally good candidates for being the referent of "Obama." (On the problem of the many, see Chapter 5.) If Jubien's challenge is to be a genuine worry for platonists, it must be shown that the problem is pressing in a way that ordinary worries about indeterminacy and reference are not. Since this is by no means clear, when faced with Jubien's challenge, most platonists are best served to deny that it is a problem over and above more familiar concerns about ensuring determinacy in our thought and talk about concrete entities. But, for those who hold it to be a persistent problem, the best strategies for addressing it are intimately connected with those needed to tackle the non-uniqueness problem we will consider in the next chapter. With this in mind, our best bet is to turn our attention to a third kind of access problem, which, for platonists who invoke propositions, is arguably more pressing than either the epistemic or semantic access problems.

§4.4 Cognitive access

In examining the epistemic and semantic access problems, our focus has been trained on mathematical entities. This is despite the fact that most platonists take abstract reality to include several other kinds of abstract entities like properties and propositions, each of which play crucial cognitive and explanatory roles. In particular, our capacity to have beliefs and desires hinges upon our capacity to "grasp" propositions. This commitment requires a far more pervasive and, in some sense, far more crucial cognitive relation between agents and proposition than the one posited between agents and numbers. In considering our cognitive tie to propositions (again, for Frege, *thoughts*), Frege (1918: 310) asks:

> How does a thought act? By being apprehended and taken to be true. This is a process in the inner world of a thinker which can have further consequences in this inner world and which, encroaching on the sphere of the will, can also make itself noticeable in the outer world . . .. One communicates a thought. How does this happen? One brings about changes in the common outside world which, perceived by another person, are supposed to induce him to apprehend a thought and take it to be true.

This platonist account of cognition and communication presupposes that propositions are public, "apprehendable" entities. Moreover, our capacity to grasp propositions is independent of our beliefs or knowledge about the existence and nature of propositions. Even those who have never reflected upon the nature of cognition will, says the platonist, spend the entirety of their rational life grasping propositions. As Frege (1918: 302) puts it: "One sees a thing, one has an idea, one apprehends or thinks a thought. When one apprehends or thinks a thought one does not create it but only comes to stand in a certain relation, which is different from seeing a thing or having an idea, to what already existed beforehand."

Plainly enough, this picture requires that agents bear a special cognitive relation of *apprehension* or *grasping* to propositions, but what exactly is this relation? And, if abstract entities are causally inactive entities, what, if anything, explains our capacity to grasp them? We can call this problem of explaining our capacity to apprehend or grasp propositions the *cognitive access* problem.

Is the cognitive access problem just a facet of the epistemic or semantic access problems discussed above? No. To see why not, notice that the stakes of the cognitive access problem are higher, since failure to overcome it would doom the entire theoretical framework of propositions and the corresponding platonist view about the nature of content. If we cannot account for agents' capacity to grasp propositions, we are not merely incapable of acquiring knowledge of or speaking about mathematical and other abstract entities. We would instead be wholly incapable of any contentful thought whatsoever. The differing stakes of these problems is reason enough to view the cognitive access problem as a different beast. Moreover, neither the epistemic nor semantic access problems take issue with the legitimacy of the relevant relations like justification and reference. They only challenge whether individuals like us can bear such relations to abstract entities. In contrast, the cognitive access problem takes issue with the grasping relation itself.[8]

Although the cognitive access problem differs from the epistemic and semantic access problems, the latter problems do still arise for propositions and other entities that we are said to grasp. Metaphysically speaking, there is no reason why Field's challenge could not be put forward as a demand for explaining our knowledge about propositions rather than mathematical entities. After all, we take ourselves to have knowledge about which propositions are asserted, which propositions are justified, and which propositions are entailed by other propositions. An analogue of Field's challenge that targets our knowledge of propositions would therefore press us to explain the reliable connection between our beliefs about propositions and the propositions themselves.

Despite this, the epistemic and cognitive access problems remain importantly different. To better clarify them, we can help ourselves to a rough distinction between knowledge *of* propositions and knowledge *about* propositions. Knowledge of the former sort is unconstrained in its subject matter. For example, when we know that it is raining in Vancouver, our knowledge is of the proposition *that it is raining in Vancouver*, which we might grasp when we come to believe that it is raining in Vancouver. In contrast, knowledge *about* propositions is more esoteric; it has knowledge pertaining to the nature of propositions as its subject matter. Some of our knowledge about propositions concerns their nature—e.g., whether they are abstract and whether more than five propositions are expressible in English. Some of it might also be fairly pedestrian in character. We know, for example, that some sentences are suitable translations of others, that someone agrees with the proposition someone else just asserted, and that no true proposition is also false. Our knowledge of propositions far outstrips our comparatively paltry knowledge about propositions, but, while the epistemic access problem threatens our knowledge *about* propositions, the cognitive access problem calls into question our far broader knowledge *of* propositions. (Our knowledge about propositions is also knowledge of propositions, so the distinction is not an exclusive one.)

The stakes of the cognitive access problem are high, since without some account of how we can grasp propositions, platonists can provide no viable explanation of attitudes and content. What, then, can platonists do to address the cognitive access problem?

For platonists who take abstractness as a primitive notion capable of explaining the remarkable features of abstracta, there is an admirably direct strategy available: assert that the grasping relation is a cognitively and metaphysically fundamental one, owing to the fact that abstract entities are, by their very nature, graspable. Viewed this way, the grasping relation between agents and propositions is comparable to other kinds of fundamental relations like *instantiation*, which unifies properties with their bearers, and *membership*, which unifies sets with their members. On such a view, our capacity to grasp propositions owes to the nature of propositions *qua* abstract entities. So, when asked how we are capable of grasping propositions, the primitivist platonist draws upon the primitive ideology of platonism: propositions are graspable *because* they are abstract entities. Or, put differently: the abstractness of propositions *explains* the fact that they, unlike concrete entities, are graspable. Without a commitment to a primitive and explanatorily robust notion of abstractness, platonists seem to be saddled with a rich ontology and series of explanatory burdens that cannot be easily discharged. But, once abstractness is taken as indefinable primitive, platonists can appeal to it in explaining the cognitive rapport between agents and propositions.

This primitivist response to the cognitive access problem faces objections similar to the ones levied against views that posit a distinctive faculty of mathematical intuition to explain epistemic access. For nominalists and others, talk of entities that are by their very nature graspable will seem like objectionable mystery mongering. Note, however, that this view of grasping is not some tentative empirical conjecture about the psychology of intuition or our perceptual capacities. It is, instead, a proposal for how we ought to treat a key cog in a powerful explanatory framework. And, unlike other proposals for explicating the talk of "grasping" that figures into platonist framework, this primitivist view does not seek to naturalize or reduce the grasping relation. Consequently, the primitivist view is unlikely to be reconciled with naturalism, given the absence of any fundamental grasping relation from our best psychological or neuroscientific theories. But, for those who accept this primitivist gambit, an ontology of propositions and an unanalyzed grasping relation delivers a theoretical framework powerful enough to justify riding roughshod over naturalism.

The primitivist also has some ways to resist the charge that grasping is wholly mysterious or entirely unconstrained. She can claim, for example, that we are perfectly familiar with our capacity to grasp propositions, since doing so is a near-constant feature of our cognitive life. She can also defend various constraints on what can and cannot be grasped. One such view, following Russell (1912), holds that we can grasp only those propositions about entities with which we are *acquainted*, where acquaintance is a cognitive relation limited to ourselves and the sense-data and universals we experience. (Other views might identify acquaintance with grasping or take one to be a species of the other.) Alternatively, she might dispense with talk of acquaintance and supply some general constraints on grasping—e.g., by holding that we can only grasp propositions about actual or presently existing individuals. But, regardless of what constraints are placed upon the grasping relation, there is ample room for primitive platonists to informatively characterize its limits and its role in our cognitive life. So, even if the grasping relation is taken as a fundamental relation akin to instantiation, it need not be mysterious or ineffable in nature. It is simply the most basic cognitive relation agents bear to propositions.

The primitivist approach provides a response to the cognitive access problem. It also furnishes platonists with an important resource for addressing the epistemic and semantic access problems. It would, after all, be a boon for platonists to show that our epistemic or semantic access to abstract entities somehow piggybacks upon our capacity to grasp propositions. One way to pursue this strategy holds, first, that our capacity to grasp propositions accounts for our capacity to refer to them. For, in grasping a proposition, we succeed in singling it out from among other propositions. Second, our capacity to grasp propositions put us in a position to know, of certain propositions, whether or not they are true and thereby accounts for our knowledge about propositions. It is plausible, for example, that merely by grasping the proposition *that Obama is both human and non-human*, we are in a position to justifiably believe this proposition to be false. Similarly, when we grasp propositions about the number seven (as opposed to grasping the number seven itself), we seem to be in a position to form justified beliefs about the truth of certain of these propositions. So, according to the primitivist platonist, our capacity to grasp a given proposition accounts for our capacity to express it rather than some other propositions. Moreover, our capacity to grasp it accounts for our justified belief in it.

The remarks above merely gesture towards a strategy on which the grasping relation allows us to address the semantic and epistemic access problems. But, of course, no story of this sort will be a simple one. If anything like the just sketched strategy is to succeed, the grasping relation will have to be ascribed controversial epistemic features that allow us to close the gap between knowledge of propositions and knowledge about propositions. Among other things, it would require that our justification for believing *that Obama is not both human and non-human* somehow puts us in a position to have knowledge *about* and not merely knowledge *of* such a proposition.

Spelling out how our ability to grasp propositions answers Field's challenge is no small matter. But, if successful, the strategy of explaining epistemic access through our capacity to grasp certain abstract entities seems distinct from and no less promising than the proposals set out in the previous section. And, once again, it illustrates the benefits of taking abstractness as a theoretical primitive—in this case, one suitable for explicating the special cognitive accessibility that platonists claim for abstract entities.

The explanatory significance of the grasping relation requires that platonists take the cognitive access problem seriously. The good news is, however, that, if the cognitive access problem can be satisfactorily addressed—perhaps through direct appeals to the nature of abstractness—the grasping relation provides another tool for addressing the epistemic and semantic access problems. For primitivist platonists who opt to explain our cognitive access to propositions by appeal to their graspability *qua* abstract entities, the result is a fruitful theory that squares with much of our ordinary thought and talk. It does, however, face a pressing challenge from naturalists who will find unreduced talk about "grasping propositions" aggravatingly opaque. At the same time, this naturalistic opposition is of little assistance in prosecuting the case in favour of nominalism. For, if propositions and grasping are to be dispensed with because of an ardent commitment to naturalistic scruples, this same commitment likely requires a commitment to the mathematical entities borne out by the indispensability argument. Alternatively, if the would-be nominalist abandons naturalism in hopes of avoiding mathematical entities, it is unclear how she might reasonably reject something like primitivist platonism, given its remarkable explanatory power and breadth. For this reason and in light of the various live options for meeting the access problems we've encountered, we are still without a compelling argument for nominalism.

§4.5 Eleaticism

The preceding causal arguments exploit worries about our epistemic, semantic, or cognitive access to causally inert abstract entities. A second kind of causal argument makes no bones about access. This second kind of causal argument is premised upon a commitment to Eleaticism, which holds causal activity and existence to move in lockstep. According to Eleatics, causal activity is a prerequisite for existence. So, if abstract entities are indeed causally inactive, Eleaticism entails that there are no abstract entities. (Eleaticism is so-called for its association with the Eleatic Stranger in Plato's *Sophist*.) It therefore places a causal constraint on reality itself: no entities can exist without making some causal contribution to the world. Put more formally, Eleaticism is the following thesis:

Eleaticism: Necessarily, *x* exists if and only if *x* is causally active.

Since the right-to-left direction of this biconditional is uncontroversial, Eleaticism's distinctive commitment is the left-to-right direction, which says that an entity exists only if it is causally active. Notice, also, that this is a necessitated biconditional, so, even if the actual world happened to include no causally inactive inhabitants, this would fall short of satisfying the Eleatic. This is because Eleaticism requires the outright impossibility of causally inactive entities, not merely the accidental causal activity of all actual entities.

The consequences of Eleaticism's proffered connection between causation and existence are widespread. Among other things, it provides a simple recipe for ontological inquiry: determine which entities are causally active and then deny the existence of any other putative entities. If, for example, Cartesian souls, macrophysical composites, and abstract entities are causally inactive, Eleaticism requires that we disavow their existence. Similarly, when asked whether there are or could be entities like epiphenomenalons—again, particles neither created nor destroyed and that enter into no causal interactions whatsoever—Eleatics will have a swift reply: these causally inert entities are impossible, since causal activity is a prerequisite for existence. By comparison, those who reject Eleaticism are unable to offer any similarly decisive answer. Instead, non-Eleatics will likely grant that such entities could exist and perhaps actually do exist, but we simply lack any good reason to posit them.

The implications of Eleaticism for the nominalist–platonist debate are more or less straightforward. If abstract entities are causally inactive, then, given Eleaticism, there can be no abstract entities. Of course, as we saw in Chapter 2, it is far from clear whether abstract entities are causally inactive. And, if we have reason to believe that certain abstracta like impure sets are causally active, Eleaticism falls short of licensing a full-scale argument against platonism. That said, there is good reason to believe at least *some* abstract entities like numbers and propositions are causally inactive. Eleaticism therefore underwrites an argument against some paradigmatic abstract entities and will prove inhospitable to most versions of platonism.

But why think Eleaticism is true? One line of argument takes Eleaticism to be motivated by arguments from access like those surveyed above.

But, despite their shared focus on causation, Eleaticism is importantly different from any thesis defensible by appeal to such arguments. To see why, notice that arguments premised on concerns about access would require us to reject entities to which Eleatics are ontologically committed. Suppose, for example, that our world comprises a plurality of causally disconnected realms but that each of these includes only causally active entities. If we endorse arguments from access, we ought to reject the existence of entities that are either causally inactive or causally isolated from us, since either type of entity would be inaccessible to us. Notice, however, that Eleatics take *causal activity* rather than *causal interaction with us* as a precondition for existence. So, while arguments from access pressure us to disavow those entities from which we are causally isolated, mere causal isolation is irrelevant to the Eleatic. Arguments based upon access therefore provide no recipe for defending Eleaticism once we properly distinguish between causal isolation and causal inactivity.

A second strategy for motivating Eleaticism appeals to Ockham's razor by arguing that causally inactive entities are never part of the simplest viable theory of the world. On this proposal, Eleaticism is a consequence of a commitment to the invariable explanatory redundancy of causally inactive entities. Put roughly, the suggestion here is that Ockham's razor will always license us to shave off causally inactive entities. Unfortunately for Eleatics, this sort of argument turns on implausible premises or falls short of its target. First, the contention that causally inactive entities are destined to be explanatorily otiose is at least as controversial as Eleaticism itself. And, while we might ultimately side with the nominalist and opt against positing causally inert mathematical entities, this would be the result of carefully weighing a host of virtues and vices. It would not be due to a surprising pre-established harmony between explanatory goodness and causal activity that this defence of Eleaticism would require. Second, since Eleaticism, if true, is necessarily true, this proposal would have to establish the impossibility of causally inactive entities. It looks, however, like the best it might do is establish that we will invariably have reason to believe theories without any causally inactive entities. This falls well short of showing there can be no causally inactive entities, especially after we acknowledge the highly tentative nature of inference to the best explanation. For this reason, souped-up appeals to Ockham's razor are also inadequate for establishing the Eleatic view on which causally inactive entities are impossible.

Perhaps the best case for Eleaticism proceeds by claiming that we owe some informative account of when entities are identical with and distinct from one another and that our best account of this kind "individuates" entities on the basis of their causal roles. If that's right, then, if some entities were causally inactive, it would be impossible to individuate them. And, following Quine's stricture against "entity without identity," we would be within our rights to conclude there are no such things.[9]

The claim that causal roles are needed to ground the identity or individuation of entities is most plausible when advanced as a thesis about properties. And, according to views like causal structuralism, properties are individuated precisely by their causal contribution to the world. (On causal structuralism, see Shoemaker (1980) and Hawthorne (2002).) On such views, any properties that play the same causal role in the world are one and the same, while properties with different causal roles are distinct. So, if one accepts causal structuralism along with some auxiliary theses (e.g., that any entity must instantiate some property), we have the makings of an argument for Eleaticism. Unfortunately for those interested in advancing the case for nominalism, this strategy for defending Eleaticism is off limits, given its commitment to properties. So, even if such an argument supported Eleaticism, it would be of little help for nominalists.

The best bet for would-be Eleatics interested in defending nominalism is to defend a kind of nominalist analogue of causal structuralism. This analogue places a causal constraint on which primitive predicates are admissible within theories. Specifically, it requires that each primitive predicate figure into the correct description of the world's causal structure and that at least one predicate is true of each entity. The nominalist thereby replicates the property-based strategy just described, but with a causal criterion for introducing and distinguishing primitive predicates rather than properties. It is unclear, however, what might motivate such a constraint on the admissibility of primitive predicates. So, while this and other metaphysical packages might be conducive to Eleaticism and nominalism, there is an evident lack of motivation for endorsing these views.

Eleaticism is a bold thesis, but the case in its favour is not convincing. The proposed tie between existence and causation cannot be defended by appeal to concerns about access, parsimony, or individuation. It also faces powerful modal objections, since, by ruling out the possibility of causally inactive entities, it rules out the possible existence of entities that seem readily conceivable. For example, it seems that there are possible worlds consisting of lonely, unchanging eternal objects or worlds with just a single slice of spacetime. But, since these are worlds without any apparent causal activity, Eleatics must deny such worlds are possible. To avoid this conflict with our modal judgments, Eleatics are likely best served to weaken the relevant notion of "causal activity" to require only that something be *possibly* though perhaps not *actually* causally active. Since the lonely, unchanging eternal objects and single slices of spacetime are causally active in richer possible worlds, the Eleatic can admit the possibility of such worlds, since these entities are causally active in this weaker sense. But even this weakened version of Eleaticism faces a modal objection: the epiphenomenalons mentioned above seem conceivable and, in turn, possible. Although such counterexamples are contentious, the absence of any strong arguments for Eleaticism leaves the view of little concern to platonists. It looks, then, like Eleatic arguments present no worrisome challenge to platonism.

Summary

This chapter examined arguments for nominalism stemming from the alleged causal inactivity, and our resulting lack of epistemic, semantic, or cognitive access, to abstract entities. After evaluating a possible causal constraint on our knowledge, Field's challenge for platonism was presented along with some leading responses. A parallel concern regarding our semantic access to abstract reality and an additional problem concerning our cognitive access to propositions were then outlined. None of these problems were shown to be insuperable, though it is unclear precisely how platonists ought to address them. For primitivists, the most promising option is to appeal directly to abstractness in explaining our ability to grasp propositions. The thesis of Eleaticism, which holds causally inactive entities to be impossible, was then introduced, but, given the paucity of arguments in its favour, was also shown to fall short of establishing nominalism.

Recommended reading

Benacerraf (1973) sets the agenda for worries about epistemic access. Field (1989: 25–30) presents a refined version of Benacerraf's argument and maps out some of its consequences for nominalism. A modified version of the epistemic access argument is defended in Cheyne (1998, 2001).

Various responses to the epistemic access problem are outlined in Lewis (1986), Balaguer (1998), Maddy (1990), Katz (1998), Linnebo (2006), and Bengson (2015). Liggins (2010) and Clarke-Doane (forthcoming) are helpful overviews of the problem and extant responses. See Field (1989: 233–242) for a counter-response to Lewis' proposal. For an overview of the epistemic access problem as it concerns modal reality, see O'Leary-Hawthorne (1996).

On the semantic access problem, see Jubien (1977), Hodes (1984), Burgess and Rosen (1997: 49–60), and Davies (2015). See Schechter (2010) for discussion of the logical analogue of the epistemic access problem.

Eleaticism sometimes travels under the name "Alexander's Dictum." It receives critical attention in Oddie (1982), Colyvan (1998), Hudson (2003), and Cowling (2015b).

Notes

1 A different strategy is to weaken the causal constraint in a way that avoids the putative counterexamples. The most promising implementation of this strategy is defended in Cheyne (1998, 2001), where the causal constraint is held to apply only to our knowledge of or justified belief in existence claims. Cheyne holds that, although we can have a kind of conditional knowledge about the features of entities that we do not causally interact with, we cannot have knowledge that such entities exist.

2 Field's own view is more extreme: he denies the truth of standard mathematics. (He does grant that some mathematical claims are vacuously true—e.g., universally quantified claims about numbers.) And, in remarking why the present challenge is properly seen to motivate nominalism rather than an agnosticism about abstracta, Field (1998: 45) says: "it seems to me undue epistemological caution to maintain agnosticism rather than flat out disbelief about such an idle hypothesis. I think that platonism has seemed a plausible position because it has been assumed that the existence of mathematical entities is *not* an idle hypothesis. But if it can be shown that the hypothesis is dispensable without loss . . ., then I think it natural to go beyond agnosticism and assert that mathematical entities do not exist."

3 More explicitly (and using some Fregean resources), Hume's principle says that for any concepts F and G, the number of entities falling under F is identical with the number of entities falling under G if and only if the entities that fall under F are in one-to-one correspondence with entities that fall under G. In this way, the abstraction principle uses the term-forming operator "the number of" to define the novel singular terms that refer to numbers and explains our knowledge of identity facts regarding such entities. On Hume's principle, see Wright (1983), Boolos (1986), and MacBride (2003).

4 For example, Potter (2004: 11) suggests that the plenitudinist view is not a genuine form of realism about mathematical entities: "A realist conception

of a domain is something we win through to when we have gained an understanding of the nature of the objects the domain contains and the relations that hold between them. For the view that bare consistency entails existence to count as realist, therefore, it would be necessary for us to have a quite general conception of the whole of logical space as a domain populated by objects. But it seems quite clear to me that we simply have no such conception."
5 For discussion, see Liggins (2010: 73–75).
6 Consider, for example, Pollock (1970: 319): "There is a characteristic phenomenological state which consists of 'seeing' self-evident [logical and mathematical] truths, and this is what we are calling 'intuition'. There is no reason to think that these intuitions are in any way mysterious. We must have some sort of mental faculty that allows us to intuit these things, and this mental faculty is presumably just as capable of physiological explanation as is our faculty of sight or hearing."
7 There is at least one principled disanalogy between these cases: reference does not seem to require a reliable connection between speakers and the entities to which they refer. We can, after all, be badly mistaken about what we are talking about even while we might nevertheless succeed in talking about it.
8 On the cognitive access problem, see Plantinga (1993: 113–117). Note, also, that the cognitive access problem arises in similar form for views on which we grasp propositions as well as instances of properties.
9 More accurately, there would be exactly one causally inert entity, but, since there is little appeal in platonisms that posit only one abstract entity, we can ignore such a view here.

5

NON-UNIQUENESS

5.1 The non-uniqueness problem
5.2 Living with non-uniqueness
5.3 Metaphysical underdetermination
5.4 Overcoming underdetermination

§5.1 The non-uniqueness problem

In addition to his canonical presentation of the epistemic access problem, Paul Benacerraf also famously poses a second problem for would-be mathematical platonists: the non-uniqueness problem, which threatens platonist views about mathematics on which numbers are identified with sets. This chapter sets outs Benacerraf's version of the non-uniqueness problem, discusses some additional instances of the non-uniqueness problem that are not distinctively mathematical, and then explores the connection between non-uniqueness and broader worries about underdetermination and theory choice. Ultimately, the non-uniqueness problem has a peculiar status: it is a persistent problem for most contemporary versions of platonism, but it falls short of constituting a full-scale argument against platonism. For, as we'll see below, certain platonist views about abstract reality do seem able to dodge the problem. Despite this, epistemic concerns regarding non-uniqueness raise what are arguably larger and more serious issues about how to develop and defend a platonist ontology. With these complexities in mind, we will assess the general implications of the non-uniqueness problem at the end of this chapter.

In Benacerraf's initial presentation, the source of the non-uniqueness problem is the theoretical richness of set theory. Once granted the vast hierarchy of sets, we have access to what David Hilbert called a "mathematician's paradise" which allows for a reduction of arithmetic and much more of mathematics to set theory. Typically, this reduction proceeds by identifying natural numbers with specific sets. If successful, the identification of natural numbers with sets yields a significant ontological advantage. Most notably, it would allow us to posit only sets rather than, say, sets and an additional category of numbers. Better still, this reduction comes with an ideological advantage, since arithmetical relations like *addition* and *exponentiation* can be analyzed in terms of sets and the barebones ideology of set theory. Metaphorically speaking, this reduction would provide a kind of "foundation" for mathematics within the ideologically modest framework of set theory. The good news, then, is that there is at least one way to reduce arithmetic to set theory. The bad news—and the source of the non-uniqueness problem—is that there is more than one way to carry out this reduction. This is because many different set-theoretic constructions satisfy the Peano axioms that characterize the natural numbers, so many different constructions suffice for modelling arithmetic.

To illustrate the availability of multiple reductions, Benacerraf (1965) rehearses two standard ways to reduce arithmetic to set theory. Owing to Johan von Neumann and Ernst Zermelo, these reductions identify the natural numbers with different set-theoretic *progressions* (alternatively, ω-sequences)— i.e., sets of sets that satisfy the Peano axioms. (On characterizing progressions, see Burgess and Rosen (1997 72–74).) According to Zermelo's proposed reduction, we identify 0 with the null set and identify any number, $n + 1$, with $\{n\}$. In contrast, on the proposed von Neumann reduction, we identify 0 with the null set and $n + 1$ with the union of n and $\{n\}$. The initial segments of these different progressions therefore run as follows:

Zermelo: $\emptyset$, $\{\emptyset\}$, $\{\{\emptyset\}\}$, $\{\{\{\emptyset\}\}\}$ ...

von Neumann: $\emptyset$, $\{\emptyset\}$, $\{\emptyset, \{\emptyset\}\}$, $\{\emptyset, \{\emptyset\}, \{\emptyset, \{\emptyset\}\}\}$ ...

Each choice seems to yield a satisfactory reduction of arithmetic to set theory, but the proposed reductions are incompatible with one another.

Evident disagreement arises once we ask questions like the following: Is the number two identical to {{∅}} or {∅, {∅}}? Does the number three have {{∅}} as a member? Since the number two cannot be identical with both {{∅}} and {∅, {∅}}, carrying out the intended reduction of arithmetic forces us into an unprincipled choice between incompatible yet equally good candidates.

The bare possibility of multiple reductions of mathematics to set theory does not, on its own, generate the non-uniqueness problem. For, if we had good reason to prefer one option on mathematical or metaphysical grounds, we would have a principled reason to endorse it over rival candidates. It would, for instance, be bizarrely unprincipled to reduce arithmetic to a hierarchy of sets founded upon, say, the singleton of the Eiffel Tower instead of the null set. But, as Benacerraf notes, the leading proposals for reduction seem equally good. Neither is mathematically preferable and, metaphysically speaking, they are on all fours, since they involve only pure sets. We are therefore faced with an especially thorny instance of underdetermination, since we lack good reason for preferring a unique reduction over its nearby rivals. Consequently, the prospects for a tenable reduction of mathematics to set theory rest upon how, if at all, we can resolve this impasse. As Benacerraf (1965: 62) puts it:

> If numbers are sets, then they must be *particular sets*, for each set is some particular set. But if the number 3 is really one set rather than another, it must be possible to give some cogent reason for thinking so; for the position that this is an unknowable truth is hardly tenable. But there seems to be little to choose among the accounts. Relative to our purposes in giving an account of these matters, one will do as well as another, stylistic preferences aside.

In focusing on the non-uniqueness problem and the prospects for reducing numbers to sets, we can reconstruct Benacerraf's argument as follows:

Singularity. The names of natural numbers like "seven" are singular referring terms.

Reductionism. Each natural number is identical with exactly one set.

Mathematical Adequacy. There are competing reductions of the natural numbers to sets that are equally mathematically adequate, so, for mathematical purposes, each progression provides an equally satisfactory reduction.

General Adequacy. There are no non-mathematical reasons for preferring one mathematically adequate reduction of the natural numbers to sets over rival reductions.

Epistemic Uniqueness. If there is no reason to prefer one specific reduction of the natural numbers to sets over rival reductions, then the natural numbers are not identical to sets.

Some brief remarks about the argument as just presented are worth noting. Singularity requires that the names of natural numbers like "1" are not covertly quantified claims referring to a plurality of entities (e.g., to both $\{\{\emptyset\}\}$ and $\{\emptyset, \{\emptyset\}\}$). Instead, they function in much the same way as our ordinary singular terms do. So, if they refer to anything, they refer to unique objects. (As we'll see below, Singularity runs contrary to various structuralist views about mathematics.) Reductionism asserts that the objects picked out by the names like "the number two" are sets rather than entities of a separate ontological category like, say, *sui generis* numbers. Taken together, Mathematical Adequacy and General Adequacy assert that no considerations, mathematical or otherwise, license a rational preference for identifying a unique progression with the natural numbers. Finally, Epistemic Uniqueness says that, if we are to identify numbers with sets, there must be some principled reason for choosing one progression over its rivals. So, given Mathematical Adequacy and General Adequacy, Epistemic Uniqueness requires that we reject Reductionism and forsake the reduction of arithmetic to set theory.

Although the most familiar guise of the non-uniqueness problem concerns the reduction of numbers to sets, this problem arises elsewhere for platonism. It recurs throughout mathematics when we turn to alternative constructions of the real numbers and other mathematicalia. (See Field (1989: 20–24).) It is also commonplace for platonist theories that rely upon other set-theoretic reductions, especially those that seek to reduce properties or propositions to sets. On such views, monadic ("one-place") properties are sets of individuals, so the property of *being a dog* is just the set of all dogs, while the property of *being a cat* is just the set of all cats. In turn, the property of *being a dog and a cat* is the intersection of these two sets (in this case, the null set) and the property of *being a dog or a cat* is the union of these sets: the set of all dogs and cats. Since not all properties are monadic, the reduction of properties to sets also requires a method for reducing relations (i.e., non-monadic properties) like *is taller than*. And, since the logical features of relations such as reflexivity and asymmetry must be captured by this reduction, relations cannot simply be identified with sets of their *relata*. Among other things, this would collapse the intuitive distinction between an entity, *a*, bearing the *is taller than* relation to an entity, *b*, and *b* bearing this same relation to *a*. For instance, if Obama is taller than Bush, then Obama bears *is taller than* to Bush, so Bush cannot, at the same time, bear *is taller than* to Obama. A suitable reduction of relations therefore requires a means for representing the intuitive "order" exhibited by relations and to mark the difference between, say, a situation in which Obama bears the relation *being taller than* to Bush and one in which Bush bears *is taller than* to Obama. In this way, any account of relations as sets must somehow "encode" the asymmetry that certain relations exhibit.

The standard strategy for capturing the ordering exhibited by relations is to introduce representational conventions regarding certain set-theoretic constructions. This practice introduces the notion of an "ordered pair," written as "<x, y>," and adopts the convention of treating x as the "first member" and y as the "second member." Relations are then held to be sets of these ordered pairs. So, for example, *is taller than* is a set that has among its members <Manute Bol, George Bush>, <Manute Bol, Bill Clinton>, <Bill Clinton, Danny DeVito>, and so on. According to this convention, the first member of the ordered pair is taller than the second. So, in a world where Obama is taller than Bush, the ordered pair, <Obama, Bush>, but not <Bush, Obama> is a member of the set identified with *being taller than*.

It is crucial to recognize here that our adopted notion of an ordered pair is a piece of theoretical shorthand—a convention for encoding certain orderings. It therefore depends upon identifying ordered pairs with certain kinds of sets chosen by stipulation. For example, on the standard Kuratowski treatment, an ordered pair, <a, b>, is the set {{a}, {a, b}} and the relevant convention holds the "first member" of the ordered pair to be the member of the singleton set. Note, however, that on alternative accounts, the ordered pair <a, b> will be identified with the set {{a, ∅}, {a, b}} and some arbitrary convention will be introduced to treat either *a* or *b* as the "first member."

As with the von Neumann and Zermelo reductions of arithmetic, there is no intrinsic feature of these sets that makes one method uniquely suited for providing a reduction of ordered pairs to sets. Moreover, our use of ordered pairs in the reduction of relations to sets is possible only because we stipulate a convention for treating various sets in certain ways in our various theoretical contexts. There is no principled metaphysical or mathematical reason for taking either the set {{a, b}, {a}} or the set {{{a}}, {{a}, b}} to be *the* ordered pair <a, b>. In turn, there is no principled reason to take these to be the sets that figure into the set-theoretic reduction of relations. As Forrest (1986b: 91) puts it: "Kuratowski's identification suffers from a grave defect if it is treated as anything more than a model-theoretic device. For it is a convention, not a discovery, that <a, b> is to be identified with {a, {a, b}} rather than, say, {{a, ∅}, {a, b}}, and serious ontology is not done by convention."

The parallel between this version of the non-uniqueness problem and the one above is straightforward enough. Relations are ordered. But, since set theory comes with no intrinsic ordering, those who would identify relations with sets can "impose" ordering only by adopting representational conventions. If, however, relations are supposed to be identical with sets of ordered pairs, the fact that we deploy arbitrary conventions in deciding which sets will serve as ordered pairs is bad news. This generates its own versions of the non-uniqueness problem. And, in these and other cases, there is no way to offer principled grounds for the relevant theoretical reductions. We are therefore saddled with a pernicious arbitrariness of the same sort Benacerraf notes.

The non-uniqueness problem also afflicts the reduction of propositions to sets. For, just as we are faced with arbitrary choices in reducing relations, we face arbitrary choices in accommodating the ordering of and relations between propositions. This is most obvious for Russellian views of propositions that identify propositions with sets of individuals and properties. Consider, for example, the sentences "May loves Ali" and "Ali loves May." These sentences are typically held to express Russellian propositions identified with ordered triples like <May, Ali, *loves*> and <Ali, May, *loves*>. But, just as with ordered pairs, these ordered triples are ultimately unordered sets treated in accordance with a stipulated convention for encoding orderings. There is no intrinsic features of these sets that makes one a mathematically or metaphysically "better" reduction than nearby options. Nor is there principled reason to hold "May loves Ali" rather than "Ali loves May" to express <May, Ali, *loves*> even if we are forced to choose between only the two ordered triples in question. As Melia (1992b: 47) puts this point:

> On [the Russellian] view, we can treat [an individual's] belief that a bears R to b as a relation between [that individual] and the ordered triple <R, a, b>. But we can just as easily treat it as a relation between [that individual] and the ordered triple <a, R, b>. Or as a relation between [that individual] and some

other permutation of a, R, and b. Now, there is no philosophical debate as to which of these treatments is *the* correct one, no philosophical debate as to whether [an individual], by believing that a bears R to b, is *really* related to <R, a, b> or <a, R, b>. Sharing the same flaws and advantages, the two treatments are equivalent. We are free to choose between the two, and it is an arbitrary matter which of them we choose.

Similar remarks apply to other views of propositions. For, as others have noted, even if we dispense with the Russellian view, we will still face the non-uniqueness problem. Suppose, for example, we follow Lewis (1986a) and Stalnaker (1984) in identifying propositions, not with ordered n-tuples of individuals and properties, but with sets of possible worlds.[1] So, for example, the proposition *that dogs bark* is just the set of all possible worlds in which dogs bark, while the proposition *that cats purr* is the set of all possible worlds in which cats purr. As with other proposed set-theoretic reductions, we are again forced into an arbitrary choice among equally good candidates. Once we note that we can equally well take propositions to be, not sets of worlds, but functions from worlds to truth-values.[2] (The same point generalizes to the case of properties.) And, since the identification of propositions with functions or sets of possible worlds are equally good, our theoretical options force us into yet another incarnation of the non-uniqueness problem.

The non-uniqueness problem also rears its head when we consider reductions that involve abstracta other than sets. For example, Jubien (2001) presents a non-uniqueness problem for views on which propositions are composed, mereologically or not, out of properties. As Jubien argues, we are forced into arbitrarily identifying certain property-theoretic composites as propositions when others would serve just as well. Similarly, King (2007) argues against extant set-theoretic views of propositions by appealing to what he calls a "Benacerraf style worry" and subsequently defends a view that identifies propositions with facts (conceived of as abstract entities).[3] Somewhat ironically, Caplan and Tillman (2013) argue that even King's view on which propositions are facts is saddled with a non-uniqueness problem, since those who accept an ontology of abundant facts are still forced into an apparently arbitrary identification of propositions with facts.

The abundance of abstract entities that comes with set theory and similarly abundant views of properties and propositions is fertile ground for non-uniqueness problems; however, non-uniqueness problems are not a distinctive product of set-theoretic reductions. They are instead a general issue for platonists with abundant ontologies, reductionist ambitions, and no principled distinctions between competing reductions. The challenge, then, is to see whether platonists can find some way to live with non-uniqueness problems or overcome the viciousness of arbitrary identifications. We turn to this challenge in the next section.

§5.2 Living with non-uniqueness

We've now presented the non-uniqueness problem in several guises. And, since many platonists accept at least some set-theoretic or property-theoretic reductions, the non-uniqueness problem is one that most platonists must grapple with. But how exactly should platonists resolve it?

Before examining some leading responses, it is worth considering whether platonists might plausibly collapse the non-uniqueness problem into the nearby problem of the many and focus their efforts on the latter problem.[4] In its usual guise, the problem of the many arises once we notice that, for a seemingly ordinary object like a cloud or a human, there is a plurality of equally good candidate objects (the many) that we might identify with the object in question. For instance, we standardly assume that, where you are located, there is only a single human. There are, however, a host of equally eligible candidates—e.g., swarms of atoms that differ only microscopically from one another—that might aptly be described as a human. Since there seems to be no principled reason to single out exactly one of these many candidates and since it is deeply counterintuitive to believe there are thousands of humans in your chair, the problem of the many is a serious worry with an intuitive affinity to the non-uniqueness problem.

The non-uniqueness problem and the problem of the many each concern arbitrariness and identification. And, since the problem of the many arises for familiar concrete objects, collapsing the non-uniqueness problem into the problem of the many would suggest that the former is not a distinctive worry for platonism. There is, however, good reason not to conflate these two problems, despite their commonalities.

First, a commitment to set theory involves a vast ontology of sets and an excess of candidates for reducing arithmetic. A potential solution to the problem of the many denies the existence of excess candidates by claiming that there is indeed only a single human "candidate" where you are located. In this way, we can avoid the arbitrariness in identification by denying the reality of putative candidates. Structurally speaking, this kind of solution simply doesn't make sense for the platonist. This is because a commitment to set theory rules out the option of disavowing abstract ontology—namely, other (sometimes overlapping) progressions—to ensure there is only a single candidate reduction. This suggests the two problems differ in at least one key respect.

Second, a standard response to the problem of the many claims that, although it is determinately true that your cat is a swarm of atoms, it is not determinate *which* specific swarm your cat is identical with. Matters seem importantly different in the abstract case. For, while we have strong independent reasons to believe that your cat is made up out of atoms, our belief that numbers are sets is wholly dependent upon our reason to believe that a successful reduction can be given. So, although our antecedent metaphysical commitments pressure us to address the problem of the many, our motivation to identify numbers with sets is contingent upon whether we can, in fact, provide a principled reduction of numbers to sets. For this reason, holding identity claims between cats and pluralities of atoms to be indeterminate is better motivated and more plausible than holding identity claims between numbers and sets to be indeterminate. In this respect, the non-uniqueness problem and the problem of the many also importantly differ.

The non-uniqueness problem and the problem of the many are related, but the former ought not be assimilated to the latter. Not only do proposals for addressing the latter go awry when applied to the former, the structure of the two problems differ in significant ways. For, as Field (1989: 24) suggests, there is a kind of "pervasive arbitrariness" that arises once we admit mathematical ontology whereas the arbitrariness and vagueness underlying the problem of the many is a contingent feature of our particular concrete world. The former seems endemic to abstract reality, but the latter owes to the murkiness of the predicates and singular terms we use. It need not persist in worlds with sufficiently sharp divisions among concreta. Having marked these salient differences, we can now turn to the platonist's prospects for addressing the non-uniqueness problem.

Deny Reductionism. Our first platonist response to the non-uniqueness problem denies Reductionism and concedes that the problem is in most, if not all, instances an intractable one. In denying Reductionism, this response simply rejects the sort of theoretical reductions sketched above and absorbs a commitment to *sui generis* kinds of abstract entities. The platonist who rejects Reductionism will, for example, grant that, while the number nine exists, it cannot be reduced to and is therefore distinct from any set. The same sort of response extends to relations and propositions that platonists might otherwise hope to reduce to sets. So, when taken as a general response to instances of the non-uniqueness problem, this denial of Reductionism leads to a view of the abstract realm on which there can be no grand reduction of all kinds of abstracta to a single kind like sets. Instead, there is a wide array of *sui generis* species of abstracta. And, although there is nothing inconsistent or incoherent about such a view, it is a remarkable fact that the theoretical reductions we actively seek in scientific inquiry are ruled out within the abstract realm. This is a somewhat remarkable contrast between the virtues pursued by our theories of concrete and abstract reality. And, for those who endorse naturalistic views about method and epistemology, forgoing parsimonious reductions in favour of admitting a wealth of *sui generis* species of abstracta will seem suspicious at best.[5]

Deny Epistemic Uniqueness. Our second response denies Epistemic Uniqueness, according to which the arbitrariness of any selection among candidate reductions requires us to reject all candidate reductions. Against Epistemic Uniqueness, this response embraces the arbitrary selection of a specific candidate as a means for securing the theoretical benefits of reduction. In doing so, this response surrenders any hope of distinguishing a uniquely qualified candidate and focuses instead on the justification for making an arbitrary choice from among rival candidates.

Importantly, this strategy does not elevate some extraneous feature of a proposed reduction to the status of theoretical significance (e.g., by holding, say, the temporal priority of Zermelo's proposal to be evidence in its favour). Instead, it proceeds by pointing out that, in the face of an arbitrary choice, considerations of ontological and ideological simplicity make it reasonable to opt for a specific reduction despite having no principled reasons to prefer it over its rivals.

For some methodological naturalists, this approach will seem quite reasonable once we properly weigh the vice of arbitrariness against the virtues of reduction. As Paseau (2009) notes, Quineans who are interested in advancing the best total theory will have no reservations about absorbing a certain measure of arbitrariness so long as it is in service to significant virtues—most notably, the simplification of ontology and ideology that comes with the reduction of mathematics to set theory. As Benacerraf (1998: 56) puts it: "Even if the realistically driven reductionist is undermined by *l'embarras du choix*, not so with the holistic Occamite, who is not beholden to any notion of 'getting it right' that transcends the best theory that survives ontic paring."

This pragmatic response to the non-uniqueness problem rejects the presupposition that adequacy in theoretical reduction requires principled reason to endorse a unique candidate. Success in our reductive ambitions merely requires success in certain stipulations and a conviction to stick to our chosen candidate across theoretical contexts. Quine (1968b: 198) suggests as much, saying:

> The subtle point is that any progression will serve as a version of number so long and only so long as we stick to one and the same progression. Arithmetic is, in this sense, all there is to number: there is no saying absolutely what the numbers are; there is only arithmetic.

Whether the denial of Epistemic Uniqueness qualifies as a "solution" to the non-uniqueness problem or as a stubborn refusal to take it seriously depends upon how one views the vice of arbitrariness. If it is merely one consideration among a smorgasbord of vices and virtues, denying Epistemic Uniqueness looks reasonable so long as the theoretical benefits are sufficiently great. If, however, arbitrariness is viewed as a mortal sin in theory choice, the denial of Epistemic Uniqueness will seem untenable. For those platonists who take questions about the taxonomy of abstract entities to concern the world's fundamental ontological categories this arbitrariness will be flatly objectionable. In contrast, some, like Quine, who simply seek to "get on with things," are far more likely to stomach the denial of Epistemic Uniqueness. So, here, as elsewhere, we find a divide between those pushed towards platonism on naturalistic grounds and platonists of a more "metaphysical" bent.

Deny Adequacy. The arbitrariness that generates the non-uniqueness problem owes to the equal merits of the various candidate reductions. One strategy for addressing the problem is, then, to argue that the merits are not, in fact, equal and that some consideration serves to break the tie between candidates. Given the many incarnations of the non-uniqueness problem, it is unclear how to pursue this ambition in a way that offers a perfectly general response to all instances of the problem. That said, one prominent version of this strategy would, following Lewis (1983a, 1986a), assert that certain sets, properties, or propositions are simply more "natural" than others. So, when it comes to assigning referents to our thought and talk and specifying which sets serve as the natural numbers, considerations of *naturalness* are what render certain candidates superior to their rivals.

Generally speaking, natural properties are those properties that comport with the sparse conception of properties. So, for example, fundamental physical properties like *mass* and *charge* are highly or perhaps even "perfectly" natural. Other properties like *being a brown dog* or *a grass stain*, which are omitted from the sparse conception, are entirely non-natural. In between perfectly natural properties and gerrymandered or wildly disjunctive ones, fall myriad other properties and relations with varying degrees of naturalness. It is, however, only the natural properties and relations that "carve at the joints of nature" and occupy key metaphysical and scientific roles. They figure into the laws of nature. They ground relations of objective resemblance. They underpin our inductive practices, distinguishing properties like *blue* from *bleen* and *green* from *grue*. Moreover, naturalness partly determines the correct interpretation of our thought and talk since natural properties and relations are more "eligible" semantic values.[6]

Since naturalness privileges certain interpretations of our thought and talk, it might also provide a recipe for tie-breaking between competing reductions. One implementation of this general strategy arises as a response to the Wittgensteinian challenge set out in Kripke (1982) of explaining why, despite the compatibility of our linguistic behaviour with a variety of interpretations, our ordinary use of the expression "plus" expresses the *addition* function rather than some function much like *addition* but, say, different when applied to remarkably large numbers. As Lewis (1983a) suggests, the relative naturalness of *addition* in comparison to other functions might render it a more eligible and therefore superior interpretation. Fully developing this response to Kripke's Wittgensteinian challenge requires spelling out a comprehensive theory of how naturalness distinguishes mathematical properties and relations, but the underlying idea should be clear enough: naturalness is a feature of the world capable of breaking otherwise intractable deadlocks in interpretation and reduction.

Our first pass at solving the non-uniqueness problem by appeal to naturalness might simply assert that one reduction is more natural than others. Unfortunately, matters aren't quite so simple. First, there is a salient disanalogy between familiar appeals to naturalness and its potential use in addressing non-uniqueness problems. Appeals to naturalness capture intuitive disparities between competing interpretations and mark apparent discrepancies between, say, *blue* and *bleen*. But, in considering the non-uniqueness problem, there is no intuitive disparity or apparent discrepancy between candidate reductions of arithmetic: unlike *blue* and *grue*, neither the von Neumann nor the Zermelo reduction *seems* more natural. So, if the naturalness strategy is to succeed, we require a kind of speculative postulation of "covert" naturalness, which would single out a unique reduction even while our ordinary judgments provide no reason to privilege it.

Second, when the interpretation of a predicate like "is charged" is underdetermined by facts about use, naturalness is thought to render one property rather than some others as its correct interpretation. For example, if we assume that properties are sets, considerations of naturalness account for why "is charged" would express the set of all charged things rather than some less natural property like the set of all charged things, give or take a few electrons. But, when presented with candidate reductions of arithmetic to set-theoretic progressions—complex sets of sets—things are far less simple. Notice that, even if one progression is more natural than other progressions and is taken to be the proper subject of our arithmetical thought and talk, its naturalness cannot, on its own, fix a uniquely correct interpretation. This is because we can employ a single progression to deliver a variety of different interpretations. There are, for example, various ways to interpret predicates like "is a prime number" or singular terms like "seven" using the various subsets of a single progression. So, although naturalness might single out which progression our thought and talk is about, this alone cannot break the tie between competing reductions drawn from this progression and its subsets. Breaking this tie therefore requires, not only that this be the most natural progression, but some further facts about naturalness that pin down a uniquely privileged interpretation of our mathematical thought and talk in terms of that progression. It might, for example, require taking naturalness to apply to interpretation functions that would map various elements of the progression onto bits of our mathematical thought and talk.

This point can be made clearer by noting, with Sider (1996), that we cannot solve the non-uniqueness problem for views that identify propositions with sets simply by claiming that certain sets are more natural than others. For, even if certain sets or ordered n-tuples are more natural than other sets or ordered n-tuples, the alleged naturalness of ordered pairs like <May, Ali, loves> and <Ali, May, loves>, leaves us with no good reason to assign one rather than the other as the proposition expressed by a given sentence like "May loves Ali." For this reason, no simple appeal to naturalness provides a solution to these paradigmatic instances of the non-uniqueness problem. And, while we might help ourselves to a richer conception of naturalness—e.g., by holding interpretation functions to be more or less natural—this would stray well beyond any familiar conception of naturalness on offer.

On such a view, naturalness far outstrips the intuitive distinction between fundamental properties like *mass* and *charge* and bizarre properties like *grueness* or *being a werewolf* or *less than one gram in mass*. The resulting conception of naturalness is therefore a remarkably rich one, distributing an ornate network of naturalness facts across abstract and concrete reality. Only those willing to stretch the notion of naturalness beyond its familiar setting should find this strategy promising.

Deny Singularity. A fourth line of response denies Singularity and, contrary to a face value interpretation, seeks to provide a semantics for arithmetical terms like "the number two" quite different from the one supplied for ordinary expressions about concreta. Implementations of this strategy often fall under the rough heading of "structuralism." They are loosely unified by a general commitment to taking arithmetic and other parts of mathematics to be concerned, not with any specific objects, but with structures such as the natural number structure characterized by the Peano axioms. For structuralists of this sort, face-value interpretations mislead us into believing that mathematical discourse concerns unique entities like the number two or the addition function. When properly interpreted, our mathematical discourse is talk about whatever entities—typically but not exclusively, sets—occupy mathematical roles like "the number two" role within various structures. On such views, Singularity is to be rejected because there is no unique object that is the number two. Instead, arithmetic and other mathematical discourse is covertly general, concerning whatever entities satisfy intended structural constraints. This sentiment, which underlies certain versions of structuralism, is aptly expressed by Benacerraf (1965: 70):

> Arithmetic is therefore the science that elaborates the abstract structure that all progressions have in common merely in virtue of being progressions. It is not a science concerned with particular objects—the numbers. The search for which independently identifiable particular objects the numbers really are (sets? Julius Caesars?) is a misguided one.

Eliminativist structuralisms are driven by this guiding insight. Roughly speaking, these versions of structuralism uphold the truth of familiar mathematical claims, but reinterpret these as general claims quantifying over domains of objects satisfying certain constraints. These domains are not taken as novel bits of ontology nor are structures themselves held to be entities in their own right. Even so, certain domains of objects, whether abstract or concrete, can be said to "realize" or "satisfy" certain structures. Consider the claim that "two is less than five." According to the eliminativist structuralist, this is properly interpreted as the claim that, for any domain of objects satisfying the relevant axioms, the object that occupies "the number two" role has the object that plays "the number three" role as a successor. Since the eliminativist structuralist denies there is a distinctive ontology of structures or a uniquely privileged entity to which "the number two" refers, the result is a markedly deflationary conception of mathematics premised upon a recipe for interpreting mathematical claims as perfectly general claims about objects and their relations to one another. Some eliminativists will go on to posit sets in order to ensure that there is a domain of objects satisfying the relevant structural constraints set out by arithmetic and other mathematical theories. But, as we'll see in Chapter 7, others might claim that concrete reality is vast enough that mathematical claims can always be interpreted in terms of concrete entities.

Eliminativist structuralism ought to be distinguished from an importantly different strand of structuralism, which pursues a very different response to the non-uniqueness problem. According to *ante rem* structuralism, structures are entities in their own right and identical with or very similar to structural universals.[7] Given their commonalities with structural universals, mathematical structures are "instantiable" or "realizable" by other entities and have constituent universals as "roles" or "offices." So, for example, there is an entity, *the natural number structure*, which is instantiable by sets or suitably many concrete objects. This structure has a constituent, *the number seven role*, which is itself instantiable by entities. And, since there is a unique entity, the natural number structure, with a unique entity that is the number seven role, the *ante rem* structuralist holds that the non-uniqueness problem is solved, not by denying Singularity, but by pointing out that there are specific entities uniquely suited to serve as the referents of our mathematical thought and talk. On such views, our talk about the number three refers to *the number three role* itself, not its myriad occupants.

Although the *ante rem* structuralist aims to deny General Adequacy, it is not clear that *ante rem* structures would, in fact, be superior to, say, set-theoretic progressions *qua* candidate interpretations. Absent an insistence that such entities are more natural than set-theoretic progressions, why think that, given the adequacy of these competing interpretations, our discourse would uniquely concern *ante rem* structures? Perhaps more worryingly, if *ante rem* structures are rightly assimilated to structural universals and such entities are composed non-mereologically, there is nothing to rule out the existence of distinct *ante rem* structures that satisfy the same constraints, but differ only by permuting their constituent universals across "spots" within these structures—e.g., by swapping the place of the number two and number twenty universals. If there are such entities, then the non-uniqueness problem re-arises even within the framework of *ante rem* structuralism. *Ante rem* structuralists will naturally hope to rule out such cases, but, in doing so, the entities they deploy in addressing the non-uniqueness problem seem like increasingly *ad hoc* metaphysical commitments.

We've now surveyed the leading platonist responses to the non-uniqueness problem with a focus on its most familiar instance, the reduction of arithmetic. Before exploring one additional proposal that professes ignorance about which reduction is correct, we will turn to a related issue for platonism that, once again, brings concerns about theory choice and arbitrariness to the forefront.

§5.3 Metaphysical underdetermination

Resolving the non-uniqueness problem forces the platonist into some substantial theoretical commitments. As we've seen, she might embrace arbitrariness and opt for a broadly pragmatic response or instead posit an especially rich conception of naturalness that guarantees one candidate reduction is superior to its rivals. Alternatively, she might abandon reductionism altogether and posit a host of different kinds of *sui generis* abstract entities. No less controversially, she might reject the apparent singularity of our thought and talk about abstract entities like numbers and propositions and adopt some form of structuralism. Whichever response she pursues, it would seem that some, perhaps negotiable, sacrifice is required. But, while the costs that accrue in addressing the non-uniqueness problem are significant, there is a problem nearby that is arguably both more pressing and of greater significance for platonism. Like the non-uniqueness problem, this problem hinges on the threat of arbitrarily endorsing one theory over rival candidates. But, where the non-uniqueness problem concerns competing proposals for reducing numbers or propositions to sets, this broader problem arises when platonists are forced to choose between many competing yet equally viable theories about the entirety of abstract reality.

The problem of underdetermination of theory by evidence is an extremely general one. Even so, it is a pressing one for platonists who believe that abstract reality has a distinctive structure and is inhabited by different species of abstract entities. As should now be clear, there is no shortage of competing platonist views and considerable variation among the kinds of abstract entities these views posit. There is also no consensus about which abstract entities are identical with or reducible to others. There is, however, a tolerably clear sense in which many platonist alternatives are *explanatorily indiscernible*. They proffer platonist explanations for the very same phenomena and differ only with respect to which species of abstracta play which explanatory role or which kinds of abstract entities reduce to which other kinds. We will have more to say about these differences below, but, given the explanatory indiscernibility of certain platonist options, a problem of metaphysical underdetermination arises for platonism. It revolves around what, if anything, could license a preference for one explanatorily indiscernible platonist rival over myriad alternatives.

This problem parallels those faced in any domain where a range of theories are equally well supported by our presently available evidence. But, while worries about underdetermination in the sciences are tempered by the possibility of acquiring additional empirical evidence, the problem facing platonists is one for which no additional empirical tie-breaking seems possible. After all, matters of empirical adequacy place little, if any, substantive constraint on platonist options. And, while some might hope that this problem is merely a run of the mill sceptical worry warmed over, it persists even if we grant that we possess substantial knowledge about abstract reality. Let us, for example, simply assume that we know that there are abstract entities and such entities play the theoretical roles standardly associated with numbers, properties, and propositions. Even granting this much about the nature of abstract reality, we are still left with a pressing question for would-be platonists: which kinds of abstract entities play which theoretical roles and what might justify our belief in one among the many competing platonist options?

In exploring this question, a bit of taxonomy will be useful. Let's call views that posit only a single kind of abstract entity *monistic* platonisms and views that admit a variety of different species of abstracta *pluralistic* platonisms. We can also distinguish *radically* pluralistic platonisms, which claim that, for any sufficiently different theoretical role—e.g., those roles associated with properties and propositions respectively—there is a unique kind of abstract entity that occupies that role.[8] Now, unless platonists accept radical pluralism and thereby reject all proposed reductions between categories of abstracta, platonists are faced with a difficult choice. Should one opt for a modest form of pluralism that seeks to construct, say, possible worlds out of sets and propositions? What about a more ambitious view that also seeks to construct propositions out of sets and properties or, alternatively, a view that takes possible worlds to be a *sui generis* kind of abstract entity and builds propositions from them using set theory? If we grant the consistency and general adequacy of these proposals, we seem to lack any principled means for adjudicating between the merits of these incompatible but explanatorily indiscernible proposals. Are we therefore forced into selecting an arbitrary candidate?

As with familiar worries about underdetermination, our already worrisome epistemic situation gets even worse once we consider the space of "unconceived alternatives"—roughly, platonist alternatives, not among the extant menu of options, but that seem no less credible for their lack of explicit defence.[9] For instance, there is likely a case to be made for as-yet-undefended heterodox views on which set-like, property-like, or proposition-like entities play various familiar theoretical roles despite being constructed in different ways or having, say, modal features unlike those usually ascribed to more familiar abstracta. Consider, for instance, set-like entities that bear an analogue of the membership relation only accidentally to their members and so, in contrast to sets, do not have their "members" essentially. Once we take unconceived platonist alternatives seriously, there are a fretfully large number of platonist options we might cook up and this number is further compounded by the diverse combinations of reductionist strategies. In any case, the end result is a panoply of platonisms each of which seems equally serviceable but none of which seem to permit non-arbitrary endorsement. So, again, what licenses us to prefer this or that version of platonism over its rivals?

§5.4 Overcoming underdetermination

The best-case scenario for the platonist is that, when faced with this underdetermination problem, one's preferred response to either the epistemic access problem or the non-uniqueness problem would yield a solution here as well. It looks, however, like few of the platonist strategies we examined provide much help in addressing the problem of underdetermination. Appeals to some sort of faculty of mathematical intuition might provide a solution to the epistemic access problem, but even if mathematical intuition justifies our belief that four is an even number, it is implausible to hold the same sort of intuition can justify the belief that mathematics is ultimately about sets rather than *sui generis* numbers or, say, *ante rem* structures. A more plausible strategy might hold that, because of our apparent capacity to grasp propositions, we are justified in believing in the existence of such entities. But even this response is quickly undermined. After all, reductionist views on which propositions are set-theoretic constructions accept the existence of propositions no more or less than views on which propositions are *sui generis* entities. They merely disagree over whether *proposition* is a fundamental category of abstract entity. Intuition and grasping are therefore of no help with the present problem.

In general, it is difficult to see how a plausible conception of *a priori* intuition, scientific knowledge, or logical knowledge might single out one version of platonism as superior to all its explanatorily indiscernible rivals. Appeals to naturalness are also of no help here. For, while naturalness might provide a means to break ties among competing interpretations or reductions, it cannot settle which kinds of abstract entities exist in the first place. We might hope, then, that theoretical virtues and vices would provide a way to break the deadlock. But, even while considerations of parsimony might suggest a preference for monistic platonism, parsimony is far from the only theoretical virtue. Other virtues like fertility and conservativeness might, for example, count against monistic views and in support of pluralist platonisms.

We might now be tempted to simply embrace the vice of arbitrariness and, like the pragmatic view considered earlier, choose one version of platonism in the absence of principled grounds. Unfortunately, this concession to pragmatism looks far less innocuous than the arbitrariness some might abide in order to deal with the non-uniqueness problem. In the present case, we would be endorsing views about the fundamental nature of the abstract realm solely for the sake of expediency and in the absence of adequate evidence. Slapdash metaphysics of this sort invites the kind of Carnapian worries that we set aside in the Introduction and, as a piece of metaphysical methodology, has little to recommend it.

Perhaps the most promising response to worries about underdetermination is plenitudinism. Recall that, in addressing the epistemic access problem, the plenitudinist claims that any consistent mathematical theory describes some portion of abstract reality. Consequently, there is a plenitude of mathematical structures rather than, say, a unique hierarchy of sets obeying a specific set of axioms. And, while plenitudinism is most familiar as a theory about mathematical entities like sets and numbers, platonists might be tempted by a generalization, according to which any consistent metaphysical theory about abstract entities describes some portion of abstract reality. On the resulting view, the ontology of the monistic platonist who accepts only properties and the ontology of the pluralist platonist who posits sets and properties each provide true but merely partial descriptions of abstract reality. Neither description does justice to the vast metaphysical plenitude of the abstract realm, which comprises all consistent theories regarding properties, propositions, and any as of yet unconceived species of abstracta. Since all consistent platonist options describe some part of abstract reality, we would no longer be forced into arbitrarily believing one theory to be correct. Instead, familiar platonist options would be on equal metaphysical footing. The underdetermination problem would, then, be dissolved by holding all extant platonist theories to be just parts of the full story about abstract reality.

Regardless of its merits as a response to the epistemic access problem, this general plenitudinism about the abstract realm is unsatisfactory. While the nature of mathematical practice suggests that the proper objects of mathematical study extend far beyond a single hierarchy of sets, there is no obvious parallel when it comes to properties, propositions, and possible worlds. Within systematic metaphysics, there is a standard presumption that, given the objective nature of abstract reality, there is a matter of fact about which particular kinds of abstract entities there are and what they are like. So, while most mathematicians would be content to admit the posits of non-standard set theories as entities no more or less real than the familiar hierarchy of ZF, metaphysicians will claim that abstracta like, say, propositions are either fundamental or constructions from other abstracta, but not both. The same goes for whether numbers and properties are sets, whether propositions are properties, and so on. Methodologically speaking, no facts about practice support generalizing plenitudinism beyond the mathematical case.

A second worry arises when we consider that most forms of platonism aim to provide explanations that are fully general. So, in appealing to properties to provide metaphysical explanations, no portion of reality falls outside of the scope of the platonist's intended explanations. But, if this generalization of plenitudinism is correct, we require that certain portions of abstract reality are isolated from one another in complex ways that preclude any fully general platonist explanations. Upon pain of paradox, there cannot, for example, be any interaction between, say, those portions of abstract reality in which propositions are set-theoretic constructions and those in which propositions are *sui generis* entities. And, if platonists hope to explain phenomena like truth and meaning in fully general terms, there would have to be propositions of both kinds that are about and true of these competing portions of reality. The threat of widespread inconsistency and flat-out incoherence is an imminent one for the plenitudinist who might hope to incorporate all consistent platonist theories within a single abstract realm. Such an unwieldy view is therefore best rejected.

The underdetermination problem, as we've posed it here, assumes that there are abstract entities occupying familiar theoretical roles standardly associated with properties, propositions, and numbers. A concessive response to this problem admits that we are simply unjustified in believing any specific platonist view. Such a response avows a thesis of *epistemic humility*, according to which we are irremediably ignorant about the kinds of abstracta there are and how these abstracta occupy their different theoretical roles.[10] We simply cannot know, says the defender of humility, whether such entities fall within ontological categories like set, property, proposition, or some altogether different categories. But, despite this ignorance, we are nevertheless in a position to know that abstract entities do occupy the roles in question. Our knowledge of the abstract realm is therefore limited to *whether* theoretical roles are occupied. It does not extend to knowledge about *which* abstract entities occupy these roles. The defender of humility therefore finds herself in an awkward but not obviously inconsistent position: she confesses ignorance about which version of platonism is true even while she claims to know that platonism of some sort is correct.[11]

Those who accept the humility thesis concede ignorance about which kinds of abstract entities there are and about which abstracta occupy which theoretical roles. Consequently, they owe no recipe for overcoming the underdetermination problem. At the same time, they can also offer a parallel response to the non-uniqueness problem. This response holds that we are irremediably ignorant about which is the correct reduction of arithmetic to sets, but that we are still justified in believing that some identification is correct. Notice, however, that this avowal of epistemic humility is importantly different from the pragmatic response we considered above. Instead of believing in a particular reduction on arbitrary grounds, the present response says that we are justified in believing that some or other reduction is true, but that the extent of our justified beliefs stops there. It therefore requires us to suspend judgment about which reduction is the right one. Of course, for the sake of theoretical expediency, the defender of humility might still treat a specific reduction as true for practical purposes. She will, however, simultaneously disavow belief in the reduction in question.[12]

Humility about the abstract realm does, of course, come with certain costs. Since we cannot know whether there are *sui generis* propositions or properties, it rules out explanatory appeals to the distinctive essences of specific kinds of abstracta. We cannot, for example, claim that some abstract entities are *instantiable* because they are properties and that what it is to be a property is just to stand in the *instantiation* relation (at least in the case of all but impossible properties). More generally, the platonist who avows humility cannot precisely identify the species of abstract entities or the fundamental relations they bear to concrete reality. After all, we can know whether instantiation, membership, and other relations hold only if we know whether there are properties or sets, and so on. So, while such platonists might still be entitled to claim that there are entities that we can treat as the objects of attitudes or entities we can treat as the grounds for resemblance, they can say frustratingly little in addition to this schematic or structural characterization of abstract reality. For nominalists, this will of course seem an implausible combination of epistemic theses.

If humility is a viable response to worries about underdetermination, platonism is defensible despite our ignorance about which version of platonism is true. And, if that's right, the specific ontological categories of abstract entities turn out to be of surprisingly limited importance. This, in turn, suggests a view even more radical than humility as final response to the underdetermination problem.

§5.4.1 Natureless abstracta

According to a *natureless* version of platonism, there are no unknowable facts about which kinds of abstract entities there are. There are merely facts about which theoretical roles abstract entities occupy.[13] On such a view, there is no sense to be made of disagreement about whether the things that occupy, say, the proposition role are sets, properties, or *sui generis* propositions. Instead, occupants of these roles are propositions in virtue of occupying the relevant theoretical role, since what it is to be a proposition is just to be a thing that plays the proposition role. Put differently: the natureless view denies that there are categoreal properties of abstract entities independent of theoretical role-properties like *being the thing that serves as the meaning of sentences* or *being the thing that explains the features of objects*.

On this natureless view, there are no further questions we can ask about the kinds or categories of abstract entities once we settle which theoretical roles abstracta occupy. So, while the humility response addresses underdetermination by denying us knowledge about the species of abstract entities over which competing platonist views disagree, the natureless view denies there is anything for us to be ignorant about. Consequently, there can be no substantive metaphysical disagreement between platonist views that agree on which theoretical roles are occupied. There is, says the natureless view, no substantive disagreement between a monistic view positing only properties and a pluralist one that posits sets, properties, and propositions.

The natureless view rules out any metaphysical difference between abstract entities that would transcend their theoretical role. On the resulting picture, distinctions between properties, propositions, and other kinds are ultimately distinctions about which entities figure into which kinds of explanations. And, although this view wards off the underdetermination problem, it is at odds with the presuppositions of most platonist theories. Among other things, the natureless view undermines any interest in reductionist proposals that seek to reduce, say, properties and propositions to sets. For, on the resulting view, there is no substantive metaphysical distinction between numbers or sets and so no motivation to minimize the ideology or ontology of the abstract realm. Once the ontological categories of abstract entities are deemed inseparable from their theoretical roles, there can be no reduction of metaphysical diversity without a reduction of theoretical roles.

The natureless view invites us to think of abstract entities as featureless nodes within a massive but explanatorily useful abstract structure. For the purposes of providing an ontology of mathematical entities, this picture is plausible enough. But, when we turn to properties and propositions, the rich interaction between these kinds of entities and concrete reality seems to demand that abstract entities have distinctive intrinsic natures. As we saw in Chapter 2, if different abstract entities are to explain why concrete entities have different features (e.g., in explaining why the universal *mass* rather than *goodness* accounts for why objects resist acceleration or why certain mental states allow us to grasp one proposition rather than another), such entities must possess different, presumably intrinsic features that account for their differing explanatory roles. And, unless such entities have distinctive intrinsic natures, it would be mysterious why one rather than another would be instantiated or grasped by the particular concrete entities to which it is specially related. For this reason, the natureless view of properties and propositions circumvents the underdetermination problem only by divesting the explanatory resources that make propositions and properties worth positing. Better, then, for platonists to avow humility about the intrinsic nature and ontological category of abstract entities than opt for the natureless view, which jeopardizes the metaphysical explanations abstracta are credited with providing.

§5.4.2 *Uniqueness and underdetermination*

We began with the non-uniqueness problem, which makes trouble for the reduction of certain abstract entities to other perhaps more basic abstract entities. We then explored a problem about underdetermination, according to which platonists are unable to provide principled reasons for endorsing a specific platonist theory over rival platonist proposals. In each case, the appeal of lapsing into outright dogmatism has been lurking in the background. Why not, then, simply endorse a specific reduction or a specific platonist ontology and get on with things? Why hyperventilate about which reduction or version of platonism to opt for, provided we have good reason to think at least some reduction or version is true?

For those untroubled by arbitrariness, dogmatism offers a simple way through each of these problems. But, for the rest of us, a clear epistemic conscience requires a principled explanation for why we might reasonably believe one competitor over its equally good rivals. So understood, platonism serves as a case study in theory choice under extreme circumstances. For when we inspect platonist options, the balance of evidence seems perfectly even between many different competitors. But, since problems regarding underdetermination afflict scientific theories that many of us are inclined to endorse, platonists can reasonably hope that parallel problems provide no compelling reason to disavow abstract entities. Indeed, it would be surprising if the fact that we are unable to decide among platonist options was reason enough to reject platonist in any form whatsoever. With this in mind, the optimistic platonist might point out that platonism actually provides a fruitful test case and a valuable proving ground for hypotheses about theory choice and the epistemic significance of arbitrariness. Viewed this way, the fertility of platonism consists not only in the metaphysical explanations it provides, but also in its methodological value: it allows us to consider, in abstraction from the murkiness of empirical scientific theories, how we ought to work through evidential impasses in theory choice. This might be true, but does little to settle how exactly platonists should combat the non-uniqueness problem. All the same, such a problem is common enough that it cannot, on its own, undercut platonism so long as platonists are content to stump for one and perhaps several of the responses we've surveyed.

Summary

This chapter introduced the non-uniqueness problem, which arises for the reduction of mathematics to set theory and for other platonist views. After presenting several responses to the non-uniqueness problem, a different and arguably more worrisome underdetermination problem was introduced. Platonist options were briefly canvassed and include plenitudinism, structuralism, pragmatism, and a thesis of epistemic humility regarding the species of abstract entities. Although it is unclear what option most platonists should prefer, worries about non-uniqueness and underdetermination provide no knockdown argument for nominalism, given the diversity of viable platonist options.

Recommended reading

The canonical presentation of the non-uniqueness problem is Benacerraf (1965). See Kitcher (1978), Balaguer (1998), Wetzel (1989), Kalderon (1996), Clarke-Doane (2008), and Paseau (2009) for responses.

On non-uniqueness problems regarding properties and propositions, see Jubien (2001), Sider (1996), Moore (1999), Melia (1992b), and Armour-Garb and Woodbridge (2012). On the connection between the non-uniqueness problem and the indispensability argument, see Baker (2003). On the taxonomy of structuralisms, see Parsons (1990), Hellman (2001b), and MacBride (2005b). On *ante rem* structuralism, see Shapiro (1997, 2008). Alternative structuralist proposals include Resnik (1997), Chihara (2004), Hellman (1989), and Kalderon (1995).

On underdetermination in philosophy of science, see Psillos (1999), Laudan and Leplin (1991), and Stanford (2006); and, on its connection to the non-uniqueness problem, see Clarke-Doane (2008).

Notes

1 This view faces several challenges. Perhaps most notably, it seems to conflate the content of sentences like "Triangles have three sides" and "The set of the real numbers is greater than the set of the rational numbers," which seem to express different propositions. Since each of these sentences are true at all possible worlds, the present view seems to require that they express the same proposition—namely, the set of all possible worlds. This problem arises because this view is an *intensional* one,

according to which any propositions that are true at all the same possible worlds are identical. In contrast, Russellian views are compatible with a *hyperintensional* view of propositions, which allows for propositions to be true at all the same possible worlds yet differ in virtue of having different structures or constituents.

2 The relevant functions are from worlds onto truth-values, where each world mapped to the truth-value "true" is a world where dogs bark and each world mapped to the truth-value "false" is a world where it is not the case that dogs bark.

3 Very roughly put, the facts King identifies with propositions are facts about the semantico-syntactic relations that hold between languages, objects, properties, and semantic relations concerning sentences. For example, the proposition that Obama swims is the fact that there is a sentence in a language that encodes a relation holding between the semantic values of its constituents—in this case, Obama and *swimming*. Note also that facts are conceived of here in a way apparently at odds with nominalism, but in a way that falls short of standard conceptions of states of affairs.

4 On the problem of the many, see Unger (1980), Lewis (1993a), and Weatherson (2003).

5 Benacerraf (1965) argues against the coherence of the *sui generis* response.

6 On possible extensions of naturalness, see Sider (1996, 2011).

7 For discussion of *ante rem* structuralism, see Shapiro (2008). On the distinction between *ante rem* structures and structural universals, see Shapiro (2008: 302) and MacBride (2005b). See also Hellman (2001b) and Parsons (1990).

8 In some cases, the distinction between monism and pluralism is a murky one. For example, on certain views of properties, propositions are not a distinct ontological category but, instead, zero-place properties.

9 On scientific realism and the problem of unconceived alternatives, see Stanford (2006).

10 Langton (1998) defends an interpretation of transcendental idealism that ascribes to Kant the thesis of Kantian Humility, according to which we can have no knowledge of the intrinsic properties of objects. On the resulting view, our knowledge of the world therefore consists entirely in knowledge of objects' extrinsic features. Lewis (2009) defends a different thesis of humility, Ramseyan Humility, arguing that we are irremediably ignorant of the fundamental properties of things.

11 Avowing humility about the various kinds of abstract entities is a surprising option for platonists, but some have come fairly close to endorsing humility about the intrinsic natures of abstracta. Lewis (1991: 33) expresses scepticism about the various non-mathematical properties of sets: "I don't say the classes are in space and time. I don't say they aren't. I say we're in the sad fix that we haven't a clue whether they are or whether they aren't. We go much to fast from not knowing whether they are to thinking we know they are not . . . . Are all singletons exactly intrinsic duplicates, or do they always differ in their intrinsic character? If they do, do those difference in any way reflect differences between the character of their members? Do they involve any of the same qualities that distinguish individuals from one another? Again we cannot argue the case one way or the other . . . ."

12 Despite their parallels, there are disanalogies between humility as applied to underdetermination and non-uniqueness. Since our justification for believing in the reduction of arithmetic to set theory is contingent upon the defensibility of the proposed reduction, worries of non-uniqueness call this defensibility into question. In contrast, platonists claim we have independent reason to believe in abstract entities, so humility about which particular abstract entities there are does not immediately call into question whether we ought to accept that there are such entities. Humility might therefore be more stable as a response to concerns about underdetermination than to concerns about non-uniqueness.

13 Other radical alternatives remain including the denial that abstract reality is built up out of objects and is, instead, a different ontological category of mere undifferentiated *stuff*. On the distinction between thing and stuff ontology, see Sider (2001: xvi–xx).

6

MODAL OBJECTIONS

6.1 Necessary existents
6.2 Necessary connections
6.3 Contingent platonism
6.4 Abstracta and actuality

Our survey of arguments against platonism has yet to turn up an especially compelling reason to disavow abstract entities. This chapter explores a final, loosely connected group of arguments against abstract entities that turn on the modal commitments of platonism. One of these modal commitments is the thesis that abstract entities like numbers and properties exist necessarily. A second and no less significant commitment is to a vast array of necessary connections between abstract entities. For example, most platonist theories hold that if an entity bears the instantiation relation to the property *being a dog*, then, of necessity, it bears the instantiation relation to the property *being a mammal* as well. Similar necessary connections hold among propositions. For, if the proposition that three dogs bark is true, then the proposition that some dogs bark must also be true. Still other necessary connections hold between properties and propositions. If, for example, something instantiates the property *being a dog*, then the proposition *that some dog exists* must be true. The motivation for positing many of these necessary connections is parasitic upon familiar and largely uncontroversial claims about what entails what. But it is only once we combine these claims about entailment with a platonist view of propositions and properties, that we quickly find ourselves committed to a plethora of abstract entities bearing myriad necessary connections to one another.

As we'll see, the acceptability of necessary connections is a point of serious controversy in modal metaphysics. And, since both necessary connections and the necessary existence of abstract entities seem crucial for satisfying the theoretical ambitions of platonism, the fate of platonism depends upon whether these are defensible commitments. With this in mind, we'll begin by presenting the case against necessary existents and then turn to the case against necessary connections. After arguing that platonism cannot be sustained without its heavy-duty modal commitments, we'll briefly examine a different question concerning actuality and platonism—namely, whether abstract entities are actual rather than merely possible entities.

§6.1 Necessary existents

The first modal argument we will consider takes aim at platonism's commitment to the necessary existence of abstract entities. It proceeds in two steps. First, it seeks to show that were abstract entities to exist, they would exist necessarily. Second, it seeks to show that no entities exist necessarily. From there, it concludes that there are no abstracta. Its key premises are therefore the following:

No Necessary Existents (NNE): No entities necessarily exist.

No Contingent Abstracta (NCA): If abstract entities were to exist, they would necessarily exist.

Let's start by focusing on the case for (NNE). Notice that (NNE) is not the thesis of *absolute metaphysical nihilism*, which says that, possibly, there are no entities whatsoever (or, equivalently: that it is not necessary that something exists).[1] Put in terms of possible worlds, absolute metaphysical nihilism ensures that there is an absolutely "empty" world—a possible world at which no entities whatsoever exist. The denial of this thesis is *absolute metaphysical anti-nihilism*, which rules out an absolutely empty possible world and requires that, necessarily, something exists. Absolute metaphysical anti-nihilism leaves open whether any specific entity or entities necessarily exist. This is because absolute metaphysical anti-nihilists can claim that there are some necessary existents or that, even if there are no necessary existents, there is nevertheless some entity or other at each possible world. So, although absolute metaphysical nihilism entails (NNE), (NNE) does not entail absolute metaphysical nihilism. For, while (NNE) guarantees that no entity inhabits every possible world, it leaves open whether there is an "empty" world, devoid of any contingent entities.

So why think (NNE) is true? Depending upon the intended sense of "necessary," some have suggested that (NNE) is intuitively plausible. As Russell (1919: 203) says: "There does not even seem any logical necessity why there should be even one individual—why, in fact, there should be any world at all . . . ." If the sense of necessity relevant to (NNE) is *logical* necessity, Russell's view is quite plausible, since no strictly logical contradiction seems to follow from the assumption that nothing at all exists. Indeed, the perennial philosophical interest in why there is anything at all owes, in part, to our inability to rule out this possibility on purely logical grounds. But, if the relevant notion of necessity is not logical necessity, the fate of (NNE) is far less certain.

For the most part, when platonists posit the necessary existence of properties and other abstracta, they are not interested in logical necessity. They are instead concerned with the very general but still restricted notion of *metaphysical necessity* and its dual *metaphysical possibility*. (Unhelpfully enough, some use the term "broadly logical possibility" to capture what others call "metaphysical possibility.") Characterizing the difference between metaphysical and logical necessity is no simple matter. Notice, however, that the laws of logic—e.g., the laws of non-contradiction and excluded middle—impose markedly weaker constraints on the world than those imposed by what we might call the "laws of metaphysics." This is because metaphysical hypotheses—e.g., that there are tropes rather than universals or that presentism rather than eternalism is true— all seem logically consistent but they are not obviously consistent with the alleged laws of metaphysics.[2]

One strategy for getting at the notion of metaphysical necessity is by drawing an analogy with the notion of physical necessity. For example, where the laws of physics like the inverse square law are necessities that govern the actual world, the "laws of metaphysics" are necessities that govern the subject matter of metaphysics, which is all of reality including both actual and merely possible worlds. Viewed in this way, metaphysical possibility is broader than physical or nomological possibility, since it is not *physically possible* for massive bodies to travel faster than the speed of light although it is presumably *metaphysically possible*. So, while nomological and metaphysical possibility are restricted modalities—i.e., less broad than logical possibility or non-alethic modalities like epistemic or doxastic possibility—they are each theoretically significant, given our interest in both what is actually as well as possibly the case.

No account of the relation between metaphysical and logical necessity is uncontroversial. But, since it is standardly assumed that nominalists and platonists are concerned with metaphysical necessity rather than logical necessity, we will follow suit here.[3] And, since our concern is with metaphysical rather than logical necessity, Russell's remark therefore provides no support for (NNE). For this reason, the best route for defending (NNE) proceeds by arguing for absolute metaphysical nihilism. If successful, this argument will, in turn, show that no entities—not even abstract ones—exist necessarily.

Why should we believe that there could be nothing whatsoever? In defending the possibility of an empty world, it is natural to look to conceivability arguments, given their familiar role in defending claims about what is possible. Generally speaking, such arguments seek to show that, given the conceivability of a scenario, we are justified in believing the scenario to be possible. Of course, details vary considerably, especially when it comes to spelling out the appropriate sense of "conceivability." Most conceivability arguments require, at a minimum, that one is able to form a positive mental representation of a scenario (though not necessarily an imagistic one) and that, upon sustained reflection, one can detect no contradiction in supposing the scenario to obtain. More demanding views require that conceivers are adequately informed about relevant empirical matters. So, for example, in attempting to determine what is possible for water, the conceiver must not be mistaken or badly ignorant about water's actual chemical composition.

For our purposes, we can set aside many of the complications that arise for conceivability arguments and focus on the peculiarities of those conceivability arguments relevant to the case at hand—namely, conceivability arguments for there being nothing at all. The key question of how, if at all, one might conceive of an empty world is not an easy one. It seems, for example, that if our positive representation of this possibility must be imagistic, no representation is likely to be apt, since any representation of nothingness would seem to involve some positive depictive elements like shape or colour. In addition, if we take our conceiving to be inherently perspectival—i.e., if in conceiving a scenario, we must conceive of it as experienced *by someone*—we can at best conceive of an almost empty world that includes a single individual experiencing nothing else. Proponents of a conceivability argument for an empty world will, however, claim that representing an empty world requires neither imagistic nor perspectival representation. Instead, it only requires that we represent there being nothing at all and that this is a plausible enough representational feat. Let us simply grant here that we can conceive, in some non-imagistic sense, that there is nothing at all. So, if we also assume a robust connection between conceivability and possibility, absolute metaphysical nihilism would follow. Notice, however, that even those who endorse strong links between conceivability and possibility might reasonably claim this to be a special case where conceivability does not guarantee possibility. For, not only does this peculiar case require successfully conceiving that absolutely no concrete entities exist, it also requires success in conceiving that there are absolutely no abstract entities either. Given that conceivability arguments are typically concerned with ways concrete reality could be, the present scenario is plausibly taken as a principled exception to the conceivability–possibility connections. For this reason, it looks as though conceivability arguments are unable to decisively establish metaphysical nihilism.

Let's turn to a second strategy for defending absolute metaphysical nihilism that appeals to principles regarding the limits of possibility. Roughly speaking, these "principles of plenitude" provide a recipe for determining what is and what is not possible. Proposed principles come in a variety of forms, differing strengths, and, depending on one's preferred modal epistemology, play different roles in our modal epistemology. Typically, however, these principles of plenitude assert that, given certain possibilities, certain other scenarios are possible. So, in light of our knowledge about the actual world, principles of plenitude justify our belief in myriad non-actual possibilities. Below, we'll consider some fairly powerful "recombination principles." Here, a weak but intuitively plausible "subtraction principle" will be our focus. This subtraction principle holds that, for any given possibility, we can "subtract" entities from that possibility and the resulting scenario will be possible as well. Potential formulations vary considerably depending upon one's view of concrete objects. A simple version holds that, for any possible world, any "contraction" consisting solely of connected duplicate sub-regions of the former, is possible. So, for example, various "contractions" of our world are, given the subtraction principle, perfectly possible as well—e.g., duplicates of the actual world with fewer planets, electrons, or regions of spacetime.

We can now put this subtraction principle to work in arguing for what we can call *concrete* metaphysical nihilism, according to which, possibly, there are no concrete entities whatsoever. Following Baldwin (1996), this delivers the subtraction argument for concrete metaphysical nihilism, which runs as follows:

A1. There could be a world with a finite domain of concrete objects.

A2. These concrete objects are, each of them, things that could not exist.

A3. The nonexistence of any one of these things does not necessitate the existence of any other such thing.

C1. There could be a world with no concrete objects.

A1 is the plausible hypothesis that the concrete world could be finite. A2 is motivated by a commitment to a subtraction principle, where the relevant principle holds the "deletion" of concrete objects like electrons or spacetime regions generates distinct possibilities. A3 is the denial that the nonexistence of "subtracted" entities somehow necessitates the existence of any "replacement" entities. Taken together, these premises suggest that a world without any concrete entities is possible. If true, this is no small discovery. But, since our interest is in the possibility of worlds without any entities whatsoever, our real concern is whether the subtraction argument can be transformed into an argument for *absolute* metaphysical nihilism and, subsequently, (NNE).

One way to strengthen the subtraction argument in order to get from concrete metaphysical nihilism to absolute metaphysical nihilism would be to show that abstract entities uniformly depend upon concrete entities. So, if there is a possible world with no concrete entities, then, at such a world, there can be no abstract entities. (On this sort of proposed dependency, see Lowe (1996).) It looks, however, like few platonists are inclined to hold that abstracta like the real numbers depend for their existence upon concrete reality. In any case, such a claim is at least as contentious as (NNE). So, absent good arguments in favour of this dependency, a more promising option is to invoke a stronger subtraction principle that applies to abstract as well as concrete entities. A subtraction principle of this sort would allow us to "subtract" abstract entities like properties, propositions, and mathematical entities and still be left with genuine possibilities.[4]

The suggestion that a possible world might be just like our own but without various properties, propositions, or numbers will strike most platonists as teetering into absurdity. And, as we'll see below, such a possibility leads to some deep questions for platonism, given the alleged necessary connections among abstract entities. It is undeniably odd, however, to think that something might be the number eight even while it is neither greater than seven nor less than ten or that something might instantiate *being a dog* without instantiating *being a mammal*. Platonists therefore seem well within their rights to reject subtraction principles that would license any piece-by-piece subtraction of abstract reality. But, even if platonists have grounds for rejecting piecemeal subtraction principles as applied to abstract reality, this leaves open the prospects for a weaker subtraction principle that rules out any piecemeal mutilation of abstract reality but permits abstract reality to be subtracted *en masse*. Such a principle would guarantee the possibility of a contraction of reality to exclusively concrete entities, but it would not generate outré possibilities according to which there are, say, no natural numbers beyond twenty-four.

At this point, platonists will likely attempt to reject such a principle by claiming that principles of plenitude apply exclusively to the concrete world. And, for those platonists who take abstractness as a primitive feature of entities, this is plausible enough. That said, the platonist's insistence that necessary connections are admissible in abstract but not concrete reality marks a deep modal disagreement, one with serious implications for platonism. Those suspicious of necessary connections between abstract entities will find fault with the platonist who restricts these principles. In particular, Humeans about modality—so-called in honour of Hume's antipathy towards necessary connections between distinct existences—will take issue with the necessary existence of abstract entities and insist that at least some weak subtraction principle holds with full generality. By doing so, they endorse a generalized version of the subtraction argument for absolute metaphysical nihilism and, in turn, for (NNE). In stark contrast, platonists will simply reiterate that the scope of principles of plenitude is rightly restricted to the concrete realm. In doing so, they claim a special modal status for abstract entities, which is made all the more plausible if *abstract entity* is taken as fundamental category, profoundly different from that of *concrete entity*.

In countering Humean opposition to the necessary connections alleged to hold among abstracta, platonists might argue as follows. Suppose that there could be nothing. If so, then it is true that there is nothing. But, if it is true that there is nothing, then the proposition *that there is nothing* exists and so something does, in fact, exist. Moreover, such a proposition would, given some auxiliary modal assumptions, be necessarily false and therefore itself a necessary existent. Therefore, the apparatus of propositions arguably guarantees both the necessary existence of propositions and the impossibility of absolute metaphysical nihilism. (For discussion, see Cameron (2006).)

Pretty clearly, an argument of this kind is not likely to convince those who are already suspicious of platonism. The nominalist and, in particular, the Humean will be unconvinced. But, for platonists, the success of explanations of truth, meaning, and possibility that invoke abstracta will be held up as a reason to believe in the necessary framework of properties, propositions, and numbers and, in turn, to reject absolute metaphysical nihilism.

Ultimately, the Humean is within her rights to reject the claimed necessary connections, but the platonist is in a parallel position, since she can reasonably reject the proposed recombination principles. We are therefore saddled with a deadlock between platonists and Humeans. Platonists will tout the explanatory generality and power of their preferred explanations, while Humeans will point to the benefits of recombination principles for modal epistemology and hold platonism to violate sacrosanct theses regarding possibility and necessity. With this deadlock in mind, we will now consider a different way to prosecute the Humean case against platonism.

§6.2 Necessary connections

In the actual world, there is exactly one entity with all the intrinsic properties of the Eiffel Tower. There could, however, have been two, fifty, or a thousand such entities. Indeed, it seems quite possible that there be infinitely many duplicates of the Eiffel Tower—e.g., in worlds of eternal recurrence where each epoch involves the construction of an indiscernible yet numerically different tower. Generally speaking, for most kinds of entities, if there could be one such entity, there could be any number of perfect duplicates of that entity.

Suppose, however, that someone insisted there could be seven or nine duplicates of the Eiffel Tower, but that it was simply impossible for there to be exactly eight duplicates of the Eiffel Tower. Such a claim seems bizarrely arbitrary and its bizarreness is compounded by the fact that, in denying what seems to be perfectly possible, an inexplicable necessary connection between entities is required. For, if this modal claim is true, then, in a world with exactly seven duplicates of the Eiffel Tower, no matter how hard one might try to build another duplicate, every effort is doomed to fail somehow. Similarly, in a world with exactly nine Eiffel Tower duplicates, no one can destroy exactly one duplicate. For, if they were to destroy one, forces will somehow conspire to destroy at least one other duplicate in order to prevent there from being exactly eight. So, no matter what any possible individuals do, necessary connections will always thwart their efforts to bring about the existence of exactly eight duplicates of the Eiffel Tower.

If we envision the totality of possible worlds as a kind of "logical space," the denial that there could be exactly eight Eiffel Tower duplicates requires an objectionable "gap" in this space. The fact that this gap in logical space is objectionable is clear enough, but it is difficult to put one's finger on precisely why it is objectionable. Fortunately, Humeans can handily explain its viciousness by appeal to what Forrest (2001) dubs "Hume's razor": the methodological injunction to avoid multiplying necessities beyond necessity. According to Hume's razor, positing necessities is theoretically burdensome, so, absent good reason to the contrary, we ought to take putative possibilities to be genuine. We ought, for example, to find fault with a theory on which it is impossible for there to be exactly eight Eiffel Tower duplicates, since we lack any reason whatsoever to discount such a possibility. Similarly, we should reject any theory on which, necessarily, there are more than four solar planets. For, just as the above suggestion regarding Eiffel Towers posits a bizarre necessary connection, this suggestion requires a remarkable necessary truth: that, no matter how things could have turned out, there would have been more than four solar planets. Without compelling reasons to the contrary, Hume's razor entreats us to reject these and other theories that posit gratuitous necessary connections between distinct existences. More generally, it takes the modal extravagance of ruling out possibilities without compelling reason to be a theoretical vice much like admitting unwarranted ontological or ideological commitments.

According to Forrest, the significance and theoretical value of Hume's razor traces back to its role in a plausible modal epistemology. As Forrest puts it: "we start with a presumption in favor of possibility and then require reasons for overcoming that presumption." So, in taking the possibility of scenarios as *prima facie* justified and genuine unless shown otherwise, Hume's razor underwrites our justified beliefs about what is and what is not possible. Hume's razor is therefore part and parcel of our general epistemology of modality as well as a guide to theory choice akin to Ockham's razor. For, when we flout it by admitting gratuitous necessities, we offend against the very principle that affords us modal knowledge in the first place.

Hume's razor is related to but distinct from a commitment to recombination principles, which serve as principles of plenitude. In their role as principles of plenitude, recombination principles aim to characterize the entirety of logical space by appealing to principles that govern transformations on possibilities that take us from one possibility to another (e.g., by duplicating or subtracting regions or objects). These principles are inadequate if they overgenerate by positing spurious possibilities or if they undergenerate by omitting possibilities that are needed to "fill the gaps" in logical space. For Humeans, the key insight into the structure of logical space is that all of its occupants are modally independent. So, taking their lead from Hume, these full-fledged recombination principles deny any necessary connections among distinct entities and take this denial to provide the recipe for determining what is and what is not possible.[5] Lewis (1986: 88) describes his preferred recombination principle as follows:

> Roughly speaking, the principle is that anything can coexist with anything else, at least provided they occupy distinct spatiotemporal positions. Likewise, anything can fail to coexist with anything else. Thus, if there could be a dragon, and there could be a unicorn, but there couldn't be a dragon and a unicorn side by side, that would be an unacceptable gap in logical space, a failure of plenitude.

The Humean ambition, in supplying a recombination principle, is to characterize the entirety of logical space.[6] On the resulting view, our knowledge of modality is roughly analogous to our mathematical knowledge. The latter proceeds from some pedestrian arithmetical knowledge and is extended outward by inferences underwritten by mathematical axioms. The former begins with our knowledge of actuality and is expanded outward by deploying a suitable recombination principle. So, granted the possibility of the dragon and unicorn mentioned above, it would be a violation of our recombination principle to accept the impossibility of a dragon and a unicorn inhabiting the same possible world or the impossibility of a unicorn existing without some other unicorn duplicate. Since these entities are distinct from one another and there can be no necessary connections between them, we know there are possible worlds of the sort in question.

Humean recombination principles and Hume's razor share in their hostility towards necessary connections, but they differ in their methodological and metaphysical consequences. For those committed to Humean recombination principles, absolutely no necessary connections between distinct existences can be admitted. This leads some proponents of Humean recombination principles to deem necessary connections "unintelligible." (See, e.g., Lewis (1986b).) In contrast, those committed to Hume's razor hold that we incur a theoretical cost in positing necessities, but that this cost might, in principle, be outweighed or otherwise worth paying. So, while proponents of Humean recombination principles have a zero-tolerance policy when it comes to necessary connections, Hume's razor permits the acceptance of certain necessary connections under the right theoretical conditions. For those who endorse Hume's razor, necessary connections remain intelligible but, like gratuitous ontology or needless complexity, they are theoretically vicious and to be avoided wherever possible.

Respect for Hume's razor does not demand the far-reaching consequences of recombination principles.[7] Better still, Hume's razor seems to be motivated, not only by plausible considerations within modal epistemology, but also by our ordinary explanatory practices. For example, in asserting that the world or some entities simply *must* be a certain way, we incur a theoretical cost since we rule out certain possibilities for the sake of our preferred theory. When repeated *ad nauseum*, this strategy hobbles the explanatory credentials of our theories: we are left with a host of parallel necessities, no account of why they hold, and only a bare insistence that they must. Ideally, we would not require promissory modal notes of this sort. Importantly this doesn't mean we ought to try and dispense with necessities altogether. Following an analogy with Ockham's razor, modal extremism that rejects the necessity of logical laws would be about as virtuous as dispensing with any and all entities in pursuing parsimony.

Hume's razor contends that we do better when we explain a plurality of apparently separate necessities as issuing from, say, a single underlying necessity. By doing so, we improve the explanatory credentials of our theories by showing them to depend, not upon a host of unrelated putative necessities, but to flow from a small range of necessary truths. We should, for example, prefer a theory with fewer axioms to its rivals, other things being equal. In this way, features like elegance and simplicity are closely bound up with Hume's razor. They jointly point in favour of theories that explain disparate necessities in terms of some more minimal range of necessities. For this reason, Humeans need not avow any stringent recombination principle. But, so long as they endorse Hume's razor, they can still take those who proliferate necessities to be poor judges of metaphysical character.

With Hume's razor in hand, we can now mount a modal case against platonism. A first pass might run as follows. Platonism posits the necessary existence of abstract entities, while nominalism avoids this commitment. So, other things being equal, Hume's razor provides grounds to prefer nominalism. Presented with this argument, an initial platonist response is predictable enough: while platonism does require the necessary existence of abstract entities, nominalism requires the necessary nonexistence of abstract entities, so both platonists and nominalists violate Hume's razor. There is, says the platonist, no advantage here for nominalists.

This response makes clear the need for a more careful accounting of posited necessities.[8] A better argument from Hume's razor therefore focuses, not merely on the necessary existence of abstract entities, but on the host of necessary connections platonists allege to hold between abstract entities. And, as noted above, these necessary connections are in vast abundance for platonists. They allegedly connect mathematical entities, properties, and propositions. So, once we note the full variety of necessary connections platonism requires, its offense against Hume's razor far outweighs that of nominalism. Worse still, the explanatory power of platonism is founded upon necessary connections and, in this way, relies explicitly upon what Hume's razor deems vicious in and of itself.

Threatened with Hume's razor, the platonist has two primary options. She can argue that the necessities among abstract entities are somehow unobjectionable and so not vicious like necessary connections among concrete entities. Alternatively, she can argue that, contrary to all appearances, Hume's razor isn't actually violated by the connections among abstract entities.

In the next section, we will explore the second option. Here, the first option warrants only brief comment. Those who pursue this option are likely to insist that abstract entities are so very different from concrete entities that the scope of Hume's razor does not extend out to the abstract realm. A response of this sort will once again place an emphasis on the distinction between the abstract and the concrete, pointing to a profound difference between these two ontological categories. And, while we've seen that platonists can employ primitive abstractness for explanatory ends, this marks a plausible limit to the utility of primitive abstractness. It is, after all, unclear why perfectly general methodological constraints like Hume's razor or Ockham's razor would bear differently on entities precisely because of their ontological category. To be sure, such principles might be outweighed by different principles when applied to different domains, but placing metaphysical restrictions upon their methodological scope seems worryingly *ad hoc*. If, like other theoretical virtues, they are guides to the truth, they are presumably guides to the truth regardless of their respective subject matters. A slightly more plausible platonist response to the argument from Hume's razor rejects such principles outright and does away with appeals to super-empirical theoretical virtues. But, as we've noted throughout preceding chapters, this comes at too steep a methodological cost; one that requires us to disavow much of what we take to be justified in both science and metaphysics. We should, then, keep our razors in hand and set aside platonist's pleas that the abstract realm warrants special treatment when it comes to modality.

Hume's razor provides a good reason to prefer nominalism over platonism provided that platonism cannot do without its myriad necessary connections. So, in the next section, we'll consider whether platonists can do without these necessary connections.

§6.3 Contingent platonism

We've presented two kinds of modal challenges for platonism. The first modal argument, drawing upon (NNE) and (NCA), sought to show that there are no necessary existents and, since abstract entities exist necessarily if at all, there are no abstract entities. The second modal argument appealed to Hume's razor as a way to break the tie between nominalism and platonism. In this section, we will consider whether platonists can admit contingency within the abstract realm and, in doing so, overturn these modal challenges. The extent to which platonists can do so will determine the extent to which each of these modal challenges can be met. If platonists can deny the necessary existence of abstract entities without grave theoretical consequences, the first modal argument can be undermined. In contrast, adequately addressing the argument from Hume's razor requires something far more demanding: platonism must be shown to be consistent and suitably motivated even after necessary connections between abstract entities are rejected. As we'll see, platonists are unlikely to succeed in this second task.

Prior to examining whether platonism and contingency can be reconciled, it is worth once again distinguishing the two kinds of necessities commonly affirmed by platonists. The first and most familiar of these asserts the necessary existence of numbers, properties, and propositions. The second kind of necessities do not require the necessary existence of any entities. They are, instead, necessitated conditionals involving one or more distinct entities.[9] Some examples: necessarily, if the number seven exists, then it has a successor, the number eight; necessarily, if the proposition that exactly three dogs exist is true, the proposition that two dogs exist is true. Both kinds of necessities count against Hume's razor. For, even if one holds that numbers and properties exist only contingently, one must nevertheless admit necessary connections by accepting necessitated conditionals of this second sort. For this reason, affirming the contingent existence of all of abstract reality does not, on its own, dispense with necessities altogether, since necessities of the second sort concern what must be the case were abstract entities like numbers or properties to exist. Granted this distinction between necessities, we can now consider four platonist views about the modal status of abstract reality.

According to *immutabilism*, abstract entities are all necessary existents and the general structure of abstract reality does not vary from world to world. For the immutabilist, abstract reality, unlike concrete reality, is invariant. The stock of mathematical entities, properties, and propositions is therefore fixed and the fundamental relations among abstract entities such as entailment are unchanged across worlds. There are, for instance, no worlds in which *that Socrates is wise* fails to entail *that someone is wise*. That said, since concrete reality varies from world to world, certain relations that abstracta stand in do vary. For example, since there are only some worlds with a blue ox, there are only some worlds where *being blue* and *being an ox* are co-instantiated. By and large, however, immutabilism takes abstract reality to be non-contingent in nature.

The chief rival to immutabilism is *systematic mutabilism*, according to which the existence of certain kinds of abstract entities depends upon specific concrete entities. For example, non-qualitative properties like *being Napoleon*, singular propositions about Napoleon, and the singleton set {Napoleon} are held to depend upon Napoleon. Such entities cannot exist in a world where Napoleon fails exist. But, since Napoleon is a contingently existing entity, systematic mutabilists deny the invariance of abstract reality and allow for *de re* dependencies of certain abstracta upon the concrete realm. Abstract reality therefore varies in a limited and systematic way from world to world but only with respect to abstract entities like haecceities, singular propositions, and impure sets that are parasitic upon concreta. The rest of abstract reality remains fixed and unchanging for the systematic mutabilist. The existence and interrelations among pure sets, general propositions, and qualitative properties are not tied to specific individuals and are therefore invariant across possible worlds.

A third view admits even more widespread contingency into abstract reality. According to *serious mutabilism*, abstract entities exist at only some worlds, but, at any worlds where there are abstract entities, all the immutabilist's alleged connections obtain between properties, propositions, and numbers. So, although abstract entities are not necessary existents, serious mutabilists still admit a host of necessary connections. They merely hold these connections to be necessitated conditionals regarding how the world must be, if abstract entities exist. Intuitively, such a view is the result of simply denying the necessary existence of abstracta, while holding all their fundamental inter-relations to be essential to them.

According to the fourth and final view, *extreme mutabilism*, there are neither necessarily existing abstracta nor necessary connections among abstract entities. Extreme mutabilism therefore eschews all the necessities the immutabilist posits regarding abstracta. For the extreme mutabilist, mathematical and metaphysical relations among abstracta are no more necessary than nomological relations governing the ties between *mass* and *acceleration*. For this reason, there are possible worlds with only a handful of numbers and others where something can instantiate the property of *being a dog* without there being any true proposition, *that something is a dog*. The extreme mutabilist also rejects the systematic dependency of the abstract upon the concrete, admitting worlds in which Napoleon exists without {Napoleon} and perhaps *vice versa*. Accepting such remarkable possibilities comes at no small cost. But, according to extreme mutabilism, these chaotic sorts of worlds are far off in logical space and so quite unlike our orderly actual world with abstracta well-behaved enough to underwrite standard platonist accounts of meaning, truth, and resemblance.

How do these four views about the contingency of abstract reality bear upon the modal challenges to platonism? If any version of mutabilism can be sustained, then platonists can reject (NCA) by pointing out that at least some abstract entities are contingent existents. And, while there are potential challenges for views on which abstract entities like haecceities and singular propositions depend for their existence upon contingency concreta, none seem decisive in undermining systematic mutabilism.[10] Platonists can therefore, in principle, admit at least some contingency among the abstract. So, apart from immutabilists, platonists have reason to reject (NCA). As such, our primary focus will be on the argument from Hume's razor. And, unlike the modal argument premised upon worries about necessary existents, the argument from Hume's razor targets necessary connections of any sort, not merely claims of necessary existence.

Consequently, it can be avoided only by opting for extreme mutabilism, since all other options remain committed to a host of necessary connections whether among abstract entities or between abstract and concrete entities.[11] So, to avoid offending against Hume's razor, all such necessary connections must be dispensed with. The remainder of this section will therefore assess the prospects for the radical contingency extreme mutabilism permits.

For the extreme mutabilist, there are no necessary connections among the abstract, among the concrete, or across the abstract–concrete divide. This opens the door to the possibility of distinct possible worlds, alike in all concrete respects, but which differ with respect to the structure of abstract reality. Suppose, for instance, that in the actual world, your last utterance involved you expressing a proposition. According to extreme mutabilism, there is a distinct possible world, indiscernible in all concrete respects, where this utterance takes place but there is no proposition for you to express. In fact, since extreme mutabilism admits worlds that are indiscernible in concrete respects but radically different with respect to abstract entities, the actual world will have myriad concrete duplicates. At one of these worlds, things are just as the nominalist claims and there are no abstracta whatsoever. At another world, things are just as the platonist claims and there are countless, systematically related abstracta. And, at many others, there is a mish-mash of abstract entities, related in more or less systematic ways. Some have properties, others have properties and propositions, some have only propositions about poutine, and so on.

An initial objection to extreme mutabilism is the charge of outright incredibility. Not implausibly, objectors might dismiss as nonsense such talk about possibilities in which the number seven exists without the number eight or in which some dogs fail to instantiate *being an animal*. These kinds of charges of meaninglessness are, however, notoriously difficult to substantiate. A more refined objection holds that the kind of contingency ascribed to, say, mathematical reality is incoherent since it runs contrary to what we know about the essences of numbers. According to this objection, what it is to be the number seven is to be something that has the number eight as a successor. More generally, this objection contends that numbers and mathematical entities have essences that connect them with other numbers and mathematical entities. So, if we are forced to believe that, at some possible world, the number seven has no successor, this conception of numbers in turn forces us to deny that such an entity is, in fact, the number seven.

Presented with this sort of objection, those who hope to sustain extreme mutabilism seem forced to deny that abstract entities like numbers have distinctive natures or essences that require them to stand in various relations to other numbers. And, if we envision abstract entities as featureless nodes with no interesting intrinsic natures and hold that such entities vary in their number and relations from world to world, the extreme mutabilist can accommodate radical contingency while still conceding that nothing can be the number seven without a successor. This merely requires us to interpret such claims as talk about analogous mathematical structures or structures in which the actual occupant of the "number seven" role occupies some different role. Unfortunately for the extreme mutabilist, this conception of abstract entities as featureless nodes is contrary to what is required by the best views of properties and propositions. For, on those views, properties and propositions are able to play their ascribed explanatory role in virtue of their distinctive intrinsic natures; they are more than merely interchangeable nodes within a structure. (See Section 2.2.5.) The dilemma for extreme mutabilists is therefore the following: how can the platonist make sense of radical contingency in the abstract realm, while retaining a view of abstract entities that can underwrite platonist explanations involving properties and propositions? There is little room for extreme mutabilists to manoeuvre in this regard, so this dilemma is a serious one.

A second objection to extreme mutabilism is still more worrisome. This is because any attempt to sustain extreme mutabilism must forgo the distinctive generality of platonist explanations. As we saw in Chapter 1, some of the best arguments for platonism turn on its capacity to provide perfectly general explanations of phenomena like truth, meaning, and resemblance. But, if platonists are forced into extreme mutabilism, there are worlds where truths obtain, where utterances are meaningful, and where entities resemble one another, but where there are no abstract entities. Any proposed platonist account of laws, causation, and modality would therefore hold only in certain well-behaved platonist worlds. So, while the platonist can claim that what it is for you to be human is for you to instantiate *humanity*, she must also countenance worlds that are alike in all concrete respects, but where you are a human without instantiating *humanity*. If platonism explains phenomena at only certain worlds, it fails to explain the perfectly general phenomena of interest. The worry for extreme mutabilism is, then, that it requires a metaphysics on which abstract entities simply cannot explain the "metaphysical" features of the world that cry out for explanation in the first place.

Faced with worries about worlds that are concrete duplicates but differ with respect to abstract entities, extreme mutabilists might be tempted to claim that abstract reality does, in fact, constrain concrete reality. The extreme mutabilist might claim, for example, that no world can be a concrete duplicate of the actual world if there are no abstract entities like properties or propositions. Unfortunately, this manoeuvre is no real help to the extreme mutabilist. It merely reinstates necessary connections between the abstract and the concrete by holding certain concrete scenarios to be impossible in the absence of certain abstract entities.

Hume's razor pushes platonists towards extreme mutabilism. But, to sustain extreme mutabilism, platonists are forced abandon the theoretical virtues and explanatory power that invite us to believe in platonism in the first place. So, once pushed to extreme mutabilism, platonism is not a theory worth saving. Consequently, those of us who carry Hume's razor in our metaphysical toolboxes ought to prefer nominalism. And, in light of our survey of arguments for nominalism, it seems that this slim but significant consideration offers us the best reason to dispense with abstract entities.

For those who insist that the balance of evidence remains in platonism's favour, Hume's razor still has consequences in deciding among platonist options. Perhaps most importantly, it suggests austere platonism is preferable to its expansive rivals. For, if one retains abstract entities, it should be done begrudgingly, given the abundance of necessary connections they require. And, since opting for expansive platonism requires, not just necessary connections among entities like properties and propositions, but a host of additional necessary connections between the abstract and the concrete, it flagrantly disregards Hume's razor. The expansive platonist will typically hold, for example, that if such-and-such concrete activities are undertaken, then entities like musical works, fictional characters, or sentence types must pop into existence. The largesse of necessary connections expansive platonism demands in accounting for the creatability and destructibility of abstracta makes the modal commitments of austere platonism seem modest in comparison. So, while Humeans should find neither austere nor expansive platonism attractive, if forced to choose one, austerity is once again preferable.[12]

§6.4 Abstracta and actuality

In the next chapter, we'll explore various ways to be a nominalist. Before doing so, let's consider one final challenge to platonism that also revolves around modal issues. This challenge arises when we focus on the connection between the nominalist–platonist debate and a parallel ontological debate between actualists and possibilists. According to possibilists, there are non-actual or "merely possible" entities like the Sino-Canadian suspension bridge or Wittgenstein's twin daughters. And, while these and other *mere possibilia* exist, they do not *actually* exist. For possibilists, reality extends beyond the actual world and includes all possible entities whether actual or non-actual. In contrast, actualists deny the existence of merely possible entities. According to actualism, everything that exists actually exists, so there are no mere possibilia. Put in terms of possible worlds, actualists claim our actual world to exhaust what there is, while possibilists take the actual world to be just one of many. Merely possible worlds and their inhabitants are therefore no less real than you, me, or the Yukon Territory.

When we consider the status of abstract and merely possible entities side-by-side, four "package deals" emerge: platonist actualism, nominalist actualism, platonist possibilism, and nominalist possibilism. The first three of these views have received able and sustained defences in a number of places. Lewisian modal realism—the most familiar version of *platonist possibilism*—is endorsed alongside a platonist metaphysics of sets (and an agnosticism about universals or tropes) in Lewis (1986).[13] *Nominalist actualism* is defended in Field (1989) and elsewhere. And, since nominalists almost universally reject possible worlds, nominalist actualism is standardly assumed to be the sole option for would-be nominalists. The third view (and the one closest to the status of orthodoxy) is *platonist actualism*. According to the platonist actualist, abstract entities like universals and propositions play the theoretical role of possible worlds, but such entities are thought to be actual entities rather than shadowy mere possibilia. The remaining package deal, *nominalist possibilism*, has received little to no sustained attention. And, while we will examine it more closely at the end of Chapter 7, our focus here is an under-appreciated challenge to the internal consistency of actualist platonism. If this challenge cannot be adequately addressed, it threatens to show that platonists are forced into admitting merely possible entities whether they want to or not.[14]

This challenge stems from the following question: are abstract entities actual or merely possible? For platonist possibilists like Lewis, the correct answer will vary depending upon which abstract entities we are interested in. The singleton set of some merely possible individual or an *in re* universal instantiated at only non-actual worlds each seem to be merely possible rather than actual. Conversely, your singleton and the universal *redness* seem plausibly counted as actual entities. Other entities like general propositions, *ante rem* universals, and sets with both actual and merely possible members seem to fall somewhere in between. (For Lewis' views on actuality and existence at a world, see Lewis (1986: 92–96) and (1983b).) Regardless of the correct verdict in these particular cases, Lewis' view suggests that it is a perfectly substantive question which abstracta are actual and which are merely possible. As such, we have no licence to simply assume that abstract entities are, by their very nature, uniformly actual or merely possible. So, in providing a metaphysics of modality, Lewis and others owe us some account of which abstracta are actual and a satisfactory explanation of why this is so. Such an explanation will presumably point to the relevant relations or properties that ensure such entities are correctly held to be part of our actual world.

What, then, should actualists say when asked about the actuality of abstract entities? If, for example, we take Peter Geach's suggestion that abstract entities like numbers are non-actual, platonist actualism looks to be in rather bad shape. Since paradigmatic abstract entities would therefore be mere possibilia, platonism would be in direct violation of actualist doctrine. On this score, Geach (1969: 165) says:

> [T]he objects of mathematics, as we shall see, if they *are* objects, are not actualities. A provisional explanation of actuality may be given thus: *x* is actual if and only if *x* either acts, or undergoes change, or both; and here I count as "acting" both the inner activities of mind, like thinking and planning, and initiation of changes in things.

Although Geach's use of "actual" might not square with its now-familiar usage, the thesis that abstracta are rightly viewed as mere possibilia rather than actual entities can't be rejected out of hand.[15] And, when pressed to account for the actuality of abstract entities, actualists are likely tempted to assert the truth of *analytic actualism*, according to which it is an analytic truth that something is actual if and only if it exists. On such a view, actuality and existence would therefore be coextensive as a matter of conceptual necessity, so no substantive explanation is needed nor can be given for why abstract entities are actual.

Unfortunately for platonist actualists, analytic actualism is implausible. We need only point out that, if analytic actualism were true, possibilism in any form would be conceptually incoherent. But, whether true or false, possibilism is perfectly intelligible even if highly controversial. There is therefore no reason to be content with analytic actualism. So, the question of why abstract entities are actual rather than merely possible remains unanswered. Platonist actualists therefore still owe some account of what unifies entities within a possible world and accounts for their actuality.

For possibilists like Lewis, an account of actuality proceeds by specifying the conditions under which entities are "worldmates" of one another. This worldmate relation is then spelled out in terms of spatiotemporal relatedness, where entities are worldmates of one another, and therefore co-actual, if and only if each part of one is spatiotemporally related to each part of the other.[16] On such a view, facts about what entities are actual or co-actual are reduced to facts about spatiotemporal relatedness.[17] But, if abstract entities are non-spatiotemporal, it looks as though they are, of necessity, merely possible. Platonist actualists cannot therefore appropriate the possibilist account of actuality; they require an alternative account of what unifies the actual world and thereby fixes whether abstracta are actual or merely possible.

The best available option for platonist actualists is to supplement the spatiotemporal account of actuality by holding certain "metaphysically special" relations like *membership*, *instantiation*, and *obtaining* to account for the actuality of abstracta like impure sets, instantiated properties, and true propositions. If properties are actual in virtue of being instantiated, singletons are actual in virtue having concrete entities as members, and propositions are actual in virtue of obtaining, platonist actualists can explain the actuality of at least these abstracta. (Of course, if such entities are spatiotemporally located, this would be another way to account for their actuality.) And, while this proposal delivers a favourable verdict in these cases, the actuality of other abstracta remains unaccounted for. Worse still, there are no non-*ad hoc* relations like *membership*, *instantiation*, and *obtaining* that might explain the actuality of other abstract entities like pure sets, uninstantiated universals, and false propositions. Since these and other abstracta are not tethered to concrete reality by any fundamental relations, there is no natural strategy for explaining why such entities are rightly deemed actual rather than merely possible.

All this leaves platonist actualists in an awkward position. Since no non-*ad hoc* account of what makes abstract entities uniformly actual is available, the platonist who hopes to avoid possibilism might be forced to prune back her abstract commitments in keeping with the best available account of what it is to be actual. She might, for example, be forced to deny the existence of uninstantiated properties and false propositions, but such efforts to satisfy the letter of actualism seem plainly *ad hoc*. There is a puzzle, then, about how platonist actualism can be sustained once we note that there is no reason to think that abstract entities are, by their very nature, actual rather than merely possible entities. There is therefore no corresponding reason to think that platonism enjoys any built-in compatibility with actualism. On the contrary, actualists must either provide a plausible account of the distinction between the actual and the merely possible or surrender any claimed superiority over possibilism. The latter option weakens platonism's claim to being a "safe and sane" metaphysics in accord with ordinary intuitions. The former is quite likely to require a higher theoretical cost than platonist actualists typically acknowledge, whether by limiting which abstracta can be admitted or by requiring the platonist to take the divide between the actual and the merely possible as fundamental.

Summary

This chapter examined modal objections to platonism which take issue with the alleged necessary existence of and necessary connections between abstract entities. These objections include arguments against admitting any necessary existents whatsoever and Humean arguments premised upon stringent recombination principles. The strongest nominalist argument against abstract entities was shown to rely upon Hume's razor, which cautions against positing gratuitous necessary connections just as Ockham's razor cautions against gratuitous ontology. After arguing that platonists are in no position to abandon the abundant necessities their theory requires, a final puzzle about the actuality of abstract entities was briefly presented.

Recommended reading

The modal status of platonism is closely examined in Rosen (2002, 2006). On nominalism and the contingency of mathematical entities see Yablo (2002), Field (1989: 167), Rosen (1993), and Hale and Wright (2001).

The recent debate over the subtraction argument begins with Baldwin (1996); though see Paseau (2006), Cameron (2006), and Rodriguez-Pereyra (1997, 2013) for subsequent contributions.

The resurgence of Humean views of modality that reject necessary connections owes largely to Lewis (1986). On Humeanism, see Armstrong (1978: 49), Forrest (2001), and Wilson (2015). On formulating principles of plenitude, see Bricker (1991), Nolan (1996), and Efird and Stoneham (2008). Dorr (2008) presents a Humean argument against platonism that relies upon a strict prohibition against necessary connections. See also MacBride (2005c). See Whittle (2010) for a response.

Questions about the nature of actuality are posed in Adams (1974). On the isolation and unification of possible worlds, see Lewis (1986: 92–96) and Bricker (1996). On the challenges in defining and defending actualism and possibilism, see Bennett (2005, 2006), Bricker (2006), Divers (2002), Lewis (1986), and Williamson (2013). Representative versions of platonist actualism include Adams (1981), van Inwagen (1986), Jubien (2009), Menzel (1990), and Stalnaker (2011).

Notes

1 Recent discussions typically use "metaphysical nihilism" to name the thesis that there could be no concrete objects whatsoever. To avoid confusion, we will call the thesis that there could be no objects at all, whether abstract or concrete, "absolute metaphysical nihilism."
2 On the notion of metaphysical modality and some challenges to the orthodox view of what is metaphysically necessary, see Rosen (2006) and Cheyne (1998). For a dissenting view, see Field (1989: 38–45).
3 Logicists are liable to have a rather different view in this regard for, if mathematical truths are logical ones, then, since there are existential mathematical truths, mathematical entities would seem to exist of logical necessity. Much here turns on the details of one's preferred brand of logicism.
4 Such a principle must also allow us to move from infinite domains (e.g., the natural numbers) to finite domains and, eventually, to empty domains. Here, we will set aside the serious complications that come with applying the subtraction principle to pluralities or sets of entities rather than concrete objects. See Paseau (2006) for discussion.
5 The relevant notion of distinctness is not mere numerical distinctness. It is the notion of "mereological distinctness" according to which entities share no parts in common. So, for example, the Humean allows that, necessarily, if there is a duplicate of you in some world, there is a duplicate of your head. This is consistent with "no necessary connections between distinct existences" because you have your head as a part.
6 For Lewis, claims about recombination are not *de re* claims: they do not require that one and the same combinatorial unit exist at different possible worlds. Instead, the principle of recombination is to be understood in terms of duplicates of individuals. Lewis (1986: 89) says: "It is right to formulate our principle of recombination in terms of similarity. It should

say, for instance, that there is a world where something like the dragon coexists with something like the unicorn . . . I should say that a *duplicate* of the dragon and a *duplicate* of the unicorn coexist at some world . . .."

7 Along with using recombination principles to defend Humean views about the laws of nature, Lewis relies upon the denial of necessary connections to argue against certain abstract entities—most notably, abstract states of affairs. See Lewis (1998).

8 "Counting" and comparing necessities or necessary connections posited by nominalists and platonists will not involve comparing their sheer number, since any familiar theory will take on commitment to a vast plurality of necessities merely by accepting mundane necessary logical truths (e.g., necessarily, if dogs bark, then dogs bark).

9 Platonists might attempt to show that the necessary connections in question are unobjectionable, since abstract entities are not, in fact, distinct, but, instead, have one another as parts. Such a strategy might succeed in limited cases—e.g., on some views, the proposition that red is a colour has the property *redness* as a part. (Notably, such views likely require non-mereological composition, which some have argued likely requires objectionable necessary connections. See Lewis (1986b).) In vastly many other cases, there are no plausible claims of overlap, so, unless platonists are willing to ascribe a remarkable mereological structure to abstract reality, their commitment to necessary connections remains objectionable.

10 Typically, these challenges revolve around negative existentials and how we might think or speak about entities that do not exist, especially when the standard explanation of thinking or speaking about entities involves singular propositions or haecceities. For discussion, see Plantinga (1983), Fine (1985), and Williamson (1998).

11 As Rosen (1993: 154) notes, in explaining the ambitions of neo-Fregean views, "We need an account of this necessary connection [between the concrete and the abstract], some way of understanding how it could possibly hold . . . . And so long as one thinks of impure sets as abstract objects in accord with the picture, this remains a mystery."

12 For worries about vagueness stemming from the creatability of abstracta, see Korman (2014).

13 See, also, Bricker (2006) and Rodriguez-Pereyra (2002).

14 Bealer (1993: 7) grants the force of arguments for both nominalism and possibilism, but endorses the conditional claim that "if actualism is

correct, so is *ante rem* [platonism]." For Bealer and others, lapsing into possibilism would therefore undermine the case for *ante rem* platonism.

15 Some defeasible evidence for taking Geach's use of "actuality" at terminological face value rather than treating his use of "actual" as synonymous with "concrete": he distinguishes these notions in speaking of "actual concrete objects" (1960: 165).

16 Lewis (1986) notes at least two concerns with such views. First, some possible worlds might be unified by "analogically spatiotemporal relations," which are similar to but distinct from spatiotemporal relations, or perhaps other external relations that aren't even *analogically* spatiotemporal. Second, some accept the possibility of worlds including spatiotemporally disconnected "island universes," which are ruled out by a spatiotemporal theory of actuality. I set aside these complications and qualifications here. See Bricker (1996) for discussion.

17 A notable exception are possibilist views that take the actual–merely possible distinction to be fundamental and posit a fundamental property, *being actual*, that only some entities instantiate. See Bricker (2006).

7

NOMINALIST OPTIONS

7.1 Nominalisms
7.2 Meaning
7.3 Truth
7.4 Commitment
7.5 Harvard nominalism revisited

§7.1 Nominalisms

This chapter provides an overview of nominalist strategies for making sense of discourse that apparently involves abstract entities. Since any metaphysical view that dispenses with abstract entities qualifies as a version of nominalism, this overview makes no claim to being an exhaustive survey. After all, nominalism could be combined with a vast range of disparate metaphysical views like idealism and solipsism. And, in addition to the options we will consider, there are myriad hybrid views that seek to "mix and match" different nominalist strategies in different domains (e.g., by treating discourse about numbers and propositions differently). Rather than cataloguing all possible options, our project is to canvas the leading versions of nominalism in an effort to see how they preserve the nominalist's "desert landscape" ontology. Our partial assessment of nominalist options is therefore primarily aimed at extracting some general lessons for would-be nominalists. I will, however, conclude by suggesting that the case for a heterodox view, nominalist possibilism, is stronger than commonly acknowledged.

The space of nominalist options can be divided up in many different ways. According to the taxonomy we'll employ, nominalist options are distinguished by their answers to three kinds of questions about claims that apparently involve abstract entities. (Here, I intend "claim" in a way neutral between beliefs and utterances, though one could, in principle, treat these quite differently.) Consider, once again, the following bits of what we will call *platonist discourse*—roughly, claims apparently involving abstract entities:

(1) There is a prime number between seven and twelve.

(2) Humility is a virtue that Xiao and Luis have in common.

(3) The meaning of "Dogs bark" is different than the meaning of "Cats bark."

The three kinds of questions we will use to divide up the space of nominalist options are as follows: (i) *Meaning*. Are these claims and other bits of "platonist discourse" meaningful? More specifically, are they descriptive claims or do they serve some non-descriptive semantic function? Additionally, are they put forward literally or figuratively in a way similar to metaphors? (ii) *Truth*. Are these claims true? If not, are they somehow specially related to some other body of true claims? (iii) *Commitment*. Does the truth of these claims require the existence of abstract entities? If not, how can the truth of these claims be reconciled with the fact that there are no abstracta?

Since most platonists affirm that claims like (1)–(3) are true, meaningful, intended literally, and committed to the existence of abstract entities, nominalists must somehow depart from the platonist's preferred answers to the above questions. And, in carving up the space of nominalist strategies, the precise point of departure from the platonist's preferred answers plays an absolutely critical role. For this reason, we will use the questions above to distinguish various strands of nominalism and to structure our survey. We will begin with radical versions of nominalism that deny platonist discourse is meaningful or put forward literally. We will then consider views that deny such claims are true and, in some cases, downplay this violence to commonsense by holding them to be specially related to certain nominalist-friendly truths. We will then assess nominalist strategies that uphold the truth and meaningfulness of these claims but deny that their truth requires a commitment to abstracta. Finally, we will conclude by exploring two outlying views and their connection to the peculiar doctrine of Harvard nominalism once jointly defended by Goodman and Quine.

§7.2 Meaning

Faced with discourse about entities one deems impossible, a kneejerk reaction is to reject the relevant discourse as meaningless. So, just as one might (understandably) be inclined to dismiss vast swathes of New Age spiritualism as meaningless, radical nominalists who view abstracta as occult creatures might allege claims like (1)–(3) to be meaningless or without "cognitive content." The resulting *non-cognitivist nominalism* expands the semantic naysaying of verificationists who deny the meaningfulness of discourse about the normative and the supernatural. But, where familiar versions of verificationism take mathematical claims to be meaningful though trivial, the non-cognitivist nominalist contends that mathematics, along with other claims involving abstract entities, is also semantically defective.

Non-cognitivist nominalism enjoys no serious plausibility. According to any remotely familiar standard of meaningfulness, claims like (1)–(3) pass with flying colours. So, either some rarefied sense of "meaning" is intended or the non-cognitivist nominalist is content to disregard our ordinary standards of meaningfulness. Setting aside the latter, less tenable option, there is little to like about the former. Even if claims like (1)–(3) are meaningless in some rarefied theoretical sense, they remain meaningful by ordinary standards. And, to the extent that they are meaningful by ordinary standards, nominalists still face the familiar challenge of explaining this meaningfulness without appeal to abstract entities. Non-cognitivist nominalists therefore gain no theoretical ground by denying the meaningfulness of these claims in only some rarefied sense, since the problems that arise for making sense of their "ordinary" meaningfulness remain and provide the same incentive for positing abstracta.

Although nominalists ought to grant that platonist discourse is meaningful, this leaves open the precise nature of their meaning. One nominalist option is to hold that these claims, while meaningful, are not representational and so not the sorts of claims that admit of truth or falsity. Instead, their meaningfulness is bound up with their cognitive role as tools for prediction and manipulation. This roughly instrumentalist strand of nominalism alleges that talk about abstract entities possesses only non-representational content.[1] (I say "roughly" here, since various conceptions of instrumentalism will qualify as non-cognitivist, depending on background assumptions about the nature of content.) The meaning of claims like (1)–(3) would therefore differ markedly from the meaning of superficially similar claims about concrete entities. For example, where pedestrian claims about concrete entities serve as literal descriptions of the world, *instrumentalist nominalism* holds that claims invoking abstract entities serve a non-representational semantic role. They function primarily as tools for the manipulation and prediction of phenomena or as "instruments" for systematizing our discourse about concrete entities. And, while meaningful representational claims can be assessed for their truth or falsity, the instrumentalist nominalist holds that claims apparently involving abstract entities are only properly assessed for their efficacy, expediency, and reliability much as we might assess instruments like telescopes and spectrometers.[2] So, while these claims are meaningful in some rather broad sense, they are without any representational much less truth-evaluable content.

Instrumentalist nominalism is an improvement over non-cognitivist nominalism. Rightly, it denies that platonist discourse is nonsense. And, in holding these claims to occupy an important though non-representational cognitive role in inference and prediction, the instrumentalist seeks to do justice to their apparent indispensability. It is, however, simply implausible to treat these claims in such marked contrast with parallel claims about concrete entities and to deny claims like (1)–(3) represent (or misrepresent) the world. If these claims were so radically different in content, we would presumably detect their differences through semantic and inferential connections. But, we seem able to speak univocally and coherently when, in the same breath, we say that numbers and geese exist or that goodness and gold coins are valuable. We also seem justified in inferring that more than two things exist if the number seven, *goodness*, and a goose exist. In these cases, our inferences and utterances suggest that claims like (1)–(3) are semantically comparable with ordinary claims about concrete entities. The alleged disanalogies in meaning that instrumentalist nominalism requires are therefore untenable.

For nominalists who suspect something is fishy about the meaning of platonist discourse, the best option is one that departs from the platonist view by denying claims like (1)–(3) are put forward literally. Instead, the *figurative nominalist* holds that claims of this kind are put forward non-literally or figuratively, in a manner comparable to metaphors. (On such views, see Yablo (2001, 2005).) So, where instrumentalist nominalists assimilate claims like (1)–(3) to mere instruments in explaining their cognitive value, the figurative nominalist assimilates these claims to metaphors and other figurative expressions. And, although one could in principle assert these claims literally, the figurative nominalist holds them to be standardly put forward in the manner of claims about butterflies in our stomach or frogs in our throat.

The suggestion that mathematical and other kinds of platonist discourse are advanced in a spirit comparable to metaphors is a surprising one. In part, this is because we are inclined to assume that we are mostly aware of the literal or figurative status of our utterances. Upon closer scrutiny, however, there is ample reason to view much of our thought and talk as unwittingly figurative. Perfectly ordinary claims about leaks within the White House and common metaphors regarding Italy being a boot are at least partly figurative, although we naturally slide into them without detecting the shift from the literal to the figurative. There is therefore no compelling argument from our naïve introspective judgments for the literal rather than figurative status of our rather peculiar talk about properties, propositions, and possible worlds. Moreover, the figurative nominalist can point to metaphors as a ready example of figurative content that has a cognitive role independent of its truth-value, since metaphors serve their communicative and cognitive function in spite of their literal falsehood (or lack of truth-value). For example, in claiming that Michigan is a mitten, one speaks falsely, but nevertheless successfully communicates that the shape of Michigan is in rough correspondence with the shape of a mitten. So, where instrumentalist nominalism requires an untenable and unfamiliar story about how theories and claims might function like instruments, figurative nominalists are in a far better position. They can draw upon the rich and ordinary phenomenon of metaphors and other non-literal claims aiding our cognitive efforts.

The view that platonist discourse is put forward figuratively is, in principle, orthogonal to the ontological disagreement between nominalists and platonists. One could, for example, endorse the view that mathematical discourse is figurative in root and branch, while remaining agnostic about whether there are abstract entities. But, for nominalists who believe there is antecedent reason to reject abstract entities, the viability of a figurative construal of platonist discourse offers a welcome option. Moreover, those who believe such discourse is figurative can appeal to features of metaphor to explain some peculiar features of discourse apparently about abstracta. As Yablo (2002: 229) argues, the value of platonist discourse, like metaphor, does not depend on "conceiving of its referential-looking elements as genuinely standing for anything." On such a view, numbers are akin to stomach-butterflies and "[s]tomach-butterflies are representational aids. They are 'things' that we advert to not (not at first, anyway) out of any interest in what they are like in themselves, but because of the help they give us in describing other things. Their importance lies in the way they boost the language's expressive power."[3]

Deference to theoretical conservatism and to the apparent significance of truth as a standard for evaluating platonist discourse suggests that, other things be equal, we ought to prefer a literal construal of it. Not only would a literal interpretation of mathematics and other abstracta-involving discourse square with our ordinary judgments about this domain, figurative nominalism also faces two other challenges in adequately explaining platonist discourse and its remarkable usefulness.

The first challenge is to explain why putative discourse about *all* abstract entities rather than about just *some* putative abstract entities is figurative. Why, after all, should we think that absolutely all claims involving abstracta are put forward figuratively rather than literally? For those who take the case for a figurative construal of discourse about abstracta to be independent of the case for nominalism, this issue need not arise. But, for nominalists hoping to make sense of platonist discourse like claims (1)–(3) in this way, the perfect alignment of the putatively abstract with the figurative is a remarkable fact that calls for explanation.

The second challenge is to explain why we are in a position to endorse nominalism and platonism as substantive, literal assertions about the world if we also have reason to believe that platonist discourse is ultimately figurative in nature. For those inclined to methodological panic, a lurking worry is that, by holding mathematical and other platonist claims to be merely metaphorical, we place ourselves in a poor position to resist a Nietzschean conception of truth on which "Truth is a mobile army of metaphors, metonyms, anthropomorphisms, in short a sum of human relations which have been subjected to poetic and rhetorical intensification, translation and decoration." Put differently: by holding what seems to be literal discourse to be covertly figurative in nature, figurative nominalists face increasing pressure to explain how metaphysical theses—e.g., regarding nominalism or platonism—could themselves be literally true.

Ultimately, these concerns fall short of supplying a reason to reject figurative nominalism outright. And, while there is no conclusive argument against the possibility of a figurative construal of discourse involving abstract entities, our deference to theoretical conservatism does suggest that, other things being equal, we ought to prefer a literal construal of platonist discourse. Not only would such an account square with our ordinary intuitions regarding truth and meaning, it handily avoids the just-noted challenges for figurative nominalism.

For nominalists who depart from platonism by denying standard assumptions about the meaning of claims like (1)–(3), three views suggest themselves: (i) non-cognitivist nominalism, which implausibly denies these claims are meaningful; (ii) instrumentalist nominalism, which denies these claims are representational but holds them to be meaningful insofar as they aid in our efforts to manipulate and predict phenomena; and (iii) figurative nominalism, which denies platonist discourse is put forward to literally describe the world. Of these options, figurative nominalism is the most plausible departure from platonism, since the cognitive value of metaphor provides an attractive starting point for explaining the value of discourse regarding abstract entities. That said, we will now turn to nominalist views on which claims like (1)–(3) are meaningful, descriptive, and put forward literally, but false even so.

§7.3 Truth

The most awkward moment in a typical exchange between a nominalist and a platonist comes when the platonist inquires about the truth of claims like (1)–(3) and other bits of platonist discourse. In the eyes of the platonist, no nominalist response is a comforting one. If the nominalist says these claims are true, the platonist will find it wildly implausible that their truth can be reconciled with the alleged nonexistence of abstract entities. If, however, the nominalist says these claims are false, the platonist will balk at the audacity of denying claims so readily assumed in everyday discourse.

A common nominalist strategy for meeting the concerns of the platonist is to offer some paraphrase of claims (1)–(3) and thereby secure the best of both worlds. According to one version of what we will loosely label as *paraphrase nominalism*, such claims are true but synonymous with nominalistically acceptable claims that require no commitment to abstract entities. For example, the paraphrase nominalist takes the claim "Two is the number of solar gas giants" to be true, but synonymous with the claim "There is a solar gas giant x and a solar gas giant y and, if anything is a solar gas giant it is identical to x or y and x is distinct from y." Since the latter claim requires no commitment to abstract entities, the paraphrase nominalist maintains that its adequacy as a paraphrase negates any obligation to posit abstract entities even while we are still permitted to accept the former claim or, on some views, hold it to be true.[4]

As usually understood, paraphrase nominalism faces a serious problem most clearly set out in Alston (1958). This problem hinges on the requirements for adequacy in paraphrase. If we require that the "target claim" to be paraphrased—here, claims invoking abstract entities—and its nominalist paraphrase be synonymous, the truth of one will entail the truth of the other. According to the paraphrase nominalist, the truth of the target claim does not, however, require commitment to abstract entities, given the availability of a suitable paraphrase. But, if we believe the truth of the target claim, when left without a paraphrase, requires commitment to abstract entities, why think that producing a synonymous claim somehow obviates our commitment to abstracta? Why, for example, should we think that our commitments "boil down" to those of the paraphrase rather than "inflate" with the target claim, which does seem committed to the number two? Put a bit differently: the worry is that, given the requirement of synonymy, there is no compelling rationale for accepting only the ontological commitments of the paraphrase rather than the synonymous target claim. For, in light of their synonymy, the truth of the paraphrase seems to require abstract entities no less than the target claim.[5]

This problem suggests that paraphrase nominalists cannot take synonymy as a criterion of adequacy for paraphrase. So, to avoid the problem at hand, it looks as though paraphrase nominalists require a more radical stance. They must hold that the target claims invoking abstract entities are false even while the nominalist paraphrases are true. And, in order, to avoid the worry above, paraphrase nominalists must relax the requirements for adequacy in paraphrase by denying the target and its paraphrase are synonymous. But, if synonymy is not our criterion for adequacy in paraphrase, what might serve as a replacement criterion?

This leaves paraphrase nominalists with two subsidiary challenges. They must provide plausible criteria of adequacy for serving as a suitable paraphrase. And, after supplying these criteria, they must actually provide suitable paraphrases for all the platonist discourse we ordinarily take to be true.[6] Neither task is an easy one. For, as we've seen in previous chapters, an ontology of sets, properties, and propositions provides remarkable gains in our capacity to express information. So, if we must dispense with quantification over these entities, it is far from obvious that we can successfully paraphrase away each and every seemingly true claim about abstracta. It seems, then, that the ambitions of paraphrase nominalism can be met only after we depart significantly from the initial thought that providing synonymous paraphrases would allow us to wiggle out of unwanted ontological commitments. Worse still, such a view no longer allows the nominalist to grant the truth of platonist discourse while avoiding any clash with face-value ordinary judgments.

The parameters of paraphrase nominalism get murky at this point. A nearby option, which we can call *replacement nominalism*, is worth making explicit here, regardless of whether it is properly counted as a paraphrase strategy. The replacement nominalist concedes that there is a uniquely apt platonist interpretation of claims like (1)–(3), but, on this most eligible interpretation, such claims are false since there are no abstracta. The replacement nominalist holds, however, that these claims can be systematically replaced with some nominalistically acceptable claims that suffice for relevant theoretical purposes. The replacement nominalist therefore holds that platonist discourse, as properly interpreted, is false, but still seeks to provide a suitable body of discourse as a replacement. A suitable replacement will, among other things, mirror the systematic inferential connections exhibited by platonist discourse. It will also mirror the assignment of truth-values that we typically ascribe to the target claims. So, although replacement nominalism does not uphold the truth of claims like (1)–(3), it supplies true surrogate claims intended to mitigate the clash of nominalism with our ordinary judgments.

To get a sense of what replacement nominalism looks like in practice, it will be useful to briefly sketch two examples of how it might be implemented. We will therefore quickly outline a fictionalist version of replacement nominalism which replaces claims about abstract entities with claims about what is true according to certain fictions. We'll then present a version of modal structuralism which pursues the same goal but uses modal claims as the intended replacements.

§7.3.1 *Replacement nominalisms*

As we saw above, figurative nominalism holds that claims like (1)–(3) and the rest of platonist discourse are put forward non-literally. Given the ties between metaphor and fiction, it should come as little surprise that some nominalists have argued that platonist discourse is properly viewed as fictional discourse. Claims (1)–(3) are, on such a view, akin to "fictional claims" like "Aquaman is king of Atlantis."[7] This is because fictional claims and platonist discourse are both, strictly speaking, false, although there are nearby claims about what is true "according to a fiction" that seem uncontroversially true. For, while "Smiley is suspicious" is false, the suitably prefixed claim, "According to *Call for the Dead*, Smiley is suspicious," is true. A fictionalist version of replacement nominalism therefore concedes that claims like (1)–(3) are false, but holds such claims to admit of systematic replacement with claims covertly "prefixed" or "prefaced" with qualifications like "According to the fiction of mathematics . . . ." or "According to the fiction that properties exist . . .." By doing so, fictionalist replacement nominalism allows us to retain useful discourse about properties and propositions. We need only recognize that, left unsupplemented, such claims are literally false, but, when made "within" a fiction, they might be true and of theoretical value.

For replacement nominalists of this fictionalist stripe, our intuitive judgments about the truth-value of platonist discourse and claims like (1)–(3) are systematically unreliable, but this unreliability admits of a simple explanation. We have a natural tendency to conflate false "unprefixed" claims about fictions and fictitious entities with counterpart claims about what is true "within" or according to a given fiction. As such, the truth-values we incline to assign to the latter are mistakenly assigned to the former. Our intuition that "Seven is prime" is true therefore owes to our systematic conflation of that claim with its counterpart and suitable replacement, "According to the fiction of standard mathematics, seven is prime."

This fictionalist version of replacement nominalism takes seriously the idea that abstract entities are useful or expedient fictions. And, in this respect, it enjoys some support from the cognitive benefits of phenomena such as idealization, which plays a notable role in our scientific practices. Despite this, it is unclear whether invoking fictions is a consistent way to sustain the thesis of nominalism. Among other concerns, many leading views about the nature of fiction take our discourse pertaining to fiction to commit us to abstract entities, whether in the form of propositions, fictions, or fictional characters. So, unless a plausible account of the semantics and metaphysics of fiction can be given without appealing to abstract entities, using the framework of fictionalism to avoid abstract entities looks to be self-defeating. If, however, a genuinely nominalist account of our talk about fictions and what is true according to them can be given, fictionalism of this sort is a noteworthy option for replacement nominalists.

Let's now consider a second version of replacement nominalism, which relies upon modal rather than fictional claims to replace our talk that is apparently about abstracta.

Worries about the finitude of the world are standardly assumed to scotch the prospects for nominalist views that would paraphrase mathematical claims in terms of claims about concrete objects. After all, our world might turn out to be one with only finitely many concrete objects. And, even if there were infinitely many such objects, a smaller world is surely possible, so we seem left with a strange view on which the truth of mathematics is contingent upon how many eels or electrons there are. The good news for replacement nominalists is that, if we seek to replace our talk about abstracta with modal claims, worries about the possible finitude of the world are irrelevant, since we can be guaranteed that *some* possible world is infinite. For the *modal structuralist* who pursues this replacement strategy, our mathematical claims are to be replaced with claims regarding the many ways the world could have been.[8] On such a view, mathematics ultimately concerns possible structures of the world, not some domain of actually existing concrete or abstract entities. And since modal structuralism is typically paired with a modalism which rejects possible worlds, it employs only the primitive ideology of modality (and some higher-order logic) to provide an ontologically lean surrogate for mathematics. For, on modal structuralism, "ordinary mathematical statements are construed as elliptical for hypothetical statements as to what would hold in any structure of the appropriate type."[9]

Presented schematically, modal structuralism has two key components. The first component asserts the possibility of certain structures—e.g., by claiming that, possibly, there are some entities that satisfy certain conditions like the Peano axioms. The second component asserts that certain truths *must* hold of these possible structures. So, for a given arithmetic sentence S, necessarily, if some entities satisfy the relevant axioms, S is true of the relevant structure. Intuitively, these two components entail that the relevant arithmetical structures could exist and that, so long as they satisfy the intended constraints (e.g., the Peano axioms), our familiar arithmetical claims must be true of them. And, since these are modal theses, they can serve as replacements of platonist discourse regardless of whether such structures actually exist.

We will briefly revisit modal structuralism later in this chapter, but two concerns about the view are worth noting here. First, given the richness of our modal discourse, the rejection of possible worlds, whether as actually-existing abstract entities or as concrete possible worlds, leaves the modal structuralist poorly positioned to make sense of much of our modal discourse.[10] When presented with claims like "There could have been more things than there actually are and none of which actually exist," modalists seem forced to expand the ideology of modality with novel operators. But the result is either a bloated modal ideology or a formalism that cries out to be interpreted via possible worlds. Second, even if modal structuralism yields adequate surrogates for mathematical discourse, it is not clear how this replacement strategy can be extended to provide a replacement for the metaphysics of properties and propositions. It is also unclear how certain of its logical resources—most notably, higher-order quantification—can be reconciled with a nominalist opposition to properties and relations. So, unlike fictionalist replacement nominalism, modal structuralism seems to admit of no clear-cut extension beyond the case of distinctively mathematical abstracta.

We've briefly introduced two ways to develop replacement nominalism—one using fictions, the other using modality. Each seeks to downplay the cost of holding claims like (1)–(3) to be false. In the next section, we'll consider a different way to divide up nominalist options and a dilemma that stems from the resulting division.

§7.3.2 *Hermeneutics and revolutionaries*

Building upon Burgess (1983), Burgess and Rosen (1997, 2005) divide nominalists into two general camps: *revolutionary nominalists* and *hermeneutic nominalists*. According to revolutionaries, when it comes to defending nominalism "the goal is reconstruction or revision: the production of novel mathematical and scientific theories to replace current theories." (Burgess and Rosen (1997: 6)) Nominalist alternatives are therefore offered as superior replacements of presently accepted theories that are errantly committed to abstract entities. In contrast, hermeneutic nominalism maintains that "the nominalist disbelief in numbers and their ilk is in the fullest sense compatible with belief in current mathematics and science." (Burgess and Rosen (1997: 6)) So, for hermeneuticists, our presently accepted theories are already nominalistically acceptable, since commitment to them doesn't require belief in abstract entities in the first place.

Whether one chooses the revolutionary or hermeneutic option, Burgess and Rosen claim the resulting nominalism will be untenable. They hold the implausibility of hermeneutic nominalism to issue from its immodest semantic thesis that claims like (1)–(3) are fully compatible with nominalism.[11] Not only does this hermeneutic thesis run contrary to standard interpretations of platonist discourse, it alleges that platonists are mistakenly "fundamentalist, taking literally what was never so meant."[12] This is no small allegation and to platonists and many nominalists it will seem to be a flatly incredible semantic hypothesis. If true, it would require something no less remarkable than what the figurative nominalist contends when she claims that mathematics is put forward as something broadly metaphorical. And, if such a remarkable claim is to be made plausible, hermeneutic nominalists would have to overcome a significant burden of proof by marshalling a wealth of linguistic evidence in its favour.

If we reject hermeneutic nominalism, we seem saddled with revolutionary nominalism. But, if nominalist views are intended to be rival alternatives to our current mathematical or scientific theories, we require some account of the standards for evaluating these alternatives. For naturalists, the only legitimate standards are those of our scientific or mathematical communities. But this delivers a high bar that nominalism is unlikely to meet. For example, if nominalist alternatives prove cumbersome, inelegant, or contrary to received scientific wisdom, the standards of science and mathematics have little reason to prefer them to prevailing platonist theories that traffic in abstracta. And, since the motivation for nominalist alternatives is the avoidance of abstracta, such theories will almost certainly require additional complexity and departures from orthodoxy that are motivated only by extra-scientific, metaphysical considerations—considerations that count for nothing in the eyes of the naturalist. According to the naturalist, failure of nominalist alternatives to outperform extant mathematical and scientific theories requires such proposals be rejected. Revolutionary nominalism therefore leaves little to no room for a commitment to naturalism.

If Burgess and Rosen are right, revolutionary and hermeneutic proposals exhaust the space of nominalist options. And, if neither is defensible, we are forced to abandon nominalism. As Burgess (1983: 101) puts this point:

> [T]he philosopher who wishes to argue for nominalism faces a dilemma. He must search for evidence for an implausible hypothesis in linguistics, or else for motivation for a costly revolution in physics. Neither horn seems very promising, and that is why I am not a nominalist.

A successful response to the above dilemma would show either that the revolutionary–hermeneutic distinction is not exhaustive or that one of the two options fares better than Burgess and Rosen claim. Setting the prospects for revolutionary and hermeneutic nominalism aside, nominalists would therefore welcome the availability of some third alternative that skirts the obstacles noted above. To this end, some nominalists have argued that there is a viable alternative that is neither hermeneutic nor revolutionary in spirit.[13] In this vein, Hellman (2001a: 703) says:

> [N]ominalistic *reconstructions* need be neither hermeneutical nor revolutionary but can be—and in most of the cases in question are—*preservationist* while attempting to solve or avoid certain epistemological, metamathematical, or metascientific problems not (or not yet) treated within science itself. . . . *Of course*, natural science takes mathematics for granted and uses it opportunistically without questioning its foundation or its interpretation. But this suggests to me that it does not worry about how to interpret mathematics *at all*, not that it accepts in any considered way a face-value, literal, platonist *reading* of mathematics . . . . Nominalism has no wish to interfere with scientific or mathematical practice. Its interests lie elsewhere.[14] (Italics from original.)

Preservationist nominalism of the sort Hellman describes seeks to avoid conflict with scientific practice. In large part, whether it can do so depends upon the claim that our best scientific theories are silent, in any epistemically significant sense, about the matters over which nominalists and platonists disagree. If this is correct, the preservationist might be able to reasonably account for the usefulness and nature of mathematical discourse in a way that eschews the existence of abstracta. But is it plausible that science is, in fact, silent on the existence of mathematical entities?

There is, I think, ample evidence that our best scientific theories do take a peculiar stance towards mathematical commitments. Consider, for instance, mathematicians' striking indifference regarding the intrinsic nature of numbers. In almost any other scientific domain, the intrinsic nature and non-formal features of entities are of profound interest and sustained investigation. It is surprising, then, that mathematicians are perfectly capable of engaging in their practice in either total disinterest or utter ignorance about where mathematical entities are and what, if any, intrinsic features they possess (e.g., whether they have parts). In fact, these very questions about the entities at the disciplinary heart of mathematics seem to fall outside the purview of standard mathematical inquiry. They seem, instead, squarely within the province of philosophy.

The peculiarity of mathematicians' disinterest in certain features of mathematical entities seems to warrant some sort of philosophical explanation.

But, while science might be silent on the *nature* of abstracta, the contention of the preservationist is that it is also silent on the *existence* of abstracta—after all, the preservationist contends that science would be undisturbed by nominalism and, in turn, the nonexistence of numbers. Here, Burgess and Rosen can plausibly claim the preservationist to have simply lapsed into revolutionary nominalism by contravening the explicit existential commitments of science. The only preservationist alternative would be to explain away scientific theories' apparent commitment to the existence of numbers, but this looks to require the kind of semantic jiggery-pokery that made hermeneutic nominalism untenable.

For precisely this reason, it looks as though Burgess and Rosen are able to push nominalists in one of two directions. They must abandon strict forms of naturalism, while still doing justice to the deliverances of science, or find the semantic wherewithal to plausibly interpret mathematical and other discourse along nominalist lines. As we'll see, however, many nominalist options are not readily lumped into just one of these categories. Instead, these options push back against both hardline naturalism and anything like a face-value interpretation of mathematical discourse.

§7.4 Commitment

Whether or not nominalists can overcome Burgess and Rosen's dilemma, there is surely something appealing about a version of nominalism that preserves the truth of claims like (1)–(3) as ordinarily interpreted but still avoids commitment to abstract entities. The primary challenge for such a view is, of course, in explaining the truth of such claims despite the absence of any abstract entities. This section briefly considers *non-committal nominalisms* that attempt to reconcile nominalism with the truth of sentences like (1)–(3) as ordinarily interpreted. (I omit this "as ordinarily interpreted" qualification throughout this section except where context requires.) Given their apparent compatibility with the deliverances of mathematics, science, and commonsense, non-committal strategies have a fair claim to being the best available versions of nominalism. As we'll see, though, non-committal views also come with contentious metaontological commitments.

Among non-committal options, one place to look is to Meinongianism, which permits quantification over entities that do not exist. Setting aside general worries about Meinongianism (of which there are many), it is unclear how to capture the nominalist thesis within a Meinonigian metaontology. For, while nominalism is typically taken to be the thesis that abstract entities do not exist, this is only because quantification and existence are typically assumed to go hand-in-hand. Roughly put, "what there is" is just "what exists" and *vice versa*. Since Meinongians reject this standard view of quantification and existence, it is an open question whether we can even capture nominalism within the resulting metaontology. Within such a framework, we might take nominalism to be a thesis about *what there is* or, instead, as a thesis about *what exists*. If it is the thesis that there are no abstract entities, Meinongians seem no better off than ordinary nominalists, since they would also be forced to deny sentences like "There are prime numbers." But, if Meinongian nominalism is the thesis that no abstract entities exist, its defender can grant the truth of sentences like "There are prime numbers" even while denying sentences like "Prime numbers exist." The latter proposal might sound more congenial to would-be nominalists, but there is no compelling reason to think it is the uniquely apt rendering of nominalism within the Meinongian metaontology. After all, the debate between nominalists and platonists has, throughout the preceding, been undertaken with the assumed equivalence between quantification and existence. Given this equivalence, both Meinongian translations of nominalism are at odds with nominalism. Absent some principled rationale for uniquely privileging one of them, a plausible conclusion to draw is that nominalism simply presupposes a non-Meinongian metaontology and cannot be transplanted into a Meinongian metaphysics. So, while Meinongians ought to be interested in the fate of the two theses above, nominalists and platonists ought to view them as orthogonal to the debate at hand. We will therefore turn to some more promising non-committal options.

For the moment, let's suppose that when platonists claim there are abstract entities, we ought to take them to be asserting something plausible. And, when nominalists deny there are such entities, we should take their claim to be no less plausible. Given this apparent disagreement, we might hope to "split the difference" and claim that, in some sense, platonists are correct and that, in some other sense, nominalists are correct. Since this disagreement seems to hinge upon ontological concerns and so partly concerns the notion of *existence*, when splitting the difference, we might therefore posit two different senses of *exists*. In one sense of *exists*, abstract entities exist, but, in the other sense, they do not.

This is a promising enough start, but we can quickly see that carrying out this strategy requires more than simply positing two different senses of *exists*. Since nominalists and platonists also disagree about sentences like "There are numbers," we would need a similar distinction to capture disagreements involving quantifiers like "There is."[15] And, even after we introduce different senses of "There is"—one platonist-friendly, the other nominalist-friendly—this strategy still remains far from complete. What, for example, should we say about the status of sentences that seem to directly entail "There are numbers" like "Two is prime." These and other sentences steeped in platonist discourse seemingly involve abstract entities but involve neither "exists" nor explicit quantification.

The best way to follow through on our initial hope of "splitting the difference" is to stop proliferating different senses of individual expressions and hold, instead, that claims like (1)–(3) and platonist discourse in general simply admit of different *uses*. Following the terminology of Dorr (2008), this strategy distinguishes between two "systematically different kinds of uses"—one "fundamental," the other "superficial"—for the following sorts of sentences:

(4) Spiders and insects share many important anatomical properties.

(5) There are properties.

(6) Everything is a material object.

Of sentences like (4), Dorr (2008: 33) says, "When we use these sentences superficially, we assert boring, well-known truths, just as we would if we had said that spiders and insects both have exoskeletons." In contrast, "anyone who seriously uttered [(6)] would very likely be using this sentence in a fundamental way. They would be making a claim about 'the ultimate furniture of reality.'" Adopting this distinction between fundamental and superficial uses, Dorr takes inferences from claims like "The number of planets is greater than one" to claims like "There are numbers" to be valid only when each claim is used superficially or when each claim is used fundamentally. But, since claims like the former are typically used superficially, any quick alethic arguments for platonism like those canvassed in Chapter 1 are unsound. We ought to accept their central premise only if we had antecedent reasons to believe that, fundamentally speaking, there are numbers.

The view that there are different uses of sentences—some committal, some not—does justice to our initial aim of splitting the difference between platonists and nominalists.[16] So, on the face it, there is much to like about this brand of noncommittal nominalism. But, as Dorr notes, platonists are likely to meet such a view with a kind of "principled incomprehension," since most platonists will maintain that there is only one familiar way to use claims like (1)–(6). On this usage, the relevant sentences, if true, entail that there are numbers and properties. Full stop. If pressed to recognize another use on which claims like (5) turn out false, platonists have little incentive or motivation to do so. For, when the platonist asserts that there are properties, she will be puzzled when the nominalists immediately asks whether she *really* thinks there are properties or whether she thinks that properties also exist *in some fundamental sense*.

Against this principled incomprehension, Dorr offers some ways platonists might get a grip on the distinction between superficial and fundamental uses. He suggests that, fundamentally speaking, there are neither analytic truths about what exists nor necessary connections among entities of which it is true to say, fundamentally speaking, that they exist. As we've seen, however, some platonists are content to take existence claims regarding abstract entities as analytic and almost all platonists will admit necessary connections. There is, then, ample reason for platonists to reject even these ways to mark the intended distinction. It would therefore be a welcome result for non-committal nominalists if there were some way to avoid the need to explicate the distinction between fundamental and superficial uses and thereby avoid platonists' principled incomprehension.

A closely related version of non-committal nominalism pursues roughly this tactic. It draws no distinction between uses of sentences like (1)–(6) in English, but it denies that ordinary English is the proper language for conducting serious ontological inquiry. Instead, it holds that, for the purposes of ontology, there is an especially natural language, Ontologese, which we ought to employ instead of English.[17] Ontologese is to be preferred on the grounds that, while the unrestricted existential quantifier of English is somewhat natural, the unrestricted existential quantifier of Ontologese is perfectly natural. So, once we recognize that naturalness distinguishes among quantifiers as well as predicates, we can see that the unrestricted existential quantifier of Ontologese offers the most perspicuous way to describe reality. When our interest is in ontology and the metaphysical structure of the world, our claims are therefore properly put forward, not in English, but in the maximally natural language of Ontologese. (Such a language is likely to look nothing like English and considerably more like first- or perhaps higher-order logic, but, here, we'll pretend that Ontologese looks and "sounds" very similar to English.)

Given the distinction between English and Ontologese, nominalists have a new resource for capturing their own view and placating platonists. According to the *Ontologese nominalist*, the unrestricted quantifier of

English includes numbers, properties, and propositions within its domain, but the unrestricted quantifier of Ontologese includes no abstract entities. And, since Ontologese is more natural than English, the most perspicuous description of reality is one on which there are no abstract entities. Put a bit differently: when correctly described in Ontologese—the language that best matches the structure of reality—it is true to say that the world comprises only concrete entities. So, while these nominalists can grant that claims like "There are prime numbers" are true sentences of English, such claims are of little interest for metaphysics and, more importantly, the parallel sentences of Ontologese are false.

The appeal of Ontologese nominalism is considerable. It acquits nominalists of having to explain the different English uses of sentences like (1)–(6). That said, it does require that nominalists defend the notion that languages can be more or less natural and that a language like Ontologese is maximally natural. For those who already deny that naturalness is a feature that divides up properties, the extension of naturalness to quantifiers or languages will seem plainly objectionable. But, for present purposes, let's assume the legitimacy of Ontologese and grant that we can evaluate sentences expressed within it.

One challenge for the Ontologese nominalist arises when we note that she holds sentences like "There are prime numbers" to be true in English. This seems to require that the domain of the unrestricted quantifier of English is broader than the domain of the unrestricted existential quantifier of Ontologese. This would, in turn, suggest that the unrestricted quantifier of Ontologese is actually a restriction of our familiar English quantifier. And, if that's right, this proposal actually seems to be no help to nominalists. After all, everyone agrees that we can restrict our domain of quantification to ensure that "There are no abstract entities" is true in English simply by restricting our domain to tables and chairs. But, plainly, our interest in nominalism is as a thesis about all of what there is, not merely about what is true of some restricted domain. Why, then, should we care if some language like Ontologese, with a quantifier more restricted than English, preserves the truth of nominalism?

One response from the Ontologese nominalist is to insist that we should care precisely because the quantifier of Ontologese is the most natural quantifier and so the most perspicuous for describing reality.[18] But, for the committed nominalists, this brute appeal to naturalness will be unsatisfying. For, even if numbers and properties fall only within the domain of a less than natural quantifier, they remain anathema to nominalism so long as they fall within the domain of any quantifier, natural or not.

A better response looks to the project of what Sider (2011) describes as "metaphysical semantics." Roughly speaking, a metaphysical semantics provides *metaphysical* truth-conditions for sentences of English (or some other language) within a fundamental language like Ontologese. These metaphysical truth-conditions need not exhibit the kind of explanatory features required by the truth-conditions that would be given in a semantics of natural language. Instead, they seek, as Schaffer (2013: 736) puts it, to "explain how the use of the language in question fits into fundamental reality." We can therefore uphold radical theses that deny the existence of abstract or even ordinary concrete objects in Ontologese while, at the same time, granting the truth of sentences in English that seem to concern these entities. This is because a metaphysical semantics for English claims about, say, ordinary concrete objects could, in principle, be given by quantifying exclusively over concrete mereological atoms. And, if so, any commitment to ordinary concrete objects expressed in English would be merely apparent. In a similar vein, claims like (1)–(6) are to be assigned metaphysical truth-conditions that involve no abstract entities whatsoever. Perhaps these metaphysical truth-conditions are enormously complicated disjunctive descriptions of fundamental particles. Or, in the case of mathematical truths, perhaps the relevant metaphysical truth-conditions are trivial, depending on nothing in particular. In either case, Ontologese nominalism leaves the face-value linguistic semantics of our ordinary claims intact, but still permits us to affirm that, metaphysically speaking, reality is wholly concrete. Better still, metaphysical semantics leaves ordinary semantics intact. This is because, in providing a linguistic semantics, we can specify the truth-conditions for sentences in English and other languages in yet another non-fundamental language in which quantification over numbers, properties, and propositions is also permitted, despite the fact that, metaphysically speaking, there are no such entities.

If this strategy is a sound one, Ontologese nominalists can rest easy. They are under no pressure to resist the truth of ordinary claims in English. But, when pressed about what reality is ultimately like, they can claim that, metaphysically speaking, there are no abstract entities. The lone requirement of metaphysical semantics is that the truth of ordinary claims be explicable in terms of what there is. And, in this respect, there is ample leeway to spell out the connections between truths of Ontologese and truths of non-fundamental languages like English. The result is, I think, the best non-committal option for nominalists, but it faces problems even so.

Along with worries about the introduction of more or less natural languages and quantifiers, there is a metaontological puzzle for Ontologese nominalists of the present variety. Suppose, when assessing the nominalist–platonist debate, the proper object of our interest is in whether there are (non-vacuously) true sentences of Ontologese that are about abstract entities. Further suppose that we've been speaking English in presenting, evaluating, and offering arguments for or against the existence of such entities. If that's right, the implications of our attitudes towards the relevant sentences of English and the arguments put forward within English are of highly uncertain relation to the status of sentences in Ontologese. Why think, for example, that, even if the indispensability argument provides good reason to believe "Numbers exist" is true in English, it has any bearing whatsoever on what is true in Ontologese? Similarly, why think that our preferred theses and patterns of arguments, which seem solely concerned with the fate of sentences in English, are of any help when we turn our attention to sentences of Ontologese?

There is ample room for doubt about whether science, parsimony, or common sense are good guides to what exists, fundamentally speaking, even if we think they are good guides to what exists in English. The worry is, then, that, if Ontologese allows us to unmoor our metaphysics from our ordinary judgments of truth and falsity, it potentially unmoors our ordinary practices for investigating and arguing about what there is. So, even if we are in a position to determine which existential claims are true in English, it is not obvious how, if at all, we can successfully determine which existential claims are true in Ontologese.[19]

Nominalists who resort to Ontologese in order to preserve ordinary discourse face a problem when it comes time to make the case for nominalism as a theory advanced, not in English, but within Ontologese. The good news for nominalists who draw upon the Humean opposition against necessary connections is that such arguments are of equal force whether advanced in English or Ontologese. But, for other non-committal nominalists, articulating a methodology for metaphysics that leaves one's preferred arguments for nominalism intact is a serious concern.

§7.5 Harvard nominalism revisited

We've now surveyed some of the leading options for sustaining a nominalist metaphysics. Before concluding, it will be useful to look back to the

Harvard nominalism of Quine and Goodman in order to better appreciate the somewhat peculiar status of our two remaining nominalist options.

Despite their subsequent and quite different changes in opinion, the nominalism jointly espoused by Goodman and Quine (1947) in "Steps towards a constructive nominalism" is noteworthy for not only its rejection of abstract entities, but for its outright hostility towards modal notions.[20] Writing later, Quine (1986) describes his early fling with nominalism as follows: "Goodman and I got what we could in the way of mathematics, or more directly metamathematics, on the basis of a nominalist ontology and without assuming an infinite universe. We could not get enough to satisfy us. But we would not for a moment have considered enlisting the aid of modality. The cure would in our view have been far worse than the disease." A similar remark, offered in Putnam's (1975) "What is mathematical truth?," further indicates the association of Quine and Goodman's early nominalism with the rejection of modality. Pun intended, Putnam (1975: 70) says: "The nominalist, good man that he is, cannot accept modal notions any more than he can accept the existence of sets." Subsequently, on account of their home institution, this dual stricture against abstract entities and modality has come to be known as "Harvard nominalism."[21]

In light of the preceding chapters, it should be fairly clear that the thesis of nominalism is properly distinguished from eliminativism about modality. We have seen, for example, modal structuralist views that seek to dispense with abstract entities by drawing precisely upon the modal resources Harvard nominalism outlaws.[22] Our interest in Harvard nominalism is not, however, focused on resuscitating the wrongheaded assumption that nominalism should be tied to modal eliminativism. Instead, our interest is in how the legacy of Harvard nominalism bears upon two remaining nominalist options, each of which has received comparatively little sustained attention: nominalist possibilism and ideological nominalism.

§7.5.1 *Nominalist possibilism*

In the eyes of the Harvard nominalist, modal ideology, whether in the form of the box and diamond of modal logic or the counterfactual conditional, resists any non-modal analysis. Harvard nominalism is therefore a two-pronged thesis. It simultaneously rejects abstract ontology and any primitive modal ideology. Consequently, it is incompatible with views like modal structuralism, which seek to dispense with abstract ontology by invoking primitive modality, and with any views that would accept abstract entities whether alongside or without primitive modality. It is, however, compatible with the modal realist proposal for reducing modal notions via quantification over concrete possible worlds. This is because the modal realist reduction of modality proceeds by taking on an expanded ontology of concrete entities. In so doing, modal realism relies upon a conception of modality radically foreign to anything that Quine and Goodman had in mind.

Recall that, according to Lewisian modal realism, there is a plurality of concrete possible worlds of the same ontological status as the actual world. And, for any way things could be, some possible world is that way. The result is a sizeable ontological commitment, but one that comes with a considerable ideological payoff: a reductive analysis of modality. Now, since Lewis himself accepts a commitment to sets (and is agnostic about universals or tropes), Lewis' own view cannot satisfy the scruples of Harvard nominalism. There is, however, a nearby alternative to Lewis' view, *nominalist possibilism*, which can dispense with sets while retaining modal realism and its reductive analysis of modality.

Nominalist possibilism rejects both the abstract ontology and the primitive modal ideology banned by Harvard nominalism. It can, however, provide metaphysical explanations akin to those of platonism by constructing ersatz sets, properties, and propositions out of the immense domain of concrete possibilia. In doing so, nominalist possibilism yields a full-scale alternative to platonism that takes concrete possible worlds as its starting point. Viewed one way, nominalist possibilism involves a "horizontal" expansion in our ontological commitments rather than a "vertical" one, requiring a distinctive ontological category of abstracta. It is therefore in direct opposition to the orthodox view, platonist actualism, which we discussed in the previous chapter.

A potential stumbling block for nominalist possibilism is the full reconciliation of nominalism with possibilism. It is commonly assumed, for example, that, by positing causally and spatiotemporally isolated worlds, nominalist possibilism will fall prey to the very same arguments that motivate nominalism in the first place. Field (1989: 75) nicely captures this common sentiment:

> In calling "possible worlds" abstract I ignore David Lewis' view ... that the actual universe is just a four-dimensional slice of a broader reality, and that the other "possible worlds" are just other four-dimensional slices of this same broader reality and hence are no more abstract than the actual universe.

> This view seems to me exceptionally implausible; in addition, it can have little appeal for the nominalist, for even if these other possible worlds are not abstract entities, the problems posed by knowledge of them and reference to them seem just as intractable as the analogous problem for numbers.

In the same vein, Burgess and Rosen (1997: 124) remark that, when it comes to concrete possible worlds, "such exotica ... are quite as repugnant to nominalists as are numbers or sets." As we've seen, however, the strongest case for nominalism owes to a Humean aversion to necessary connections, not to any epistemic worries about our access to causally isolated realms. And, since Lewisian modal realism, once purged of sets and other abstracta, can uphold the Humean stricture against necessary connections, nominalist possibilism is motivated independently of worries about epistemic access. So, contrary to the sentiments expressed above, there is no internal tension between nominalism and possibilism so long as one takes the Humean route in defending nominalism.

The more serious challenge for nominalist possibilists consists in recovering the explanatorily powerful framework of sets, properties, and propositions by appeal to concrete possibilia rather than abstract entities. Fortunately, prospects are surprisingly good in this regard. One option is to simply appropriate the general features of modal structuralism, but, instead of using primitive modal operators, allow for quantification over a plurality of concrete possible worlds. Roughly speaking, the resulting modal realist brand of modal structuralism replaces claims about the structure of an actually existing abstract realm with corresponding modal claims about the ways in which merely possible concrete entities are, in fact, structured. In this way, possibilism provides nominalists with a means for overcoming a perennial stumbling block of nominalist reconstruals of mathematics: the possibility that our actual world is a finite one. The main concern with such a strategy is, however, its lack of generality. For, while it provides a ready-made account of mathematical discourse, it is not clear how it can account for discourse about properties and propositions.

A second, more general option builds upon Lewis' own proposal for reducing the singleton relation of set theory to the nominalistically acceptable devices of mereology and plural quantification. Very roughly, this package of ideological and logical resources allows us to dispense with any distinctive set-theoretic ideology provided that we have ontology rich enough to allow concrete entities to play the role of singleton sets.[23] And, as Nolan (2002) suggests, a nominalist possibilist can, in principle, do away with distinctively set-theoretic ontology once given sufficiently many concrete possible worlds. And, if this strategy can be carried out, the nominalist possibilist is in an enviable position. She can first recover the resources of set theory. Then, given these resources and concrete possible worlds, she can develop a theory of properties and propositions that mirrors Lewis' own view but dispenses with any abstracta. There are, then, at least two avenues by which nominalist possibilists can provide a comprehensive replacement for abstract ontology while also helping themselves to the other theoretical benefits that come with modal realism.[24]

It will come as little surprise that the strongest resistance to modal realism stems from its commitment to concrete possible worlds.[25] For those moored to common sense ontology, modal realism remains simply incredible. The same concern, of course, applies to nominalist possibilism. But, if one takes seriously the careful weighing of theoretical virtues and vices, both Lewisian modal realism and nominalist possibilism are live metaphysical options. And, in the case of nominalist possibilism, a commitment to concrete possible worlds affords both a reduction of modality and a viable replacement for the platonist's framework of sets, properties, and propositions. Nominalist possibilism therefore represents an alternative to platonism, equally matched in explanatory strength but without the ideological and ontological costs that attend abstract entities. So, for those who hope to use an expanded ontology to avoid platonism or already admit concrete possible worlds, nominalist possibilism has a strong claim to being the best of the available options.

§7.5.2 Ideological nominalism

For those unwilling to posit concrete possible worlds, one final but no less radical alternative remains. This last option avoids any novel ontological commitments, but posits a richer metaphysical structure by taking on additional primitive ideology. According to the *ideological nominalist*, true sentences apparently involving abstract entities are to be replaced, with the help of novel ideology, by sentences that involve no quantification over the abstract. In its most familiar guise, ideological nominalism accomplishes this with the help of a predicate functor language—*functorese*, for short—that matches the expressive resources of a first-order language with quantifiers but relies exclusively on predicates and operators—most notably, predicate functors, which are devices for generating predicates from other predicates. (On functorese, see Turner (2011).) For, as Quine (1960) describes this strategy, "a general, finite battery of such auxiliary operators can be assembled that will enable us always to coax variables thus into positions where we can dispense with them."

Simplifying considerably, functorese allows us to translate familiar claims like "x loves y" into something other than its familiar rendering in first-order logic like ExEyL(x, y). With the help of predicate functors, the ideological nominalist translates such claims into zero-place predicates by introducing, among other functors, a "derelativization" operator. This operator, Der, turns a dyadic relation like "loves," which in first-order logic would have two arguments places, into a one-place predicate "(Der L)" with only a single argument place. When applied a second time, Der takes us from the sentence "(Der L)x" to "Der Der L," which can be understood as "something loves something," but that involves no quantification and so seemingly no ontological commitments.

A gaggle of additional operators are required to accommodate asymmetry in predicates. So, for example, an inversion operator, Inv, takes us from "Der Der L" ("something x loves something y") to "Inv Der Der L" ("something y loves something x"). Still more operators are needed to accommodate other kinds of complexity as in the case of reflexive predicates. And, despite the foreign nature of these functors and their ideological cost, they provide a direct strategy for dispensing with quantification in a nevertheless extremely powerful language.

Though Quine discusses the intriguing features of functorese, he denies that it provides a means for minimizing ontological commitments, since he holds that any theory must be forcibly recast into first-order logic before being evaluated for its ontological commitments. Sentences of functorese therefore have precisely the same ontological commitments as their translations in first-order logic. (See Quine (1960).) While we owe much to Quine's insights regarding ontology and ideology, we need not hold his views as sacrosanct. And, if we reject his commitment to the canonical status of first-order logic for assessing ontology, functorese offers both a radically different view of the world's metaphysical structure and also a natural way for nominalists to dispense with abstracta.

The good news is, then, that there is ample reason to reject Quine's conception of first-order logic as the final arbiter of ontology. After all, views on which modal or temporal logic are interpreted via quantification over possible worlds or non-present times seem quite different from competing views that invoke only primitive modal or temporal operators. Since these are substantive ontological disagreements, we should deny that such views are equivalent even if they seem equivalent when forcibly recast into first-order logic. We must, then, take potential trade-offs between ontology and ideology seriously. Consequently, a view that would invoke functorese to dispense with all quantification delivers a profoundly different metaphysics from one that retains familiar first-order quantifiers. And, while I know of no good argument for pursuing a nihilist view that rejects all ontological commitments, ideological nominalism, which uses functorese to dispense with quantification over abstract entities, remains well worth considering. If successful, it has a fair shot at matching the explanatory power of platonism while doing without an abstract realm or concrete possible worlds. Viewed one way, ideological nominalism is a radical extension of the Quinean strategy of replacing properties with primitive predicates. But, where Quine's "ostrich nominalism" uses ideology only to avoid properties, the ideological nominalist employs primitive predicates to dispense with even abstract objects like sets and propositions as well.

To see what such a view might look like, consider, once again, a broadly structuralist view of mathematics. According to such a view, the subject matter of mathematics consists of one or more structures, which can be aptly characterized by lengthy existentially quantified claims satisfying various logical constraints. Equipped with functorese, the ideological nominalist can replace these lengthy existentially quantified claims with zero-place predicates with no ontological commitments. So understood, functorese is alleged to capture the content of mathematics in wholly ideological terms. And, if this strategy can be carried over to the case of propositions and other putative abstracta (i.e., if structural characterizations can be provided and then translated into functorese), ideological nominalists have a general recipe for replacing abstract reality while, at the same time, upholding the meaningfulness and truth of mathematical claims. So understood, ideological nominalism contends that our familiar talk about the abstract realm gets something right about the world's metaphysical structure, but goes wrong in taking this structure to be ontological rather than ideological.

Challenges to ideological nominalism stem from at least two sources. First, in our discussion of predicates throughout the preceding chapters, we focused exclusively on those with adicities of one or more. And, while monadic predicates and relations with higher adicities are commonplace, the underlying metaphysics of ideological nominalism hinges on the coherence of invoking zero-place predicates. This is because functorese is, in principle, a means for converting strings of quantifiers to predicates that apply to nothing at all. At first pass, this is fretfully odd. Notice, however, that some take propositions to be zero-place properties which are instantiated by nothing at all. Following this analogy between properties and propositions, ideological nominalists might try and give sense to the notion of a zero-place predicate as simply a predicate that need not apply to an entity, but instead applies *simpliciter*. Alternatively, sentences of functorese might be interpreted as covertly one-place predicates that uniformly and trivially apply to a single entity, the world. Perhaps there are still other options available, but, regardless, there is a distinctive metaphysical oddness to zero-place predicates. This oddness is, however, of uncertain theoretical significance. Its peculiarity requires ideological nominalists to say more about the structure of such radical ideology, but, even so, these sorts of worries are not yet a decisive strike against the view.

A more serious concern regarding ideological nominalism surfaces when we try to integrate functorese claims "about" abstract entities within a broader theory that also admits quantification over concrete entities. If the domains of the abstract and the concrete were fundamentally discrete and we required no substantive connections across the abstract–concrete divide, we could simply use functorese to describe the abstract realm and then use a separate language like first-order logic to describe the concrete world. There is, however, a wealth of "mixed" talk of concrete objects instantiating properties, sets having members, and minds bearing propositional attitudes that must be captured. And, in such cases, we seem to require a mish-mash of functorese, to dispense with abstracta, and quantification, to allow us to capture facts about abstract–concrete interaction in a single breath—e.g., when we say that there is a proposition that Edie and Gomer each believe. Unfortunately, it is not obvious how we can consistently render this mixed talk in a way that does violence to neither functorese nor first-order logic. If we convert all claims that seem to involve abstract entities into functorese, we threaten to miss out on certain inferential connections. (E.g., from the fact that Edie and Gomer each believe P, we should be able to infer there are at least two things that believe P.) So, while functorese is a handy tool for dispensing with quantification over abstract entities like propositions when our target discourse is suitably isolated, there is no simple recipe for making sense of facts straddling concrete reality and what platonists take to be the abstract realm.

Figuring out how, if at all, mixed claims can be accommodated is the central challenge for would-be ideological nominalists. But, given the limited attention ideological nominalism has received, any provisional assessment of the prospects for meeting this challenge would be hasty. If, however, this challenge can be overcome or its significance suitably downplayed, ideological nominalism emerges as the best nominalist option that does without concrete possible worlds. Interestingly enough, there is also reason to believe that it can be reconciled with the ambitions of Harvard nominalism. For, although most ideological nominalists will simply help themselves to primitive modal operators, the prodigious ideology of functorese suggests a different Harvard-friendly strategy: use non-modal primitive ideology to replicate the expressive resources of modal realism and then use this non-modal primitive ideology to generate a reductive analysis of modal ideology. Roughly speaking, such a view would describe concrete possible worlds using functorese and then help itself to analyses of modal operators in a manner parallel to that of the modal realist. The resulting view is undoubtedly a strange one, but, even so, it is yet more evidence that metaphysical structure is more than ontology alone.

Summary

This chapter outlined a working taxonomy of nominalist alternatives. This taxonomy divides up the space of options on the basis of the ascribed meaning, truth, and ontological commitments of claims that seem to require abstract entities. Views that deny the meaningfulness of platonist discourse were seen to enjoy little plausibility, while figurative nominalism, according to which such claims are not put forward literally, fared somewhat better. Views that offer up paraphrases or replacements in their place were briefly surveyed. Along with hermeneutic nominalism, other views that invoke subtle metaontological commitments to avoid platonism, while upholding the truth of our ordinary claims, were considered. Finally, two under-appreciated and oft-neglected options—nominalist possibilism and ideological nominalism—were briefly sketched. For those of us sympathetic to modal realism, the former is the best available option, although the latter enjoys considerable promise.

Recommended reading

On nominalist options, see Burgess and Rosen (1997, 2005) and Melia (2008). On the varieties of fictionalism, see Field (1980), MacBride (1999), Sainsbury (2009), and Kroon (2011). Stephen Yablo has several rich discussions of the connection between ontology and figurative thought and talk, especially regarding abstract entities. See Yablo (2000, 2001, 2002, 2005). On paraphrase and its relation to ontology, see Alston (1958), Van Inwagen (1990), and von

Solodkoff (2014). On modal structuralism, see Putnam (1967) and Hellman (1989). For discussion of general strategies for nominalizing scientific theories, see Dorr (2010). Relevant recent work in metaontology can be found in Azzouni (2004), Dorr (2005), Chalmers (2009), Sider (2011), and Korman (2015a, 2015b). On the Lewisian metaphysics of sets and the prospects for nominalist possibilism, see Lewis (1991, 1993b) and Nolan (2002). On Harvard nominalism and Quine's later views, see Quine (2008) and Burgess (2008) along with the original Goodman and Quine (1947) paper. For discussion of functorese and its implications for ontology, see Quine (1960), Dasgupta (2009), and Turner (2011).

Notes

1. The nominalist strategy set out in Field (1980) is sometimes labelled as a version of instrumentalism (as, e.g., in Yablo (2001)), but takes mathematical claims to have literal content. Their distinctive and valuable contribution to theories consists in their *conservativeness*—roughly speaking, standard mathematics yields no novel consequences when added to scientific theories that are non-mathematical in nature. Since their value consists in their conservativeness and claims need not be true to be conservative, the Fieldian nominalist grants the pragmatic value of mathematics without accepting the truth of standard mathematics.
2. Historically, this brand of nominalism has its closest affinity with certain formalist views in the philosophy of mathematics on which mathematical theories are series of rules for manipulating symbols and lack any representational content. On formalism, see von Neumann (1964).
3. On some of the more peculiar features of platonist discourse, see Yablo (1998: 259).
4. One way to spell out the paraphrase strategy without conceding the truth of target sentences draws upon what propositions sentences *really* express. Since such a view is of little appeal to nominalists (or itself requires some further paraphrase), I leave it aside here. See van Inwagen (1990: 108–114).
5. Talk of paraphrase in metaphysics is far from univocal. On different conceptions about its role and the constraints of adequacy, see Keller (forthcoming).
6. There are certain "one size fits all" paraphrase strategies worth considering. As Dorr (2008: 37) notes, we might try to paraphrase a given sentence of platonist discourse, *S*, as follows: "If there were abstract entities,

S would be the case." On the prospects for this and other "one size fits all" strategies, see Dorr (2010).

7 Varieties of fictionalism are legion. They vary with respect to the particular entities they purport to dispense with and in their preferred semantic and metaphysical underpinnings. Some fictionalisms are therefore properly assimilated to non-figurative nominalism, while others belong in a category of their own. Here, our interest is only with how fictionalism plays out within the ambit of replacement nominalism. On fictionalist options and the revolutionary–hermeneutic distinction, see Yablo (2001: 85). On fictionalism, see MacBride (1999) and Kroon (2011).

8 On modal structuralism, see Hellman (1989), Putnam (1967), Kalderon (1995, 1996), and Burgess and Rosen (1997: 124–172).

9 Hellman (1989: 54). Hellman argues elsewhere that his view is a distinctive brand of "preservationist" nominalism. Here, we're considering perhaps a different view that employs modal structuralist resources to carry out the strategy of replacement nominalism.

10 For discussion, see Hazen (1976), Melia (2003: 81–98), and Nolan (2002: 51–76).

11 Competing forms of hermeneutic nominalism differ with some focusing on the semantic content of mathematical and scientific theories and others focusing on the attitudes we bear towards these theories. See Burgess and Rosen (2005).)

12 Burgess (2004: 23).

13 Cf. Chihara (2004: 506).

14 Burgess (2004: 23) suggests any "third way" for nominalists will collapse upon one of two horns: "[I]t is sometimes said that a nominalist interpretation represents 'the best way to make sense of' what mathematicians say. I see in this formulation not a third alternative, but simply an equivocation, between 'the empirical hypothesis about what mathematicians mean that best agrees with the evidence' (hermeneutic) and 'the construction that could be put on mathematicians' words that would best reconcile them with certain philosophical principles or prejudices' (revolutionary)."

15 Some deny the Quinean equivalence of quantification and talk about what "exists" even while rejecting Meinongianism. On such views, see Azzouni (2004).

16 Note, however, that Dorr does not intend the superficial use of (5) to be non-literal nor is the truth of superficial uses of sentences like (4) and (5) something that requires no explanation. On the contrary, the truth of the

superficial uses must be explicable in terms of how the world is, fundamentally speaking. Dorr therefore holds that, for any true superficial claim, there is a "a sentence which, when taken in a fundamental sense, says how things would have to be for the original sentence to be true in a superficial sense." Cf. Sider (2011) on the project of "metaphysical semantics" discussed below.

17 See Dorr (2005), Cameron (2010), Sider (2009, 2011), and Korman (2015a).

18 Note that entities that fall within the scope of the Ontologese quantifier exist in the most fundamental sense of "exist," but this leaves open whether the entities are properly viewed as "fundamental" entities. One might, for example, hold that both fundamental and derivative entities exist in the fundamental sense of "exist."

19 Proponents of non-committal nominalism might respond to this challenge by claiming that ontologists have been speaking (perhaps to our surprise) Ontologese all along. If that's right, then our preferred arguments require no radical repair or revision. At the same time, if nominalists and platonists have been speaking Ontologese all along, we face worries about semantic immodesty akin to those pressed by Burgess and Rosen against hermeneutic nominalism. It is puzzling, for example, why platonists would attempt to draw support from ordinary standards of assertion or familiar claims in science if, all along, they were advancing a thesis in Ontologese rather than English. As Korman (2015b) points out, if ontologists were already steeped in Ontologese, it would be puzzling how we or they might recognize the distinction between claims put forward in English and those in Ontologese.

20 Quine retained his stricture against intensional entities like universals and propositions, but eventually accepted the existence of sets. In contrast, Goodman came to endorse an idiosyncratic thesis, which he called "nominalism," that rejected any theories that admit distinct entities generated from the same basic entities—e.g., set theory and certain non-extensional mereologies.

21 This usage is also taken up by another Harvard philosopher: Parsons (1990: 315). See Burgess (2008) for discussion.

22 Of course, some nominalists might seek to argue for modal eliminativism as a consequence of rejecting abstract entities. Nominalists of this sort are likely to claim that modality requires abstract possible worlds, so, once we reject abstracta, we are duty-bound to throw out the modal baby with the abstract bathwater.

23 This strategy assumes the ontology of modal realism, the apparatus of classical extensional mereology coupled with mereological universalism, and the

admissibility of plural quantification, which admits irreducible quantification over many entities in addition to singular quantification. Within the main text of Lewis (1991), Lewis defends a view on which the singleton relation between entities like Socrates and their respective singletons like {Socrates} is a primitive relation of which frustratingly little can be said. Lewis (1991: appendix; 1993b) defends a "structuralist" view of the singleton relation on which talk about *the* singleton relation is properly understood as covertly quantified talk regarding any relations that satisfy certain logical and metaphysical constraints. There is, therefore, no unique, metaphysically special singleton relation; there are merely relations that satisfy the constraints required to be singleton relations. And, since the remaining ideology of set theory is mereological, this structuralist view dispenses with any primitive set-theoretic ideology. This structuralist approach faces a powerful objection: since it requires quantification over relations and relations are typically understood set-theoretically (i.e., as sets of ordered pairs), it presupposes the very sets it purports to eliminate. As Lewis notes, this objection would be compelling were it not for the technical results given in an appendix to Lewis (1991) co-written with John Burgess and Allen Hazen. These results show how mereology, plural quantification, and a sufficiently vast ontology of mereological simples allow us to simulate quantification over relations. For Lewis, the distinctive mathematical ontology of sets is not up for elimination, since it would involve a substantive revision to mathematics. Lewis' version of structuralism about the singleton relation therefore effects an ideological elimination of the primitive singleton relation without dispensing with sets. As Nolan (2002) argues, however, this view can, when granted some auxiliary assumptions (most notably, that there is a proper class of possible worlds), be extended to dispense with the ontology of sets as well. An alternative option that relies upon non-classical mereology is considered in Forrest (2002).

24 There are other potential benefits that come with nominalist possibilism. For example, Lewis (1983c) and Bricker (2006) suggest that modal realism offers an attractive account of descriptive content by taking concrete possibilia to be the objects of general thought.

25 Another concern is that modal realists are best served to view possible worlds as abstract rather than concrete entities and, in this way, simply cannot escape a commitment to platonism. See Lewis (1986: 86) and Cowling (2014a).

CONCLUSION

Where do things now stand in the debate between nominalists and platonists? Perhaps unsurprisingly, it depends largely upon what kind of nominalism or platonism one is interested in. While the last chapter set out a variety of nominalist options, previous chapters distinguished platonist alternatives in no small number of ways. Among other things, we saw that platonists differ considerably in their views about the diversity, modal status, and intrinsic nature of abstracta. In concluding, we can briefly mark some of the most significant of these divisions.

(i) *Naturalistic vs Non-naturalistic.* For naturalistic platonists, our best scientific theories serve as our exclusive guides to what there is. The case for abstract entities therefore depends entirely upon the role of such entities within these theories. And, while naturalistic platonists rely upon the indispensability argument, non-naturalistic platonists take the best case for abstract entities to proceed, at least in part, on the strength of extra-scientific considerations—e.g., our ordinary intuitions or the metaphysical usefulness of abstracta. This distinction between naturalistic and non-naturalistic platonism aligns with most platonists' preferred responses to nominalist objections. For example, when it comes to addressing epistemic concerns about abstract entities, naturalistic platonists typically hold our mathematical knowledge to be part and parcel of our broader scientific knowledge, whereas non-naturalistic platonists usually take our epistemic access to flow from *a priori* knowledge or some kind of rational intuition.

(ii) *Austere vs Expansive*. Where austere platonism admits only paradigmatic abstracta like mathematical entities, properties, and propositions, expansive platonism posits a broader range of abstract entities such as musical works, directions, GDPs, and fables. Both varieties of platonism further sub-divide in a multitude of ways. Some austere platonists posit only sets or only properties; others accept both and more besides. The most profligate austere platonists are probably plenitudinists who, in attempting to explain our epistemic access to abstract reality, hold all consistent mathematical theories to be true of some portion of the abstract realm. In-house disagreement among expansive platonists is even more pervasive as it concerns whether certain entities exist, whether certain entities are abstract, and whether certain entities might actually be reduced to sets, properties, or other "austere" abstracta. Generally speaking, however, expansive platonism strays from austere platonism by admitting abstracta that are created, located in space or time, or are merely contingent existents. For austere platonists, abstract reality is far more likely to be immutable, "outside" of spacetime, and non-contingent in nature.

(iii) *Primitivist vs Reductionist*. While reductionism claims that the abstract–concrete distinction can be explained in non-circular terms, primitivism admits it as a basic piece of metaphysical theory. Since there is a host of competing reductionist proposals, there is a range of importantly different views about what abstractness consists in. For some reductionists, abstractness is simply a lack of spatiotemporal location. For others, abstractness consists in lacking causal powers, intrinsic qualitative properties, or some other feature. Disagreement among reductionists in turn leads to disagreement about whether certain entities ought to be counted as abstract. For example, some maintain that Aristotelian universals are concrete since they are located, while others might deny this. Primitivists are, of course, required to take sides on whether such entities are abstract or not, but they are also better positioned to invoke abstractness in providing metaphysical explanations. The primitivist can, for instance, claim that abstract entities are graspable or exist necessarily *in virtue of being abstract* but, at the same time, they can deny that abstractness admits of any further explanation. For the reductionist, no parallel move is available if what it is to be abstract is just to be, say, without spatiotemporal location or without causal powers.

The above distinctions crosscut one another in various ways. And, given other internecine platonist disagreements about the modal status and intrinsic nature of abstract entities, we are left with too many platonist alternatives to offer any swift summary judgment. It seems, however, that two leading camps emerge from within the broad church of platonism.

The first camp is driven by a commitment to the "specialness" of abstract entities, which is manifested by their explanatory value within metaphysics and most naturally paired with an austere primitivist view. Platonists of this stripe concede that abstracta are radically different from concrete entities, but point out that their distinctive nature is precisely what accounts for their explanatory power and our special epistemic access to them. Since these platonists are driven primarily by non-scientific considerations, they eschew all but the most permissive forms of naturalism. Here, we can call them *metaphysical platonists*.

The second camp is motivated by a disdain for those who would ride roughshod over the letter of science and deny the truth of sentences like "There are prime numbers." This kind of platonism stems from a strict form of naturalism and a considerable deference to our best scientific theories. Since this second camp is not motivated by the promise of metaphysical explanations of resemblance and modality, they have little use for a primitive notion of abstractness. And, while they might accept an expansive ontology of abstract species, types, sonatas, and so on, platonists of this sort will actively distance their view from versions of platonism on which we "peer" into abstract reality through something like *a priori* rational intuition. Since those in this camp depart from the metaphysical package associated with the historical tradition of platonism, it is unsurprising that they often prefer to be labelled as *anti-nominalists* instead.

Other platonist options fall between the two rough categories of metaphysical platonism and anti-nominalism. But these two quite different strains of platonism face distinctive challenges, which are inherited by many of the views that fall between them.

Metaphysical platonism is a bold hypothesis about the structure of reality, promising a wealth of resources for solving perennial philosophical problems. As a philosophical artifact, it is of profound value and interest. Its credibility is, however, notably limited by its apparent departure from naturalism in postulating primitive notions and entities alien to our best physical theories. It is a metaphysical theory in the truest (and, for some, most pejorative) sense and faces all the epistemic burdens that come with straying beyond the ambitions of contemporary science. In contrast, anti-nominalism aligns itself with our best scientific theories and, by doing so, purports to be a modest, sensible doctrine. Unfortunately, in cutting ties with metaphysical platonism, it offers little to no guidance about the ontological status and features of posits like numbers and propositions. And, since the anti-nominalist view teeters into a kind of quietism about the metaphysical nature of abstract entities, it is increasingly unclear why the anti-nominalist ought to retain the abstract–concrete distinction in the first place.

The stark difference between these two brands of platonism is reflected in their diverging responses to familiar nominalist arguments. Metaphysical platonists will address worries about epistemic, semantic, or cognitive access by leaning heavily on the distinctive character of abstract entities. In contrast, anti-nominalists will seek to assimilate our access to abstracta to our broader scientific knowledge of the world. And, while metaphysical platonists can wheel out elaborate views about the nature of abstracta to allay concerns about non-uniqueness, anti-nominalists are more likely to reject these concerns as hair-splitting. Unlike metaphysical platonists, they can comfortably opt for a kind of pragmatic indifference.

As I suggested in Chapter 6, the strongest nominalist argument takes aim at all versions of platonism by invoking Hume's razor, which cautions against unduly multiplying necessities. Since it takes issue with the profusion of necessary connections required by any coherent version of platonism, it is a problem for metaphysical platonists and anti-nominalists alike. That said, efforts to overturn this argument drive metaphysical platonism and anti-nominalism yet further apart. Where the anti-nominalist will reject Hume's razor as a piece of anti-naturalist dogmatism, the metaphysical platonist will plead that abstract entities enjoy a special ontological status that exempts them from the reach of Hume's razor. Neither response is obviously unacceptable, but, for the Humeans among us, neither is preferable to nominalism.

As we've seen, nominalist options are legion. But strategies for choosing among them are likely to mirror our rough division between metaphysical platonism and anti-nominalism. For those who are interested in upholding the virtues that drive anti-nominalism while still dispensing with numbers, some non-committal version of nominalism will seem most appealing. But, if one hopes instead to explain away the apparent virtues that drive anti-nominalists, figurative nominalism is also a live option. For those more interested in providing metaphysical explanations, any viable nominalism must replace abstract entities with either a largesse of ideology or additional concrete entities. Those skittish about excess ontology should carefully consider the merits of ideological nominalism or some variety of modal structuralism, while those of us who view concrete possible worlds as a "philosopher's paradise" are better served to replace abstract entities with concrete possibilia. And, since we have seen that the best argument for nominalism need not impugn concrete possible worlds, no nominalist argument need drive us from the paradise Lewis has created for us.[1]

As should come as no surprise: one's choice among nominalist options—or between nominalism and platonism, for that matter—happens downstream, after deciding what it is we want from our metaphysical theories. How exactly we ought to make that decision is far from clear, but once made, the preceding chapters should provide a good idea of the challenges nominalists and platonists should expect to face.

Note

1 See Hilbert (1925). Cf. Wittgenstein (1978: 7).

GLOSSARY

abstract entities Contrasted with *concrete entities*. Roughly, entities such as numbers, properties, and propositions, which are typically held to exist necessarily and lack spatiotemporal locations or causal powers.
actualism The thesis that there are only actually existing entities.
***ante rem* entities** Contrasted with *in re* entities. Entities such as numbers and propositions, which lack spatiotemporal location. Sometimes called "transcendent" entities.
austere platonism Contrasted with *expansive platonism*. The view that abstract entities exist but are limited to properties, propositions, and mathematical entities, which are necessarily existing, causally inactive entities without spatiotemporal locations.
concrete entities Contrasted with *abstract entities*. Roughly, entities such as electrons, eagles, and estuaries, which are typically held to exist contingently, occupy spatiotemporal locations, and stand in causal relations.
duplication The sharing of all qualitative intrinsic properties.
Eleaticism The thesis that, necessarily, a given entity exists if and only if it is causally active.
eliminativism The thesis that there is no substantive or theoretically worthwhile abstract–concrete distinction. On such a view, no entities are concrete or abstract.

expansive platonism Contrasted with *austere platonism*. The view that, in addition to properties, propositions, and mathematical entities, there are also abstract entities like fictional characters, musical works, and GDPs, where such entities seem to be contingently existing, spatiotemporally located, and causally active.

fictionalism A strategy for treating discourse about some entities—e.g., claims about numbers or possible worlds like "Seven is prime"—as comparable to discourse about fictional entities—e.g., claims like "Aquaman is the ruler of Atlantis."

Hume's razor The methodological injunction to avoid multiplying necessities and, in particular, necessary connections between distinct entities.

ideology The commitments of theories, distinct from ontology, required for describing the world. Examples include primitive predicates and unanalyzed operators like the box and diamond of modal logic.

indiscernibility The sharing of all qualitative properties, whether intrinsic or extrinsic.

impure sets Sets with concrete entities as members (or as members of members, etc.).

***in re* entities** Entities located in spacetime, typically used to distinguish views on which universals are located in spacetime. Sometimes called "immanent" or "Aristotelian" entities.

intrinsic property Contrasted with *extrinsic property*. A property an object instantiates in virtue of how it is rather than how other objects are or how it is related to other objects.

logicism The thesis that mathematics is, in some sense, reducible to logic—e.g., in virtue of mathematical knowledge being logical knowledge.

mereology The logic and metaphysics of the part–whole relation.

metaphysical nihilism The thesis that, possibly, there are no entities whatsoever. The *absolute* version of this thesis is unrestricted in scope; the *concrete* version concerns only concrete entities.

methodological naturalism The thesis that the methodology of the natural sciences is correct and uniquely authoritative and that the commitments of our best scientific theories neither require nor admit of extra-scientific justification.

modality Feature of the world concerning different "modes" of truth like necessity and possibility. Modal notions are commonly analyzed in terms of possible worlds.

modal realism The thesis that there are concrete possible worlds in addition to the actual world. A version of *possibilism*.

naturalism The thesis that the findings and methodology of science are authoritative. See *methodological naturalism* and *ontological naturalism*.

naturalness A feature of properties, quantifiers, or languages that makes them metaphysically "privileged"—e.g., natural properties are those that figure into fundamental physical laws or guarantee objective resemblance between their bearers.

nominalism The thesis that there are no abstract entities.

non-qualitative property Contrasted with qualitative property. A property that depends upon or is necessarily connected to specific individuals—e.g., a "haecceity" like *being Socrates* or a property like *being taller than Socrates*.

Ockham's razor The methodological injunction to avoid multiplying entities beyond necessity in theories. Often held to justify belief in simpler theories over otherwise equally good rivals.

Ontologese A maximally natural language posited and deployed when undertaking metaphysical inquiry.

ontological category Fundamental distinction among entities, required for providing a comprehensive metaphysical theory.

ontological naturalism The thesis that our best scientific theories are authoritative in determining what exists.

ontology Ontological commitments of a theory are, roughly speaking, those entities that must exist for the theory to be true. Also used as the name for inquiry into what there is.

parsimony The theoretical virtue of minimizing theoretical commitments. See Ockham's razor.

Peano axioms Axioms that define arithmetic in terms of the natural numbers and a relation, *successor*, among them. They assert, along with mathematical induction, that every natural number has a unique successor, that natural numbers with the same successor are identical and that there is a natural number which is not the successor of any natural number (i.e., zero).

platonism The thesis that there are abstract entities.

plenitudinism The thesis that all consistent mathematical theories describe some portion of mathematical reality in virtue of the existence of a plenitude of different mathematical structures.

possibilism The thesis that there are merely possible entities in addition to actually existing ones.

primitivism Contrasted with *reductionism* and *eliminativism*. The thesis that the abstract–concrete distinction is theoretically basic and that the notion of *abstract entity* is a primitive notion, resisting further analysis.

properties Abstract entities that are identical with or explain the features of entities—e.g., *being blue* or *being an ox*. Held on various views to be universals, tropes, or sets of entities.

propositions Abstract entities commonly held to be the meaning of sentences, the primary bearers of truth-values, and the objects of cognitive attitudes

pure sets Sets with no concrete entities as members (or members of members, etc.). The hierarchy of pure sets is built upon the empty or "null" set.

Pythagoreanism The thesis that there are only abstract entities.

qualitative parsimony The parsimony theories exhibit in virtue of minimizing the number of kinds of commitments.

quantitative parsimony The parsimony theories exhibit in virtue of minimizing the number of commitments.

reductionism The thesis that the abstract–concrete distinction admits of reductive analysis by providing necessary and sufficient conditions for being abstract (or, alternatively, being concrete). Contrasted with *primitivism* and *eliminativism*.

sets Abstract collections often held to be the fundamental subject matter of mathematics. Some collections have several members—e.g., {Pluto, Mars, Venus}—while singleton sets like {Socrates} have exactly one member. The null or empty set, $\emptyset$, has no members.

singular terms Expressions—most notably, proper names or definite descriptions like "Edie" or "the comfiest couch,"—typically defined in terms of their syntactic or semantic function of referring or purporting to refer to some entity.

sparse property See *naturalness* and *properties*.

theoretical virtues Features like parsimony, fertility, and conservativeness that make theories superior to their rivals.

tropes Particularized property instances held by some to play the role of properties.

types Abstract entities, similar to or identical with properties, that have tokens—e.g., there are two tokens of the letter type "o" in the word "loot."

universals Abstract entities typically held to play the role of properties.

REFERENCES

Abbott, F.E. (1885) *Scientific Theism*. Boston: Little, Brown, and Company.
Adams, R.M. (1974) "Theories of actuality." *Noûs*, 8: 211–231.
— (1981) "Actualism and thisness." *Synthese*, 49: 3–41.
Alspector-Kelly, M. (2001) "On Quine on Carnap on ontology." *Philosophical Studies*, 102: 93–122.
Alston, W. (1958) "Ontological commitments." *Philosophical Studies*, 9: 8–17.
Armour-Garb, B. and Woodbridge, J.A. (2012) "The story about propositions." *Noûs*, 46(4): 635–674.
Armstrong, D.M. (1978) *Universals and Scientific Realism, Vols I and II*. Cambridge: Cambridge University Press.
— (1983) *What Is a Law of Nature?* Cambridge: Cambridge University Press.
— (1997) *A World of States of Affairs*. Cambridge: Cambridge University Press.
Arntzenius, F. and Dorr, C. (2012) *Space, Time, & Stuff*. Oxford: Oxford University Press.
Azzouni, J. (2004) *Deflating Existential Consequence*. Oxford: Oxford University Press.
Baker, A. (2003) "The indispensability argument and multiple foundations for mathematics." *Philosophical Quarterly*, 53: 49–67.
— (2005) "Are there genuine mathematical explanations of physical phenomena?" *Mind*, 114: 223–238.

— (2009) "Mathematical explanation in science." *British Journal for the Philosophy of Science*, 60(3): 611–633.

Balaguer, M. (1998) *Platonism and Anti-Platonism in Mathematics*. Oxford: Oxford University Press.

— (2015) "Platonism in metaphysics." In *The Stanford Encyclopedia of Philosophy*, http://plato.stanford.edu/archives/spr2016/entries/platonism/.

Baldwin, T. (1996) "There might be nothing." *Analysis*, 56(4): 231–238.

Bealer, G. (1982) *Quality and Concept*. Oxford: Oxford University Press.

— (1987) "The Philosophical Limits of Scientific Essentialism." *Philosophical Perspectives*, 1: 289-365.

— (1993) "Universals." *Journal of Philosophy*, 90(1): 5–32.

— (1998) "Propositions." *Mind*, 107: 1–32.

Benacerraf, P. (1965) "What numbers could not be." *Philosophical Review*, 74: 47–73.

— (1973) "Mathematical truth." *Journal of Philosophy*, 70: 661–679.

— (1998) "What mathematical truth could not be." In M. Schirn (ed.), *Philosophy of Mathematics Today*. Oxford: Clarendon Press, pp. 9–59.

Benacerraf, P. and Putnam, H. (1964) *Philosophy of Mathematics: Selected Readings*. New Jersey: Prentice-Hall.

Bengson, J. (2015) "Grasping the third realm." *Oxford Studies in Epistemology*, 5: 1–38.

Bennett, K. (2005) "Two axes of actualism." *Philosophical Review*, 114: 297–326.

— (2006) "Proxy 'actualism'." *Philosophical Studies*, 129: 263–294.

— (2009) "Composition, colocation, and metaontology." In D. Chalmers, D. Manley, and R. Wasserman (eds), *Metametaphysics*. Oxford: Oxford University Press, pp. 38–76.

Bliss, R. (2013) "Viciousness and the structure of reality." *Philosophical Studies*, 166(2): 399–418.

Boolos, G. (1986) "Saving Frege from contradiction." *Proceedings of the Aristotelian Society*, 87: 137–151.

Bradley, F.H. (1897) *Appearance and Reality*. London: Swan Sonnenschein.

Bricker, P. (1991) "Plenitude of possible structures." *Journal of Philosophy*, 88: 607–619.

— (1996) "Isolation and unification: the realist analysis of possible worlds." *Philosophical Studies*, 84: 225–238.

— (2006) "Absolute actuality and the plurality of worlds." *Philosophical Perspectives*, 20: 41–76.

— (2008) "Concrete possible worlds." In T. Sider, J. Hawthorne, and D. Zimmerman (eds), *Contemporary Debates in Metaphysics*. Oxford: Blackwell, pp. 111–134.

— (2014) "Ontological commitment." In *The Stanford Encyclopedia of Philosophy*, http://plato.stanford.edu/archives/win2014/entries/ontological-commitment/.

Bueno, O. (2013) "Putnam and the indispensability of mathematics." *Principia*, 17(2): 217.

Burge, T. (1992) "Frege on knowing the third realm." *Mind*, 101: 633–650.

Burgess, J. (1983) "Why I am not a nominalist." *Notre Dame Journal of Formal Logic*, 24: 93–105.

— (1998) "Occam's razor and scientific method." In M. Schirn (ed.), *Philosophy of Mathematics Today*. Oxford: Oxford University Press, pp. 195–214.

— (2004) "Mathematics and *Bleak House*." *Philosophia Mathematica*, 12: 18–36.

— (2008) "Cats, dogs, and so on." *Oxford Studies in Metaphysics*, 5: 56–78.

Burgess, J. and Rosen, G. (1997) *A Subject with No Object*. Oxford: Oxford University Press.

— (2005) "Nominalism reconsidered." In S. Shapiro (ed.), *Oxford Handbook of Philosophy of Mathematics and Logic*. Oxford: Oxford University Press, pp. 460–482.

Cameron, R. (2006) "Much ado about nothing: a study of metaphysical nihilism." *Erkenntnis*, 64: 193–222.

— (2008) "Turtles all the way down: regress, priority and fundamentality." *Philosophical Quarterly*, 58: 1–14.

— (2010) "How to have a radically minimal ontology." *Philosophical Studies*, 151: 249–264.

Campbell, K. (1990) *Abstract Particulars*. Oxford: Blackwell.

Candlish, S. (2007) *The Russell/Bradley Dispute and its Significance for Twentieth-Century Philosophy*. London: Palgrave Macmillan.

Caplan, B. and Matheson, C. (2006) "Defending musical perdurantism." *British Journal of Aesthetics*, 46: 59–69.

Caplan, B. and Tillman, C. (2013) "Benacerraf's revenge." *Philosophical Studies*, 166: 111–129.

Carmichael, C. (2010) "Universals." *Philosophical Studies*, 150(3): 373–389.

Carnap, R. (1950) "Empiricism, semantics, and ontology." *Revue Internationale de Philosophie*, 4(2): 20–40.

Chalmers, D. (2009) "Ontological anti-realism." In D. Chalmers, D. Manley, and R. Wasserman (eds), *Metametaphysics*. Oxford: Oxford University Press, pp. 384–423.

Cheyne, C. (1998) "Existence claims and causality." *Australasian Journal of Philosophy*, 76: 34–47.

— (2001) *Knowledge, Cause, and Abstract Objects*. Dordrecht: Kluwer.

Chihara, C. (1973) *Ontology and the Vicious-Circle Principle*. Ithaca: Cornell University Press.

— (2004) *A Structural Account of Mathematics*. Oxford: Clarendon Press.

— (2008) "Quine's lecture on nominalism from the perspective of a nominalist." *Oxford Studies in Metaphysics*, 4: 79–98.

Church, A. (1950) "On Carnap's analysis of statements of assertion and belief." *Analysis*, 10: 97–99.

— (1951) "The need for abstract entities in semantic analysis." *Proceedings of the American Academy of Arts and Sciences*, 80: 100–112.

Clarke-Doane, J. (2008) "Multiple reductions revisited." *Philosophia Mathematica*, 16: 244–255.

— (forthcoming) "What is the Benacerraf problem?" In F. Pataut (ed.), *New Perspectives on the Philosophy of Paul Benacerraf*. Dordrecht: Spring.

Cohnitz, D. and Rossberg, M. (2006) *Nelson Goodman*. Chesham: Acumen.

Colyvan, M. (1998) "Can the Eleatic principle be justified?" *Canadian Journal of Philosophy*, 28: 313–335.

— (2003) *The Indispensability of Mathematics*. Oxford: Oxford University Press.

— (2006) "Scientific realism and mathematical nominalism: a marriage made in hell." In C. Cheyne and J. Worrall (eds), *Rationality and Reality*. Dordrecht: Springer, pp. 225–237.

Cowling, S. (2011) "The limits of modality." *Philosophical Quarterly*, 61: 473–495.

— (2013) "Ideological parsimony." *Synthese*, 190: 889–908.

— (2014a) "The way of actuality." *Australasian Journal of Philosophy*, 92: 231–247.

— (2014b) "Instantiation as location." *Philosophical Studies*, 167: 667–682.

— (2015a) "Non-qualitative properties." *Erkenntnis*, 80: 275–301.

— (2015b) "Advice for Eleatics." In C. Daly (ed.), *Palgrave Handbook of Philosophical Methods*. London: Palgrave MacMillan, pp. 306–330.

— (forthcoming) "Intrinsic properties of properties." *Philosophical Quarterly*.

Currie, G. (1982) *Frege*. Brighton: Harvester Press.

Daly, C. and Langford, S. (2009) "Mathematical explanation and indispensability arguments." *Philosophical Quarterly*, 59: 641–658.

Dasgupta, S. (2009) "Individuals: an essay in revisionary metaphysics." *Philosophical Studies*, 145: 35–67.

Davies, J. (2015) "How to Refer to Abstract Objects." Dissertation, University of Toronto.

Devereux, D. (1994) "Separation and immanence in Plato's theory of forms." *Oxford Studies in Ancient Philosophy*, 12: 63–90.

Devitt, M. (1980) "Ostrich nominalism or mirage realism?" *Pacific Philosophical Quarterly*, 61: 433–449.

Divers, J. (2002) *Possible Worlds*. London: Routledge.

Dorr, C. (2005) "What we disagree about when we disagree about ontology." In M. Kalderon (ed.), *Fictionalism in Metaphysics*. Oxford: Oxford University Press, pp. 234–286.

— (2008) "There are no abstract objects." In T. Sider, J. Hawthorne, and D. Zimmerman (eds), *Contemporary Debates in Metaphysics*. Oxford: Blackwell, pp. 32–64.

— (2010) "Of numbers and electrons." *Proceedings of the Aristotelian Society*, 110: 133–181.

Dretske, F. (1977) "Laws of nature." *Philosophy of Science*, 44: 248–268.

Dummett, M. (1956) "Nominalism." *Philosophical Review*, 65: 491–505.

— (1973) *Frege: Philosophy of Language*. London: Duckworth.

— (1991) *Frege: Philosophy of Mathematics*. London: Duckworth.

Eddon, M. (2011) "Intrinsicality and hyperintensionality." *Philosophy and Phenomenological Research*, 82: 314–336.

— (2013) "Fundamental properties of fundamental properties." *Oxford Studies in Metaphysics*, 8: 78–104.

Effingham, N. (2013) *An Introduction to Ontology*. Cambridge: Polity.

— (2015) "The location of properties." *Noûs*, 49(4): 846–866.

Efird, D. and Stoneham, N. (2008). "What is the principle of recombination?" *Dialectica*, 62: 483–494.

Ehring, D. (2011) *Tropes*. Oxford: Oxford University Press.

Eklund, M. (2013) "Carnap's metaontology." *Noûs*, 47: 229–249.

Everett, A. (2013) *The Nonexistent*. Oxford: Oxford University Press.

Field, H. (1980) *Science Without Numbers*. Princeton: Princeton University Press.

— (1989) *Realism, Mathematics & Modality*. London: Blackwell.

Fine, G. (1980) "The one over many." *Philosophical Review*, 89: 197–240.
— (1993) *On Ideas*. Oxford: Oxford University Press.
Fine, K. (1977) "Properties, propositions and sets." *Journal of Philosophical Logic*, 6: 135–191.
— (1985) "Plantinga on the reduction of possibilist discourse." In J. Tomberlin and P. van Inwagen (eds), *Alvin Plantinga*. Dordrecht: D. Reidel, pp. 145–186.
Forrest, P. (1982) "Occam's razor and possible worlds." *The Monist*, 65: 456–464.
— (1986a) "Ways worlds could be." *Australasian Journal of Philosophy*, 64: 15–24.
— (1986b) "Neither magic nor mereology: a reply to Lewis." *Australasian Journal of Philosophy*, 64: 89–91.
— (2001) "Counting the cost of modal realism." In G. Preyer (ed.), *Reality and Humean Supervenience*. London: Rowman and Littlefield, pp. 93–103.
— (2002) "Nonclassical mereology and its application to sets." *Notre Dame Journal of Formal Logic*, 43: 79–94.
Forster, P. (2011) *Peirce and the Threat of Nominalism*. Cambridge: Cambridge University Press.
Fraenkel, A., Bar-Hillel, Y., and Levy, A. (1973) *Foundations of Set Theory*. Amsterdam: Elsevier.
Frege, G. (1884) *The Foundations of Arithmetic*. J.L. Austin (trans.), Oxford: Blackwell.
— (1918) "The thought" In P. Geach and R.H. Stoothoff (trans.), *Gottlob Frege*. Oxford: Basil Blackwell, pp. 351–372.
Geach, P.T. (1969) *God and the Soul*. London: Routledge.
Gödel, K. (1964) "What is Cantor's continuum problem?" In S. Feferman, et al. (eds), *Kurt Gödel: Collected Works II*. Oxford: Oxford University Press, pp. 254–270.
Goldman, A. (1967) "A causal theory of knowing." *Journal of Philosophy*, 64: 357–372.
Goodman, N. (1956) "A world of individuals." In J.M. Bochenski, et al. (eds), *The Problem of Universals*. South Bend: Notre Dame Press, pp. 13–31.
— (1972) "Seven strictures on similarity." In N. Goodman, *Problems and Projects*. Indianapolis: Bobbs-Merrill, pp. 23–32.
Goodman, N. and Quine, W.V. (1947) "Steps toward a constructive nominalism." *Journal of Symbolic Logic*, 12: 105–122.
Gould, P. (2014) *Beyond the Control of God?* New York: Bloomsbury.
Hale, B. (1987) *Abstract Objects*. Oxford: Basil Blackwell.

— (2013) *Necessary Beings*. Oxford: Oxford University Press.
Hale, B. and Wright, C. (1994) "A Reductio ad Surdum? Field on the contingency of mathematical objects." *Mind*, 103: 169–184.
— (2001) *Reason's Proper Study*. Oxford: Oxford University Press.
Hale, S. (1988) "Spacetime and the abstract/concrete distinction." *Philosophical Studies*, 85–102.
Hallett, M. (1986) *Cantorian Set Theory and Limitation of Size*. Oxford: Oxford University Press.
Harman, G. (1997) "Pragmatism and reasons for belief." In C.B. Kulp (ed.), *Realism/Antirealism and Epistemology*. Lanham: Rowman and Littlefield, pp. 123–148.
Hart, W.D. (1977) "Mathematical knowledge." *Journal of Philosophy*, 74(2): 118–129.
Harte, V. (2008) "Platonic metaphysics." In G. Fine (ed.), *Oxford Handbook of Plato*. Oxford: Oxford University Press, pp. 191–216.
Hawley, K. (2010) "Mereology, modality and magic." *Australasian Journal of Philosophy*, 88(1): 117–133.
Hawthorne, J. (2002) "Causal structuralism." *Metaphysics*, 15: 361–378.
Hawthorne, J. and Sider, T. (2002) "Locations." *Philosophical Topics*, 30(1): 53–76.
Hazen, A. (1976) "Expressive completeness in modal language." *Journal of Philosophical Logic*, 5(1): 25–46.
Hellman, G. (1989) *Mathematics Without Numbers*. Oxford: Oxford University Press.
— (2001a) "On nominalism." *Philosophy and Phenomenological Research*, 62(3): 691–705.
— (2001b) "Three varieties of mathematical structuralism." *Philosophia Mathematica*, 9(2): 184–211.
Hilbert, D. (1925) "On the infinite." In P. Benacerraf and H. Putnam (eds), *Philosophy of Mathematics: Selected Readings*. New Jersey: Prentice-Hall, pp. 183–201.
Hirsch, E. (2009) "Ontology and alternative languages." In D. Chalmers, D. Manley, and R. Wasserman (eds), *Metametaphysics*. Oxford: Oxford University Press, pp. 231–259.
Hodes, H. (1984) "Logicism and the ontological commitments of arithmetic." *Journal of Philosophy*, 81(3): 123–149.
Hoffman, J. and Rosenkrantz, G. (2003) "Platonistic theories of universals." In Michael J. Loux and Dean W. Zimmerman (eds), *Oxford Handbook of Metaphysics*. Oxford: Oxford University Press.

Hofweber, T. (2009) "Ambitious, yet modest, metaphysics." In D. Chalmers, D. Manley, and R. Wasserman (eds), *Metametaphysics*. *Oxford:* Oxford University Press, pp. 260–289.

Hudson, H. (2003) "Alexander's Dictum and Merricks' Dicta." *Topoi*, 22: 173–182.

Hull, D. (1976) "Are species really individuals?" *Systematic Zoology*, 25: 174–191.

Hylton, P. (2001) *Quine*. London: Routledge.

— (2003) "The theory of descriptions." In N. Griffin (ed.), *Cambridge Companion to Bertrand Russell*. Cambridge: Cambridge University Press, pp. 202–240.

Jackson, F. (1977) "Statements about universals." *Mind*, 86(343): 427–429.

Jubien, M. (1977) "Ontology and mathematical truth." *Noûs*, 11(2): 133–150.

— (1989) "On properties and property theory." In G. Chierchia, B. Partee, B., and R. Turner (eds), *Properties, Types, and Meaning*. Dordrecht: D. Reidel, pp. 159–175.

— (1997) *Contemporary Metaphysics: An Introduction*. London: Blackwell.

— (2001) "Propositions and the objects of thought." *Philosophical Studies*, 104: 47–62.

— (2009) *Possibility*. Oxford: Oxford University Press.

Kalderon, M. (1995) "Structure and the Concept of Number." Dissertation, Princeton University.

— (1996) "What numbers could be (and, hence, necessarily are)." *Philosophia Mathematica*, 4: 238–255.

Kaplan, D. (1968) "Quantifying in." *Synthese*, 19(1): 178–214.

— (1995) "A problem in possible worlds semantics." In W. Sinnott-Armstrong, D. Raffman, and N. Asher (eds.), *Modality, Morality and Belief*. Cambridge: Cambridge University Press, pp. 41–52.

Katz, J. (1998) *Realistic Rationalism*. Cambridge: MIT Press

Keller, J. (forthcoming) "Paraphrase and the symmetry objection." *Australasian Journal of Philosophy*.

Kim, J. (1970) "Events as property exemplifications." In M. Brand and D. Walton (eds), *Action Theory*. Dordrecht: D. Reidel, pp. 310–326.

King, J. (2007) *The Nature and Structure of Content*. Oxford: Oxford University Press.

King, J., Soames, S., and Speaks, J. (2014) *New Thinking About Propositions*. Oxford: Oxford University Press.

Kitcher, P. (1978) "The plight of the platonist." *Noûs*, 12: 119–136.

Klement, K. (2010a) "Russell, his paradoxes, and Cantor's theorem: part I." *Philosophy Compass*, 5(1): 16–28.

— (2010b) "Russell, his paradoxes, and Cantor's theorem: Part II." *Philosophy Compass*, 5(1): 29–41.

Korman, D. (2014) "The vagueness argument against abstract artifacts." *Philosophical Studies*, 167: 57–71.

— (2015a) *Objects*. Oxford: Oxford University Press.

— (2015b) "Fundamental quantification and the language of the ontology room." *Noûs*, 49(2): 298–321.

Kraut, R. (2010) "Universals, metaphysical explanations, and pragmatism." *Journal of Philosophy*, 107: 590–609.

Kripke, S. (1980) *Naming and Necessity*. Cambridge: Harvard University Press.

— (1982) *Wittgenstein on Rules and Private Language*. Cambridge: Harvard University Press.

Kroon, F. (2011) "Fictionalism in metaphysics." *Philosophy Compass*, 6: 786–803.

Kuhn, T. (1977) "Objectivity, value judgment, and theory choice." In T. Kuhn, *The Essential Tension*. Chicago: University of Chicago Press, pp. 320–339.

Langton, R. (1998) *Kantian Humility*. Oxford: Oxford University Press.

Laudan, L. and Leplin, J. (1991) "Empirical equivalence and underdetermination." *Journal of Philosophy*, 88: 449–472.

Leftow, B. (1990) "Is God an abstract object?" *Noûs*, 24(4): 581–598.

Leng, M. (2010) *Mathematics and Reality*. Oxford: Oxford University Press.

Lewis, D. (1973) *Counterfactuals*. Cambridge: Blackwell.

— (1983a) "New work for a theory of universals." *Australasian Journal of Philosophy*, 61: 343–377.

— (1983b) "Individuation by acquaintance and by stipulation." *Philosophical Review*, 92: 3–32.

— (1983c) Postscript to "Counterpart theory and quantified modal logic." In D. Lewis, *Philosophical Papers: Volume I*. Oxford: Oxford University Press, pp. 39–46.

— (1986a) *On the Plurality of Worlds*. Oxford: Blackwell.

— (1986b) "Against structural universals." *Australasian Journal of Philosophy*, 64(1): 25–46.

— (1986c) "Events." In D. Lewis, *Philosophical Papers: Volume II*. Oxford: Oxford University Press, pp. 241–269.

— (1990) "Noneism or allism?" *Mind*, 99: 23–31.

— (1991) *Parts of Classes*. Oxford: Blackwell.
— (1993a) "Many but almost one." In K. Campbell, J. Bacon, and L. Reinhardt (eds), *Ontology, Causality and Mind*. Cambridge: Cambridge University Press, pp. 23–38.
— (1993b) "Mathematics is megethology." *Philosophia Mathematica*, 1: 3–23.
— (1998) "A world of truthmakers?" *Times Literary Supplement*, 4948, 13 February, p. 30.
— (2009) "Ramseyan humility." In D. Braddon-Mitchell and R. Nola (eds), *Conceptual Analysis and Philosophical Naturalism*. Cambridge: MIT Press, pp. 203–222.
Liggins, D. (2008) "Quine, Putnam, and the 'Quine–Putnam' indispensability argument." *Erkenntnis*, 68(1): 113–127.
— (2010) "Epistemological objections to platonism." *Philosophy Compass*, 5(1): 67–77.
Linnebo, Ø. (2006) "Epistemological challenges to mathematical platonism." *Philosophical Studies*, 129: 545–574.
Linsky, B. and Zalta, E. (1994) "In defense of the simplest quantified modal logic." *Philosophical Perspectives*, 8: 431–458.
Lipton, P. (2004) *Inference to the Best Explanation*. London: Routledge.
Loux, M. (1998) *Metaphysics: A Contemporary Introduction*. London: Routledge.
Lowe, E. J. (1995) "The metaphysics of abstract objects." *Journal of Philosophy*, 92: 509–524.
— (1996) "Why is there anything at all?" *Aristotelian Society Proceedings Supplement*, 70: 111–120.
MacBride, F. (1999) "Listening to fictions: a study of Fieldian nominalism." *British Journal for the Philosophy of Science*, 50(3): 431–455.
— (2003) "Speaking with shadows: a study of neo-logicism." *British Journal for the Philosophy of Science*, 54: 103–163.
— (2005a) "The particular–universal distinction: a dogma of metaphysics?" *Mind*, 114: 565–614.
— (2005b) "Structuralism reconsidered." In S. Shapiro (ed.), *Oxford Handbook of Philosophy of Mathematics and Logic*. Oxford: Oxford University Press, pp. 563–589.
— (2005c) "Lewis' animadversions on the truthmaker principle." In H. Beebee and J. Dodd (eds) *Truthmakers*. Oxford: Oxford University Press, pp. 117–140.
— (2011) "Relations and truthmaking." *Proceedings of the Aristotelian Society*, 111: 161–179.

Maddy, P. (1990) *Realism in Mathematics*. Oxford: Oxford University Press.
— (1992) "Indispensability and practice." *Journal of Philosophy*, 89(6): 275–289.
— (1997) *Naturalism in Mathematics*. Oxford: Oxford University Press.
Mag Uidhir, C. (2013) "Art, metaphysics, and the paradox of standards." In C. Mag Uidhir (ed.), *Art & Abstract Objects*. Oxford: Oxford University Press, pp. 1–26.
Malament, D. (1982) "Review of Field's *Science Without Numbers*." *Journal of Philosophy*, 79(9): 523–534.
Marshall, D. (2012) "Analyses of intrinsicality in terms of naturalness." *Philosophy Compass*, 7(8): 531–542.
— (2013) "Analyses of intrinsicality without naturalness." *Philosophy Compass*, 8(2): 186–197.
Maurin, A. (2012) "Bradley's regress." *Philosophy Compass*, 7(11): 794–807.
McMullin, E. (1976) "The fertility of theory and the unit for appraisal in science." In R.S. Cohen, et al. (eds), *Essays in Memory of Imre Lakatos*. Dordrecht: D. Reidel, pp. 395–432.
Meinong, A. (1960) "On the theory of objects" (translation of *Über Gegenstandstheorie*, 1904). In R. Chisholm (ed.), *Realism and the Background of Phenomenology*. Glencoe: Free Press, pp. 76–117.
Melia, J. (1992a) "Against modalism." *Philosophical Studies*, 68(1): 35–56.
— (1992b) "An alleged disanalogy between numbers and propositions." *Analysis*, 52: 46–48.
— (2000) "Weaseling away the indispensability argument." *Mind*, 109: 455–479.
— (2003) *Modality*. Chesham: Acumen.
— (2005) "Truthmaking without truthmakers." In H. Beebee and J. Dodd (eds) *Truthmakers*. Oxford: Oxford University Press, pp. 67–84.
— (2008) "A world of concrete particulars." *Oxford Studies in Metaphysics*, 4: 99–124.
Menzel, C. (1990) "Actualism, ontological commitment, and possible world semantics." *Synthese*, 85(3): 355–389.
Merricks, T. (2015). *Propositions*. Oxford: Oxford University Press.
Moore, J. (1999) "Propositions, numbers, and the problem of arbitrary identification." *Synthese*, 120: 229–263.
Nolan, D. (1996) "Recombination unbound." *Philosophical Studies*, 84(2): 239–262.
— (1997a) "Impossible worlds: a modest approach." *Notre Dame Journal for Formal Logic*, 38(4): 535–572

— (1997b) "Quantitative parsimony." *British Journal for the Philosophy of Science*, 48(3): 329–343.
— (1999) "Is fertility virtuous in its own right?" *British Journal for the Philosophy of Science*, 50(2): 265–282.
— (2001) "What's wrong with infinite regresses?" *Metaphilosophy*, 32(5): 523–538.
— (2002) *Topics in the Philosophy of Possible Worlds*. London: Routledge.
— (2014) "Hyperintensional metaphysics." *Philosophical Studies*, 171(1): 149–160.
— (2015) "The unreasonable effectiveness of abstract metaphysics." *Oxford Studies in Metaphysics*, 9: 61–88.
— (forthcoming) "It's a kind of magic: Lewis, magic and properties." *Synthese*.
Normore, C. (1987) "The tradition of medieval nominalism." In J. Wippel (ed.), *Studies in Medieval Philosophy*. Washington: Catholic University of America Press, pp. 201–217.
Oddie, G. (1982) "Armstrong on the Eleatic principle and abstract entities." *Philosophical Studies*, 41(2): 285–295.
Okasha, S. (2001) "Darwinian metaphysics: species and the question of essentialism." *Synthese*, 131: 191–213.
O'Leary-Hawthorne, J. (1996) "The epistemology of possible worlds: a guided tour." *Philosophical Studies*, 84: 183–202.
Oliver, A. (1993) "Classes and Goodman's nominalism." *Proceedings of the Aristotelian Society*, 93: 179–191.
Olson, K. (1987) *An Essay on Facts*. Stanford: Center for Study of Language and Information Press.
Parsons, C. (1971) "Ontology and mathematics." *Philosophical Review*, 80: 151–76.
— (1990) "The structuralist view of mathematical objects." *Synthese*, 84: 303–346.
— (1995) "Platonism and mathematical intuition in Kurt Gödel's thought." *Bulletin of Symbolic Logic*, 1: 44–74.
Parsons, T. (1980) *Nonexistent Objects*. New Haven: Yale University Press.
Paseau, A. (2006) "The subtraction argument(s)." *Dialectica*, 60(2): 145–156.
— (2009) "Reducing arithmetic to set theory." In Ø. Linnebo and O. Bueno (eds), *New Waves in the Philosophy of Mathematics*. London: Palgrave Macmillan, pp. 35–58.
Peirce, C.S. (1976) *The New Elements of Mathematics*. C. Eisele (ed.) Atlantic Highlands: Mounon Publishers.

Penner, T. (1987) *The Ascent from Nominalism*. Dordrecht: D. Reidel.
Penrose, R. (1989) *The Emperor's New Mind*. Oxford: Oxford University Press.
Pincock, C. (2011) *Mathematics and Scientific Representation*. Oxford: Oxford University Press.
Plantinga, A. (1974) *The Nature of Necessity*. Oxford: Clarendon Press.
— (1983) "On existentialism." *Philosophical Studies*, 44: 1–20.
— (1993) *Warrant and Proper Function*. Oxford: Oxford University Press.
Pollock, J. (1970) *Knowledge and Justification*. Princeton: Princeton University Press.
Potter, M. (2004) *Set Theory and its Philosophy*. Oxford: Oxford University Press.
Priest, G. (1995) *Beyond the Limits of Thought*. Cambridge: Cambridge University Press.
— (2005) *Towards Non-Being*. Oxford: Oxford University Press.
Psillos, S. (1999) *Scientific Realism*. London: Routledge.
Putnam, H. (1967) "Mathematics without foundations." *Journal of Philosophy*, 65: 5–22.
— (1971) *Philosophy of Logic*. New York: Harper and Row.
— (1975) "What is mathematical truth?" In H. Putnam, *Mathematics, Matter, and Method*. Cambridge: Cambridge University Press, pp. 60–78.
— (1995) *Pragmatism: An Open Question*. London: Blackwell.
— (2012) "On mathematics, realism, and ethics." *Harvard Review of Philosophy*, 18(1): 143–160.
Quine, W.V. (1937) "New foundations for mathematical logic." *Journal of Symbolic Logic*, 2(2): 86–87.
— (1948) "On what there is." *Review of Metaphysics*, 2: 21–38
— (1951) "Ontology and ideology." *Philosophical Studies*, 2: 11–15.
— (1953) "Two dogmas of empiricism." *Philosophical Review*, 60: 20–43.
— (1956) "Quantifiers and propositional attitudes." *Journal of Philosophy*, 53(5): 177–187.
— (1960) "Variables explained away." *Proceedings of the American Philosophical Society*, 104(3): 343–347.
— (1962) "Paradox." *Scientific American*, 206(4): 84–95.
— (1968a) "Ontological relativity." *Journal of Philosophy*, 65: 185–212.
— (1968b) "Existence and quantification." In W.V. Quine, *Ontological Relativity*. New York: Columbia University Press, pp. 91–113.
— (1969) "Natural kinds." In N. Rescher, et al. (eds), *Essays in Honor of Carl G. Hempel*. Dordrecht: Springer, pp. 41–56.

— (1976a) "Whither physical objects?" In R. Cohen, et al. (eds), *Essays in Memory of Imre Lakatos*. Dordrecht: D. Reidel, pp. 497–504.

— (1976b) "Three grades of modal involvement." In W.V. Quine, *The Ways of Paradox and Other Essays*. Cambridge: Harvard University Press, pp. 158–176.

— (1981a) "Things and their place in theories." In W.V. Quine, *Theories and Things*. Cambridge: Harvard University Press, pp. 1–23.

— (1981b) "Five milestones of empiricism." In W.V. Quine, *Theories and Things*. Cambridge: Harvard University Press, pp. 67–72.

— (1986) "Reply to Parsons." In E. Hahn and P. Schilpp (eds), *The Philosophy of W.V. Quine*. La Salle: Open Court.

— (2008) "Nominalism." *Oxford Studies in Metaphysics*, 4: 3–21.

Ramsey, F. (1925) "Universals." *Mind*, 34: 401–417.

Resnik, M. (1997) *Mathematics as a Science of Patterns*. Oxford: Oxford University Press.

Richard, M. (1981) "Temporalism and eternalism." *Philosophical Studies*, 39 (1): 1–13.

Rodriguez-Pereyra, G. (1997) "There might be nothing: the subtraction argument improved." *Analysis*, 57(3): 159–166.

— (2002) *Resemblance Nominalism*. Oxford: Oxford University Press.

— (2013) "The subtraction arguments for metaphysical nihilism." In T. Goldschmidt (ed.), *The Puzzle of Existence*. London: Routledge, pp. 197–214.

— (2015) "Nominalism in metaphysics" In *The Stanford Encyclopedia of Philosophy*, http://plato.stanford.edu/archives/sum2015/entries/nominalism-metaphysics/.

— (forthcoming) "Indiscernibility universals." *Inquiry*.

Rosen, G. (1993) "The refutation of nominalism (?)" *Philosophical Topics*, 21: 149–186.

— (2001) "Nominalism, naturalism, epistemic relativism." *Philosophical Topics*, 25: 60–91.

— (2002) "A study in modal deviance." In J. Hawthorne and T. Gendler (eds), *Conceivability and Possibility*. Oxford: Oxford University Press, pp. 283–307.

— (2006) "The limits of contingency." In F. MacBride (ed.), *Identity and Modality*. Oxford: Oxford University Press, pp. 13–39.

— (2014) "Abstract objects." In *The Stanford Encyclopedia of Philosophy*, http://plato.stanford.edu/archives/fall2014/entries/abstract-objects/.

Russell, B. (1903) *The Principles of Mathematics*. Cambridge: Cambridge University Press.
— (1905) "On denoting." *Mind*, 14(56): 479–493.
— (1912) *The Problems of Philosophy*. New York: Henry Holt and Company.
— (1919) *Introduction to Mathematical Philosophy*. London: George Allen and Unwin.
Sainsbury, R.M. (2009) *Fiction and Fictionalism*. London: Routledge.
Schaffer, J. (2003) "Is there a fundamental level?" *Noûs*, 37: 498–51
— (2009) "On what grounds what." In D. Chalmers, D. Manley, and R. Wasserman (eds), *Metametaphysics*. Oxford: Oxford University Press, pp. 347–383.
— (2010) "Monism: the priority of the whole." *Philosophical Review*, 119: 31–76.
— (2012) "Necessitarian propositions." *Synthese*, 189(1): 119–162.
— (2013) "Metaphysical semantics meets multiple realizability." *Analysis*, 73(4): 736–751.
Schechter, J. (2010) "The reliability challenge and the epistemology of logic." *Philosophical Perspectives*, 24: 437–464.
Shapiro, S. (1997) *Philosophy of Mathematics*. New York: Oxford University Press.
— (2008) "Identity, indiscernbility, and *ante rem* structuralism." *Philosophia Mathematica*, 16: 285–309.
Shoemaker, S. (1980) "Causality and properties." In P. van Inwagen (ed.), *Time and Cause*. Dordrecht: D. Reidel, pp. 109–135.
Sider, T. (1996) "Naturalness and arbitrariness." *Philosophical Studies*, 81: 283–301.
— (2001) *Four-Dimensionalism*. Oxford: Oxford University Press.
— (2009) "Ontological realism." In D. Chalmers, D. Manley, and R. Wasserman (eds) *Metametaphysics*. Oxford: Oxford University Press, pp. 384–423.
— (2011) *Writing the Book of the World*. Oxford: Oxford University Press.
— (2013). "Against parthood." *Oxford Studies in Metaphysics*, 8: 237–293.
Simons, P. (2010) "Relations and truthmaking." *Aristotelian Society Supplementary*, 84(1): 199–213.
Sober, E. (1975) *Simplicity*. Oxford: Clarendon Press.
— (1993) "Mathematics and indispensability." *Philosophical Review*, 102: 35–57.
Stalnaker, R. (1984) *Inquiry*. Cambridge: MIT Press.
— (2011) *Mere Possibilities*. Princeton: Princeton University Press.
Stanford, P.K. (2006) *Exceeding Our Grasp*. Oxford: Oxford University Press.
Steiner, M. (1975) *Mathematical Knowledge*. New York: Cornell University Press.

Strawson, P.F. (1959) *Individuals: An Essay in Descriptive Metaphysics*. London: Methuen.
Swoyer, C. (1996) "Theories of properties: from plenitude to paucity." *Philosophical Perspectives*, 10: 243–264.
— (2008) "Abstract entities." In T. Sider, J. Hawthorne and D. Zimmerman (eds.), *Contemporary Debates in Metaphysics*. Oxford: Blackwell.
Szabó, Z. (2003) "Nominalism." In M. Loux and D. Zimmerman (eds), *Oxford Handbook of Metaphysics*. Oxford: Oxford University Press, pp. 11–45.
Thomasson, A. (1999) *Fiction and Metaphysics*. Cambridge: Cambridge University Press.
— (2015) *Ontology Made Easy*. New York: Oxford University Press.
Tooley, M. (2009) "Causes, laws, and ontology." In H. Beebee, et al. (eds), *Oxford Handbook of Causation*. Oxford: Oxford University Press, pp. 368–386.
Turner, J. (2011) "Ontological nihilism." *Oxford Studies in Metaphysics*, 8: 3–54.
Unger, P. (1980) "The problem of the many." *Midwest Studies in Philosophy*, 5: 411–467.
Uzquiano, G. (2015) "Modality and paradox." *Philosophy Compass*, 10(4): 284–300.
Van Cleve, J. (1994) "Predication without universals: a fling with ostrich nominalism." *Philosophy and Phenomenological Research*, 54: 577–590.
van Inwagen, P. (1977) "Creatures of fiction." *American Philosophical Quarterly*, 14: 299–308.
— (1986) "Two concepts of possible worlds." *Midwest Studies in Philosophy*, 11: 185–213.
— (1990) *Material Beings*. Ithaca: Cornell University Press.
— (2004) "A theory of properties." *Oxford Studies in Metaphysics*, 1: 107–138.
— (2009) "Being, existence, and ontological commitment." In D. Chalmers, D. Manley, and R. Wasserman (eds), *Metametaphysics*. Oxford: Oxford University Press, pp. 472–506.
Vogel, J. (1990) "Cartesian skepticism and inference to the best explanation." *Journal of Philosophy*, 87: 658–666.
Von Neumann, J. (1964) "The formalist foundations of mathematics." In P. Benacerraf and H. Putnam (eds), *Philosophy of Mathematics*. Cambridge: Prentice-Hall, pp. 61–65.
von Solodkoff, T. (2014) "Paraphrase strategies in metaphysics." *Philosophy Compass*, 9(8): 570–582.
Weatherson, B. (2003) "Many many problems." *Philosophical Quarterly*, 53: 481–501.

Wetzel, L. (1989) "That numbers could be objects." *Philosophical Studies*, 56: 273–292.
— (2009) *Types and Tokens*. Cambridge: MIT Press.
Whittle, B. (2010) "There are brute necessities." *Philosophical Quarterly*, 60: 149–159.
Williamson, T. (1998) "Bare possibilia." *Erkenntnis*, 48: 257–273.
— (2002) "Necessary existents." In A. O'Hear (ed.), *Royal Institute of Philosophy Supplement*. Cambridge: Cambridge University Press, pp. 269–87.
— (2013) *Modal Logic as Metaphysics*. Oxford: Oxford University Press.
Wilson, J. (2014) "No work for a theory of grounding." *Inquiry* 57: 535–579.
— (2015) "Hume's Dictum and metaphysical modality: Lewis's combinatorialism." In B. Loewer and J. Schaffer (eds), *Blackwell Companion to David Lewis*. Oxford: Blackwell, pp. 138–158.
Wittgenstein, L. (1978) *Remarks on the Foundations of Mathematics*. In G.H. von Wright, et al. (eds), Oxford: Blackwell.
Wright, C. (1983) *Frege's Conception of Numbers as Objects*. Aberdeen: Aberdeen University Press.
Yablo, S. (1998) "Does ontology rest on a mistake?" *Proceedings of the Aristotelian Society*, 72: 229–261.
— (2000) "Apriority and existence." In P. Boghossian and C. Peacocke (eds), *New Essays on the A Priori*. Oxford: Oxford University Press, pp. 197–228.
— (2001) "Go figure: a path through fictionalism." *Midwest Studies in Philosophy*, 25: 72–102.
— (2002) "Abstract objects: a case study." *Philosophical Issues*, 12: 220–240.
— (2005) "The myth of the seven." In M. Kalderon (ed.), *Fictionalism in Metaphysics*. Oxford: Oxford University Press, pp. 88–115.
Zalta, E. (1983) *Abstract Objects*. Dordrecht: D. Reidel.

INDEX

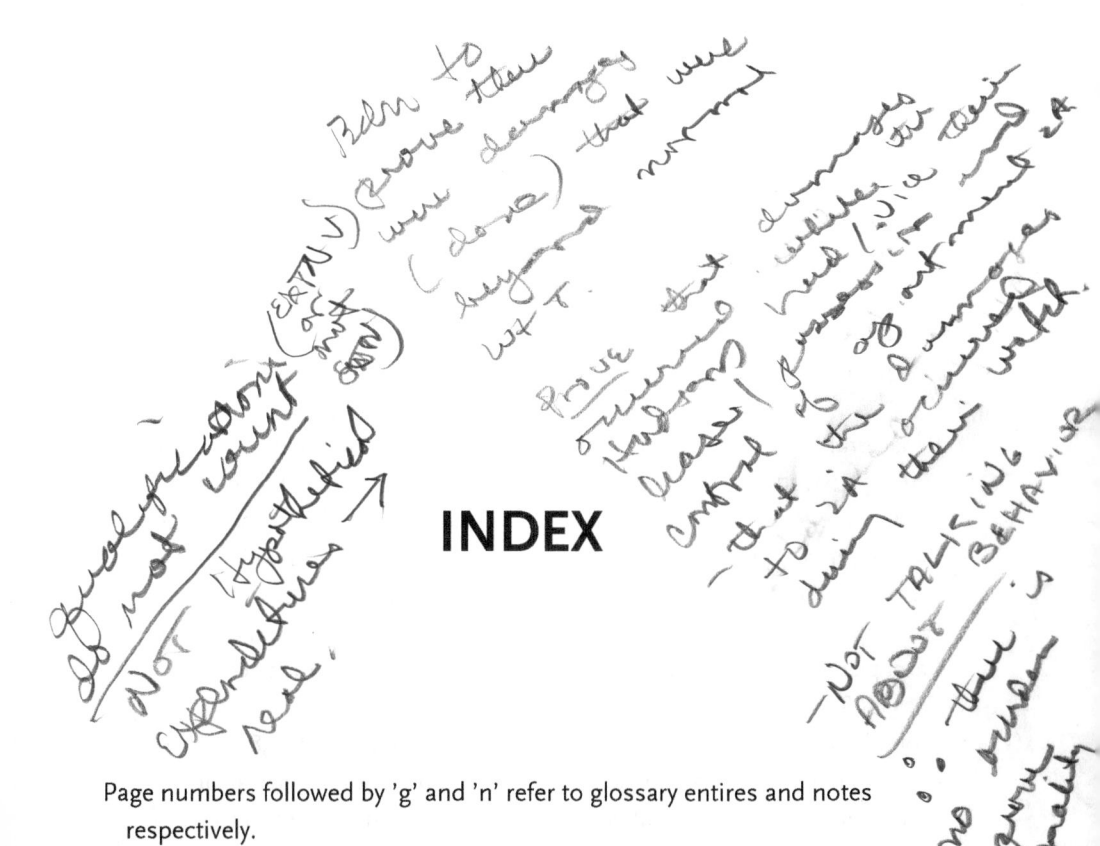

Page numbers followed by 'g' and 'n' refer to glossary entries and notes respectively.

Abbott, F.E. 10–11
abstract-concrete distinction:
  accessibility 2, 72, 94, 95, 96, 98, 100, 101; boundary-setting 3–4; causation 2, 74, 79–82, 83, 94, 95, 96, 98, 99, 100, 101, 156; eliminativism 70, 97–102, 252g; location 2, 74, 76–9, 84, 94, 95, 96, 98, 101; mind-independence 2–3, 76, 98; necessity 82–4, 94, 95, 96, 97, 98, 100, 101; and nominalism 102–3; and the platonist-nominalist debate 6–8, 9, 16, 24; primitivism 70, 92–7, 100, 101, 103, 155, 255g; standard view 70–3, 98–9; see also reductionism
abstract entities: arguments for see case for platonism and abstract entities; defined 252g; expansive platonism 4–5, 6, 78, 81–2, 101, 206, 248, 253g; see also abstract-concrete distinction
Abstraction, Way of 75–6
actualism 207–10, 252g
alethic arguments 26, 63, 68n32;
  Fregean 38, 42–4, 47; and non-committal nominalism 230; Quinean 38, 39–42, 47, 63; truthmaker theory 38, 44–7
ante rem entities: defined 252g; structuralism 176–7, 179; universals 34, 78, 94, 101, 103, 208
anti-nominalism 18, 249–51
Aristotelian entities see *in re* entities
Armstrong, D.M. 65n11, 79, 124, 132

austere platonism: and causal inactivity 82, 252g; defined 252g; and expansive platonism divide 5–6, 19, 44, 73, 97, 206, 248, 252g; and primitivism 70, 94, 95, 96, 97, 101, 103, 249

Benacerraf, P. 74, 115, 131, 132–6, 162, 163–5, 167, 171, 175
Bradley's regress 121–7
Burgess, J. 53, 142, 148, 225–6, 228, 237, 244n14

Carnapian ontology 13–15, 77, 180
Carnap, Rudolph *see* Carnapian ontology
case against platonism and abstract entities 17; actualist-possibilist debate 207–10; cognitive access argument 150–5; Eleaticism 131, 155–9, 252g; epistemic access argument *see* epistemic access argument; necessary connections *see* necessary connections; necessary existents 189, 190–6, 210; non-uniqueness problem *see* non-uniqueness problem; paradoxes as 106, 107–14, 127; parsimony argument 106, 107, 114–20, 126–7, 157, 200, 210; regress arguments 106, 107, 120–7; semantic access argument 147–50
case for platonism and abstract entities 2, 16, 25–6, 63; alethic arguments 38–47, 68n32; direct semantic arguments 26, 27–9; explanatory semantic arguments *see* explanatory semantic arguments; indispensability arguments *see* indispensability argument; lawhood 62; modality explanation 57, 60–1; resemblance 57, 58–60, 205
categoreal structure 23–5, 98, 99; *see also* ontological category(ies)
causal concerns 17; cognitive access argument 150–5; Eleaticism 131, 155–9, 252g; epistemic access argument *see* epistemic access argument; semantic access argument 147–50
causal structuralism 158
causation: and the case against abstract entities *see* causal concerns; in eliminativism 99; general abstract feature 2–3, 5, 16, 72; and necessity 83, 95; in primitive platonism 94, 95, 96, 101; reductive analysis 15, 70, 73, 74, 79–82, 84, 100, 103
challenges to platonism and abstract entities *see* case against platonism and abstract entities
cognitive access 2, 72, 94, 95, 96, 97, 100, 101, 150–5
conceivability arguments 192–3
concrete entities: defined 252g; in truthmaker theory 45, 46; *see also* abstract-concrete distinction
confirmational holism 49, 53, 54, 55
conservativeness 114, 115, 116, 117, 180, 219, 243n1
contingent platonism 201–6

direct semantic arguments 26, 27–9
Dorr, C. 230, 231, 243n6
duplication 86, 89, 188n11, 196–7, 206, 252g

Eleaticism 131, 155–9, 252g
eliminativism 70, 97–102, 175–6, 252g; see also modal eliminativism
eliminativist structuralism 175–6
epiphenomenalons 82, 156, 159
epistemic access 2, 76, 98, 248; see also epistemic access argument
epistemic access argument: formulation of 131–8; implications of 147; platonist response to 138–46, 179
existence monism 89–90, 123
expansive platonism: abstract entities for 4–5, 6, 78, 81–2, 101, 206, 248, 253g; and austere platonism 5–6, 19, 44, 73, 97, 206, 248, 252g; and Fregean alethic argument 44; location and causation 78, 81–2; and primitivism 96, 97, 101
explanatory semantic arguments 26, 63; as abductive argument 29–30; and Bradley's regress 123; nominalist response 35–8; properties 32–5, 36; propositions 30–2, 65n12
extreme mutabilism 203, 204–6
extrinsic properties 86–7, 187n10

fictionalism 222–3, 253g
Field, H.: epistemic access challenge 135–8, 140, 141–2, 143, 145, 146, 148, 152, 155, 159; on the indispensability case for platonism 48, 52; instrumentalism 243n1; on metaphysical necessity 211n2; nominalist actualism 207; non-uniqueness problem 165, 170; on possible worlds 236–7
figurative nominalism 217–20, 222, 226, 242
Forrest, P. 82, 167, 197
Fregean alethic arguments 38, 42–4, 47
Frege, Gottlob 2, 3, 74, 80, 139, 150, 151; see also Fregean alethic arguments
functorese 238–9, 240–1, 242
fundamentality: abstract-concrete distinction 89–92

Geach, P. 208
Gödel, K. 144, 145
Goodman, N. 22n12, 74, 107, 109, 113, 216, 235, 236

Hart, W. D. 135
Harvard nominalism 216, 234–5, 236, 242
Hellman, G. 227, 244n9
hermeneutic and revolutionary nominalism 225–8
Hume's razor 195–201, 202, 203–4, 206, 210, 237, 253g
humility thesis 182–3

ideological nominalism 235, 238–42, 251
ideological parsimony 37, 93, 94, 116, 117–18, 119, 120, 126, 171

ideology: and the abstract-concrete distinction 74, 92–3, 94, 95, 97, 98, 101, 102, 103; Bradley's regress, platonist response 125, 126, 127; defined 36, 253g; ideological nominalism 235, 238–42, 251; modal 37, 225, 235, 242; in modal structuralism 224, 225; objective view of 37–8; parsimony 37, 74, 93, 94, 116, 117–18, 119, 120, 126, 171; set theoretic reductions 163
immanent entities *see in re* entities
immutabilism 202; *see also* mutabilism
impure sets: actualism and 209; defined 34, 253g; epistemic access to mathematical knowledge 143; mutabilism 202, 212n11; and primitivism 94, 96, 97, 101; reductive analysis 78, 81, 83, 85, 89, 92, 156
indiscernibility 86–9, 253g
indispensability arguments: and confirmational holism 49, 53, 54, 55; enhancements 55–7; expressive and explanatory indispensability 54–7; naturalistic platonists 247; nominalist response 48, 51, 52–3, 55, 56, 57; and ontological naturalism 48–9, 50, 51–2, 53, 54, 55, 56, 63, 155; and traditional platonism 50
infinite regresses 120–7
in re entities 34, 35, 78, 83, 92, 101, 207, 248, 253g
instrumental nominalism 216–17, 218, 220

interactional paradoxes 110–12
intrinsic property(ies) 86–8, 89, 94, 184, 187n10, 227, 248, 253g; *see also* duplication
intuition 143–5, 146

Jubien, M. 148–9, 150, 168

Kaplan's paradox 111–12
King, J. 168
Kripke, S. 148, 173

lawhood argument for platonism 62
Lewis, D.: on the abstract-concrete distinction 74–5, 88–9, 98, 104n1; epistemic humility 188n11; on Field/epistemic access to abstract entities 137; on Kaplan's paradox 112; modal realism 61, 207–8, 209, 236, 237; non-uniqueness problem 168, 172, 173; on parsimony 118; recombination principles 198, 211n6, 212n7
location, abstract-concrete distinction 2, 74, 76–9, 84, 94, 95, 96, 98, 101
logicism 138–41, 146, 211n3, 253g

Maddy, P. 50–1, 53, 141–2, 143
many, problem of 169–70
mathematical entities: actuality of 208; alethic case for platonism 41, 43, 44, 45–7; Carnapian view 13; categoreal structure 24–5, 98; epistemic access 2, 76; *see also* epistemic access argument; extreme mutabilism 204–5; ideological nominalism 240;

indispensability case for platonism 48, 49–51, 52, 54, 55, 56, 57, 155; modal structuralism 224–5; non-uniqueness theses 162, 163–5, 170, 171–2, 174, 175–6; preservationist nominalism 227–8; Pythagorean theorem 1, 3, 4, 6, 7, 26, 72; research programmes 9; semantic access 147–50; semantic case for platonism 26, 28; terminology 4, 21n5
Meinongian nonexistent entities 39–40, 228–9, 244n15
Melia, J. 55, 117, 167–8
mental entities 2–3, 24
mereology: abstract-concrete distinction and 84–6, 87, 91, 99; and contingent platonism 212n9; defined 253g; distinctness of 211n5; and nominalist possibilism 237–8; non-uniqueness problem 168
metaphysical nihilism 190–1, 192, 193–4, 195, 253g
metaphysical underdetermination 162, 164, 174, 177–85
methodological naturalism 115–16, 141–3, 146, 171–2, 253g
mind-(in)dependence 2–3, 6, 30, 31, 76, 98
modal constancy 70, 71, 104n1
modal eliminativism 37, 235, 242
modality: and abstractness 84; case for platonism 57, 60–1; defined 253g; eliminativism 37, 235, 242; Harvard nominalism 235, 242; ideological nominalism 238, 242; *see also* necessity

modal objections: actualist-possibilist debate 207–10; contingent platonism 201–6; Eleaticism 158–9; necessary connections *see* necessary connections; necessary existents 189, 190–6, 210
modal realism 207–8, 236, 237–8, 254g
modal structuralism 224–5, 235, 237, 251
monistic platonism 178, 180–1, 184
mutabilism 202–6

naturalism: defined 254g; methodological 115–16, 141–3, 146, 171–2, 253g; vs. non-naturalistic platonism 247–8, 249–50; *see also* ontological naturalism
natural knowledge 141–3
naturalness 172–5, 177, 180, 231, 254g, 323
necessary connections: contingent platonism 201–6; Humean objections to 195–201, 202, 203–4, 206, 210, 237, 253g; platonist modal commitment to 189–90
necessary existents 189, 190–6, 210
necessity: abstract-concrete distinction 82–4, 94, 95, 96, 97, 98, 100, 101; truthmaker theory 44–7; *see also* necessary connections; necessary existents
nihilism *see* metaphysical nihilism
nominalism: and the abstract-concrete distinction 82, 99, 102–3; and the alethic case for platonism 40, 42, 45, 46, 47; defined 2,

254g; and indispensability theory 48, 51, 52–3, 55, 56, 57; and metaphysical arguments for platonism 57, 60–1, 62; objections to (nominalist-platonist debate) 12–16; ontological and categoreal basis 2, 24–5, 69; and the semantic case for platonism 27, 28, 31, 33, 35–8; significance and history (of nominalist-platonist debate) 6–12; terminology 18–19; see also case against platonism and abstract entities; nominalist options
nominalist actualism 207
nominalist options: choice between 250–1; fictionalist replacement nominalism/fictionalism 222–3, 253g; figurative nominalism 217–20, 222, 226, 242; hermeneutic and revolutionary nominalism 225–8; ideological nominalism 235, 238–42, 251; instrumental nominalism 216–17, 218, 220; modal structuralism 224–5, 251; nominalist possibilism 235–8; non-cognitive nominalism 216, 217, 220; non-committal nominalism 228–34, 250; Ontologese nominalism 231–4; paraphrase options 220–2; preservationist nominalism 227–8; radical nominalism 215–16; replacement nominalism 222–5
nominalist possibilism 17, 207, 208, 215, 235–8, 242
non-cognitive nominalism 216, 217, 220
non-committal nominalism 228–34, 250
non-naturalistic platonism 247–8, 250
non-qualitative property(ies) 83, 86, 87, 89, 202, 254g
non-uniqueness problem: defined 162–9; platonist responses 170–7; and the problem of the many 169–70; and underdetermination 162, 164, 174, 177–85

Ockham's razor 107, 114–15, 116, 117, 119, 157, 199, 200, 210, 254g
Ontologese 231–2, 233, 234, 254g
ontological category(ies): abstract-concrete distinction 24–5, 28–9, 71, 200; abstract entities as 41, 183, 184–5, 188; metaphysical fundamentality 23–4, 172, 254g; and non-uniquenes 182, 183, 184–5; possible worlds as 61; properties and propositions 4, 24, 34, 58, 59, 65n12, 187n8
ontological naturalism: cognitive access 153, 155; defined 254g; and indispensability arguments 48–9, 50, 51–2, 53, 54, 55, 56, 63, 155; and nominalism 226, 228; and parsimony 171
ontological parsimony 116, 117–18, 118–19, 120, 127, 171
ontology: defined 254g
ostrich nominalism 36, 126, 240

paradoxes 35, 106, 107–14, 127, 139
paraphrase nominalism 220–2

parsimony 37, 93, 94, 106, 114–20, 126–7, 171, 180, 254g; *see also* Ockham's razor
Paseau, A. 105n14, 171
Peano axioms 139, 163, 175, 224, 254g
Peirce, C.S. 10
Plato 20n1, 32, 90, 120, 196
platonism: alternatives to *see* nominalist options; defined 254g; expansive platonist view of abstract entities 4–5, 6, 78, 81–2, 101, 206, 248, 253g; objections to (nominalist-platonist debate) 12–16; significance and history (of nominalist-platonist debate) 6–12; terminology 18–19; *see also* abstract-concrete distinction; case against platonism and abstract entities; case for platonism and abstract entities
plenitudinism 139–41, 146, 180–2, 186, 248, 254g
pluralistic platonisms 178, 180, 184
possibilism 207–10, 215, 235–8, 242, 254g
predicate functor language/ functorese 238–9, 240–1, 242
predicates 32–3, 34, 35, 36–7, 76, 93, 107–9, 126, 127, 239, 240–1
preservationist nominalism 227–8
primitivism 92–7, 100, 101, 103, 248–9, 255g
properties: actuality 209; alethic arguments 41, 42, 43, 44, 45; austere and expansionist platonism 5, 248; causal structuralism 158; cognitive access to 2, 132, 146, 150, 153; defined 255g; duplication 86, 89, 188n11, 196–7, 206, 252g; in ideological nominalism 241; immutabilism 202, 203, 204, 205, 206; and infinite regress 121, 123, 124–5, 126; location 10, 19, 78, 83; metaphysical case for platonism 58–60, 61, 62; metaphysical underdetermination 178–9, 181, 182, 183, 184; modal structuralism 225; necessary connections 189–90, 196, 200, 202, 206; necessary existents 191, 194, 196, 201, 202; non-relationality thesis 70–1; non-uniqueness problem 165–7, 168, 169, 172–3, 174, 175; Ontologese 232, 233; ontological disagreement 69; and paradox 107, 108–11, 112, 113, 114; and parsimony 116, 117–18, 119, 126–7; platonist commitment 4, 8, 24, 25; primitivism 93, 94, 95, 101; Quine's ostrich nominalism 36, 240; reductive analysis of the abstract-concrete distinction 78, 79, 80–1, 82, 83, 84–9, 90, 91; semantic arguments 30, 32, 33–5, 36, 38
propositions: in the actualist-possibilist debate 207, 209; and anti-nominalism 250; Bradley's regress 122; cognitive access 2, 132, 146, 150–5, 159; defined 255g; eliminativism 98, 99, 101; in ideological nominalism 240, 241; metaphysical underdetermination

177, 178, 179, 180, 181–2, 183, 184; mind-independence 3; necessity 82–3, 189–90, 194, 195–6, 200, 201–2, 203, 204, 205, 206; and the nominalist-platonist debate 7, 8, 9–10; non-uniqueness problem 165, 167–8, 172, 174; and ontological categories 4, 23–4, 65n12, 187n8; and paradox 107, 110–12, 114; parsimony 117, 119; primitivism 94, 95; pro-platonist arguments 25, 30–2, 41–2, 43, 45, 46, 61, 62, 63; and standard view of the abstract-concrete distinction 2, 72
pure sets 34–5, 90, 164, 202, 209, 255g
Putnam, H. 10, 11, 48–9, 115, 148, 235
Pythagoreanism 20n2, 105n11, 117, 255g

qualitative parsimony 118–19, 120, 127, 255g
qualitative properties 86, 87, 88, 89, 202, 248; *see also* duplication; indiscernability
quantitative parsimony 118–19, 120, 255g
Quinean alethic argument 38, 39–42, 47, 63
Quine, W. V.: and the case for platonism 35–6, 37, 38, 48, 49, 53; *see also* Quinean alethic argument; on functorese 238–9; methodological naturalism 141; and the non-uniqueness problem 172; on paradoxes 107, 108, 109, 113; and parsimony 117, 119; spatiotemporal location 74, 77; *see also* Harvard nominalism

radical nominalism 215–16
razor arguments 106, 114–17, 119, 120, 127; *see also* Hume's razor; Ockham's razor
reductionism 70, 103; Abstraction, Way of 75–6; academic interest in 74–5; causation 79–82; complexity 84–6; defined 255g; and eliminativism 97, 99, 100–2; Example, Way of 75; fundamentality 89–92; indiscernability and duplication 86–9; location 76–9; necessity 82–4, 94; and primitivism 94–5, 248–9
regress arguments 120–7
replacement nominalism 222–5
resemblance: as metaphysical case for platonism 57, 58–60, 205
revolutionary and hermeneutic nominalism 225–8
Rosen, G. 53, 142, 148, 212n11, 225–6, 228, 237
Russell, B. 40, 79–80, 123–4, 153, 167–8, 191, 192; *see also* Russell's paradox
Russell's paradox 107–9, 110, 111, 113, 139

Schaffer, J. 90, 233
semantic access argument 147–50
semantic arguments: direct 26, 27–9; *see also* explanatory semantic arguments
serious mutabilism 203
sets: actuality 207–8, 209; best scientific theories 50–1; defined 34–5, 255g; entities (terminology)

18; epistemic access 143, 144; Harvard nominalism 235, 245n20; ideological nominalism 240, 241; and nominalist possibilism 236, 237–8; and paradox 107–10, 111, 112, 113, 114; parsimony 115, 119; platonist options 68n31, 248; pure 34–5, 90, 164, 202, 209, 255g; *see also* impure sets; non-uniqueness problem

Sider, T. 37, 98–9, 100, 101, 174, 188n13, 233

singleton sets 34, 164, 166, 188n11, 202, 207, 209, 237

singular terms 40, 42–3, 44, 165, 170, 174, 255g

sparse property(ies) 35, 91, 109, 173, 255g

systematic mutabilism 202

theoretical virtues 106, 114–15, 116, 117, 255g

Third Man argument 120, 121, 124

transcendent entities *see ante rem* entities

tropes 34, 35, 78, 105n15, 124–5, 126, 255g

truthmaker theory 38, 44–7

types 4, 23, 31–2, 65n11, 249, 255g

underdetermination 162, 164, 174, 177–85

universals: in categoreal structure 24; defined 255g; entities (terminology) 18; location in spacetime 10, 19, 34, 78, 83, 248; nominalist-platonist debate 19; platonist actualism 207–8, 209; Plato's Third Man argument 120, 121; predication 32–3; in Quinean alethic argument 42; structural 84, 85, 86, 90, 176–7; universal theory of properties 34, 35, 84, 101

von Neumann, J. 163, 166, 173

Zermelo, E. 163, 166, 173; *see also* Zermelo-Fraenkel set theory

Zermelo-Fraenkel set theory (ZF) 108, 110, 181

Taylor & Francis eBooks

Helping you to choose the right eBooks for your Library

Add Routledge titles to your library's digital collection today. Taylor and Francis ebooks contains over 50,000 titles in the Humanities, Social Sciences, Behavioural Sciences, Built Environment and Law.

Choose from a range of subject packages or create your own!

Benefits for you
- Free MARC records
- COUNTER-compliant usage statistics
- Flexible purchase and pricing options
- All titles DRM-free.

Benefits for your user
- Off-site, anytime access via Athens or referring URL
- Print or copy pages or chapters
- Full content search
- Bookmark, highlight and annotate text
- Access to thousands of pages of quality research at the click of a button.

REQUEST YOUR FREE INSTITUTIONAL TRIAL TODAY — Free Trials Available. We offer free trials to qualifying academic, corporate and government customers.

eCollections – Choose from over 30 subject eCollections, including:

Archaeology	Language Learning
Architecture	Law
Asian Studies	Literature
Business & Management	Media & Communication
Classical Studies	Middle East Studies
Construction	Music
Creative & Media Arts	Philosophy
Criminology & Criminal Justice	Planning
Economics	Politics
Education	Psychology & Mental Health
Energy	Religion
Engineering	Security
English Language & Linguistics	Social Work
Environment & Sustainability	Sociology
Geography	Sport
Health Studies	Theatre & Performance
History	Tourism, Hospitality & Events

For more information, pricing enquiries or to order a free trial, please contact your local sales team:
www.tandfebooks.com/page/sales

Routledge — Taylor & Francis Group | The home of Routledge books

www.tandfebooks.com